SECONDS
OUT

WOMEN *and* FIGHTING

ALISON DEAN

COACH HOUSE BOOKS, TORONTO

first edition

Published with the generous assistance of the Canada Council for the Arts and the Ontario Arts Council. Coach House Books also acknowledges the support of the Government of Canada through the Canada Book Fund and the Government of Ontario through the Ontario Book Publishing Tax Credit.

LIBRARY AND ARCHIVES CANADA CATALOGUING IN PUBLICATION

Title: Seconds out : women and fighting / Alison Dean.
Names: Dean, Alison (Alison V.), author.
Identifiers: Canadiana (print) 20210184698 | Canadiana (ebook) 20210184876 | ISBN 9781552454190 (softcover) | ISBN 9781770566668 (EPUB) | ISBN 9781770566675 (PDF)
Subjects: LCSH: Martial arts—Social aspects. | LCSH: Boxing—Social aspects. | LCSH: Boxing for women. | LCSH: Women martial artists. | LCSH: Women boxers. | LCSH: Violence in women.
Classification: LCC GV1101 .D43 2021 | DDC 796.8082—dc23

Seconds Out is available as an ebook: ISBN 978 1 77056 666 8 (EPUB); 978 1 77076 667 5 (PDF)

Purchase of the print version of this book entitles you to a free digital copy. To claim your ebook of this title, please email sales@chbooks.com with proof of purchase. (Coach House Books reserves the right to terminate the free digital download offer at any time.)

For my parents

Tell me, what else should I have done?
Doesn't everything die at last, and too soon?
Tell me, what is it you plan to do
with your one wild and precious life?

– Mary Oliver, 'The Summer Day'

What kind of beast would turn its life into words?
What atonement is this all about?
– and yet, writing words like these, I'm also living.

– Adrienne Rich, 'Twenty-One Love Poems: VII'

CONTENTS

★

INTRODUCTION

'Hit me,' I tell her. 'It's okay. I won't break.' Asking someone to punch a stranger in the face without anger or provocation is like administering an on-the-spot personality test. The young woman across from me is in her late teens. She's soft-spoken and has a look that is both earnest and apologetic. This is no seedy back alley or mid-life crisis. This is just a drill. We are wearing boxing gloves and mouthguards and we're both here to learn. Despite her reticence to strike, I know there is some part of her that wants to do it. I've been to every class since the day she joined the gym; for weeks now, she has kept coming back.

While many of us are socially programmed *not* to fight, there's *something* that leads a person to a martial arts dojo or combat sports gym. It might be the workout, but you can get exercise a lot of ways. Sometimes people try it once and never come back. But as a regular at an MMA gym and an assistant kickboxing coach, I have seen a lot of new people come through. I can't necessarily predict the ones who will stick around, but I will say this: in many cases, regardless of how a new student reacts to their first taste of training – from learning fighting stance, to taking lessons on how to throw the first basic punches or kicks – they show up again the next day, and the day after that, and the day after that. Sometimes a person gets hooked immediately, even if on the outside they seem uncomfortable, insecure, unco-ordinated, or psychologically incapable of crossing the line to punch someone else on command (at the beginning, anyway). I understand this compulsion. I was one of those people.

As is so often the case, I make my way here standing on the shoulders of women who came before. Writers like Katherine Dunn and Sarah Deming began tracking (started writing about, and in

Deming's case, also competing in) boxing decades ago. At well over two hundred Muay Thai fights, Sylvie von Duuglas-Ittu has competed the most of any westerner in Thailand and has been thoughtfully chronicling her training and her place as a woman in martial arts. There are many others who have lent their bodies and their voices to the discussion, both historically and today. L.A. Jennings and Wendy L. Rouse have done an admirably thorough job of fleshing out comprehensive histories of women in combat sports training and competition. This book veers away from a strict historical account, however. I am starting with one close, limited, subjective history (my own) as a gateway to asking questions about other fighters and other stories. How do fighters – of all genders – navigate training, and the spaces of combat sports, now?

A fundamental question lingers throughout. What is a fighter? The more I seek the answer, the more disappointing the responses appear. Even in many of the most interesting and thoughtful accounts of and reflections on combat sports and martial arts culture, the concept of a 'fighter' is not male by default but male *by definition*. Maybe this isn't a surprise, or maybe I should have seen it coming. Regardless, it doesn't ring true. In what follows, I go beyond the stories and themes I see so often repeated in narratives about fighting and competition. Instead of simply asking what fighting shows us about being a man, as so many others have done, I'm changing the terms of the conversation in order to more accurately reflect reality, rather than popular – or some people's preferred – perception. The two terms, *man* and *fighter*, are not synonymous, no matter how many people try to tell us they are.

I have wins, and losses. But even a win isn't an end, and like a lot of people, my fight is as much outside of the ring as in it. This is why I have chosen to explore different questions, not only those applicable to women but those asked with a wider range of social and embodied experiences in mind. How do assumptions about femininity and masculinity shape cultural assumptions about fighting and self-defence? What does the often-repeated phrase 'mental toughness' mean to fighters and coaches? What's really behind the preoccupation with worrying about women getting cut or bruised in the face? How does self-defence signify when the lines between inside and outside the ring get blurred? How do we negotiate being 'coachable' as students, given the dangers of being submissive to authorities and institutions that don't necessarily have our best interests at heart? What are the verbal, psychological, and physical languages with which fighters and coaches communicate? How are different bodies regulated in combat competition and training? How do we both learn from and fight against the systems that form us? What does it mean to have – or lose – empathy in order to fight? And if it's okay for men to cry all the way to, from, and in the MMA cage or the boxing ring, then why do I feel like such a failure if I get frustrated and tear up in training?

When I first stepped into a gym to try a kickboxing class, I had no idea where it would lead. As an academic in my thirties, emerging from the all-consuming project of completing my PhD, I was weak and out of touch with my body after years of physical inactivity. I had no experience with anything resembling a martial art and I disliked group exercise as a rule. An introvert in a public-facing career, I thought taking a kickboxing class would help me learn to be more assertive and I might get some exercise in the process. I got a lot more than I bargained for. The process of learning to fight has changed who I think I am, and what I feel I am capable of. In fact, it shows me how much and how often both of those categories can shift. I was holding the bar too low.

I am a planner. I rarely act rashly; it feels unbearable when I say or do the wrong thing. I want so badly to be in control, to have some power over the world around me and my place in it. And yet, as a woman, I am also constantly told how vulnerable I am. Combat training is, in many ways, about controlling both ourselves and others. We train to be perfect. We use mirrors, coaches, training videos, and exhaustive repetition in order to gain mastery over ourselves. But all of that work is necessary because when you step into the ring, you give up control. No matter who you are or how well you prepare, anything can happen in a fight. I did not think I would like that uncertainty, that letting go, and yet I have found that stepping into that intense situation offers a rare presence, focus, and immediacy – a kind of freedom. Coming to terms with my own power (which includes negotiating and challenging my own limitations) changes the way I move through the world, both inside and outside the ring.

This book is about how fighting changed my life. Though women have trained in martial arts for hundreds of years, combat sports are becoming increasingly popular with women. For many, this kind of training represents more than a fitness trend; it is part of a process of empowerment. This is not, as some detractors suggest, a loss of femininity. If fighting causes the erosion of some mythical womanly 'goodness,' then so be it. That fictional woman is not a model of gender or sex I would want to subscribe to anyway. In my life (for better or worse), I seem to have sought out historically masculine spaces, from the academy to the ring. I consciously and unconsciously mine these cultures to find elements I can adapt for myself. I want to take on these challenges, but I want to do them *my* way, and on my own terms.

Women who train to fight have to find their own ways to negotiate these spaces, ideally with their eyes open. Gender, race, class, sexuality, and ability all play a central part in determining a person's relationship to violence, and they inform the ways we respond to training, from self-defence to combat sports, with all the blur and overlap that connects them. There is a very real tension between practice and life outside the gym. Women live with the seeming inevitability, the constant looming threat, of violence or rape. This fact, among others, means that we move through the world differently than the majority of the men who teach and train beside us. When we bring our embodied histories and experiences into male-dominated combat sports and consider what it means to be there, however, our very presence has the potential to shed new light on notions of control, boundaries, and conflict.

By offering a look at the people, spaces, philosophies, rituals, and challenges of fighting sports like kickboxing, Muay Thai, boxing, and Brazilian Jiu-Jitsu – combat sports that commonly feed into what we know now as MMA – I talk about the world that female fighters of all disciplines, ages, and experience levels are stepping into, and (in the best cases, I think) how women are remaking these spaces and the culture around them.

★

WARM-UP

I pull up to a strip mall in Northern California and park my car at the base of a stately eucalyptus tree flanked by flowering plants, palm trees, and a scattering of pickup trucks. I dig my oversized gym bag from the trunk of my silver Honda and head toward the MMA gym located on a corner of the strip. My bag is bulky and heavy on my shoulder, and I nudge it forward a little with my hip as I walk. Entering the airy, brightly lit gym, I wave and call out greetings to the people around me – stragglers from the class before, people who will be attending a different class at the same time, or those who will be training alongside me in the kickboxing class. As I'm checking myself in on the gym's iPad, I glance into the boxing ring located to the right of the door. Two people are sparring up on the square pedestal. Their extra gear and water bottles are piled along the outer edges of the ropes, and a few classmates and coaches stand on the ground below, yelling encouragement and advice up to fighters. I approach the mat and take off my shoes. In spaces where Mixed Martial Arts, Brazilian Jiu-Jitsu, or wrestling are practised, there can be no outdoor shoes on the mat, as a rule. Bare feet are one thing, but grapplers often have their bodies and faces pressed into this mat as they train.

This is, to varying extents, a specific, if not a sacred, kind of space. Some people stop and bow as they enter the mat, facing outward, bending at the waist to acknowledge the space of the dojo. They pay respect to their sensei or coach and to what will be practised here. I was never trained to bow, but I make note of the border as I cross it. As I do so, I greet Mowgli, my coach's dog. No one is better acquainted with the invisible wall between life as we know it and the perimeters of the gym mat than this ball of fur. Patient, devoted, and obedient,

Mowgli is intimately aware of the limits of his world. No dogs are allowed on the mat. He lies on the ground, impassive face resting gingerly just along the safe side of the border, eyes trained on his master, Sam Radetsky, who is in his own element on the blue padded flooring within. I pet Mowgli, twirl his ears between my finger and thumb, and whisper sweet nothings before stepping across the threshold, where he can't follow. Some of his hair always sneaks a ride on my clothes, but the rest stays put. Barefoot, I tread across the room, noting the give of the slightly soft grappling mat under my feet. This synthetic floor is a version of home to me now, too. And although it was an adjustment to go without shoes in public, I have come to prefer it. Having spent their entire lives wrapped in warm socks in cold climates, my feet and I are just getting to know each other now that I have let them loose. I try to keep them clean, intact, and healthy, because they spend so much time out in the world. In return, they (mostly) do what I ask of them.

I find the spot where I will get ready. I change into my training clothes, usually black compression sport leggings and a cut-off T-shirt. I take my messy curls and pull them into a bun secured with doubled elastics, or wind them into a French braid to keep them contained. I sit cross-legged on the floor. First, I pull a roll of kinesiology tape from my bag. I roll my left pant leg up to mid-thigh and fasten three pieces in a criss-crossing U around my left knee, in the hope that it will make the chronically weak joint a little more secure. Then, I pull a roll of white sports tape out of my gym bag. I take my left foot in my hands and wrap the tape once, twice, three times around my big toe, which has been perpetually jammed (or broken, or both) for more than a year. The tape gives it a little extra solidity, so it doesn't snag on mat corners or other people's body parts. A toe that has lost its own spatial awareness is a clumsy thing and re-injures easily. I feel like the tape helps it to stay focused. Next, I wrap the same tape around my left wrist, to give it extra protection. It's not hurting today, but the extra layers help me to hit a little harder without the constant worry of re-injury. Once, twice, three times around my wrist. At the end, I use my thumbnail, or my teeth, to tear the tape and press the edges down. Later, I will have to pry all of this tape off my body before stepping into the shower; it will be wet and gummy with sweat. But for now, it is doing its part to keep me whole.

Next, I reach into the duffel and grab my hand wraps. When I am organized, I keep these rolled tight in neat individual round discs, so they stay smooth for easy unrolling and wrapping. The heavy cloth, 180 inches long and two inches wide, comes in all different colours and patterns. Today, I have opted for basic black, but in the pocket of my gym bag I have bundles in all different colours. There is no single right way to wrap them. Some people put extra wrapping on their wrist; some like to keep their palm bare; whereas others cover wrist, palm, and the spaces between with the cloth. Some wrap their thumbs. Others don't. I didn't used to, but when I'm boxing rather than kickboxing, I go for the extra protection.

When I am ready to wrap, I take the first bundle by the end and flick it forward. Like a rhythmic gymnast's ribbon, it pours itself out onto the mat. If my wraps are all wrinkled or knotted, the simple pleasure of drawing that line is lost. I wrap my hands using a hybrid of two methods I was taught, repeating familiar steps. I take the end, with the loop for the thumb, and fold it slightly wider than the width of the knuckles on my left hand. I fold it over three times to create a pad that I then hold against my knuckles and press down with my thumb. From there, I wind the cloth around my hand, around my wrist multiple times; loop it between my knuckles, around my wrist, under and around my thumb, and then back around again. I want it tight on my wrist, and pulled taut up to my knuckles, so that my hand is contained. The cloth between my fingers will keep them from knocking together when I hit things, and the extra wrist support should help protect my inconveniently narrow stems on impact. I pull the fabric around and through, around and over and across, and over, and across, until I can secure it tightly around my wrist with the Velcro end. I pick up the other wrap and repeat the same process on the right.

Once I am dressed, wrapped, and ready, I move around a little to warm up, and then start to stretch. My hips and hamstrings are always unreasonably tight, no matter how often I stretch them. As I take pigeon pose, I sink deep into the stretch, hold it, and drop my head, momentarily checking out from the sounds of talking, laughing, and people hitting leather bags or grunting and rolling around me. I use this moment to get my head in order. With one leg bent in front of me and the other one straight against the mat behind me, I focus on keeping my hips square and breathing more deeply. I close my eyes, press my body down, rest my head forward on my forearms, and take in the slightly stale smell of the mat underneath me, the texture of the cloth gently binding my hands, the smooth feeling of my tights against my stretching hips and thighs, which have suddenly come alive. I breathe the familiar air of the gym, with its sounds whirling around me, a mix of conversations, laughter, bodies breathing hard in exertion, time clocks beeping, and leather smacking against leather.

When I finally lift my head and open my eyes, it's as if I have just conjured my surroundings. Everything that came before this moment has disappeared. I'm not the woman who stood in front of a university classroom and lectured earlier today, or the former wife who got off a phone call with her ex right before walking in. None of that belongs here.

This is my world now. Smiling as I shift my gaze up to the people around me, I am a part of its landscape. Right where I belong.

CHAPTER 1

★

AN EDUCATION

In the fifth grade, I decided to play volleyball. I was four-foot-something, feather-light, and mortally afraid of the ball. Despite that winning formula, I tried out for the school team. I don't think I played a single game. The next year, I tried again, and kept a permanent spot on the bench. From then until the beginning of university, I practised as much and as often as I could, often attending two practices in an evening. I was too short to be anything but a setter, and for most of that time, not even strong enough to consistently serve the ball over the net. But I thought the sport was beautiful, even balletic. I wanted to feel that beauty from the inside out.

When volleyball outgrew me after high school (in height as well as skill), my athletic life ground to a halt. I had only played the sport for the love of it, and no other physical activity held my interest. For over fifteen years, I mostly avoided exercise. I was healthy and able enough for my sedentary lifestyle. I'd go dancing with friends on the weekend or take long walks when travelling ... but that was it. If I measured my fitness at all, it was determined by whether my clothes fit. The idea of group exercise made me anxious, and the deeper I got into my own intellectual work, the more introverted I became. Those years were mostly spent in school, curled up in front of computers or reclining with books. For the bulk of my adult life, I focused on living inside my head, not my body. I believed they were somehow separate.

The first day of PhD orientation, I met the three other people entering the doctoral program. I became fast friends with Meg, a quietly contained Vancouverite studying food culture in Asian-Canadian literature, and Sarah, a US Southerner who specialized in the eighteenth-century author Eliza Haywood. After a stint working in art gallery education and administration, I had decided to return to school with the idea of studying the ways we talk about, and conceive of, photography. My interest began with the study of agency and intimacy in portraiture, which quickly dovetailed into analyzing images of violence, torture, and atrocity.

Graduate programs have a spotty rate of completion; it's a four- to ten-year commitment, and a lot can happen in that time. For five years of coursework, comprehensive exams, research, dissertation writing, and PhD defences, the three of us supported each other while Sarah and I repeated our mantra: 'If they want to get rid of us, they will have to claw these PhDs from our cold, dead hands.' In retrospect, this was our own grad student version of a macho fighter's 'I will die in this ring' speech. We were rallying ourselves for a fight.

Throughout that time, I was often single-minded in my focus, with what felt like no room for hobbies or even physical activity. I poured my energy into my work. Between two undergraduate degrees, a master's degree, and a PhD, I spent about eleven years immersed in study. Through my academic life, I learned how to think, how to ask questions, and how to learn. I developed intellectual and emotional skill sets to carry me through. That process made me who I am today. But one of the invisible but central tenets built into the Ivory Tower is a set of values based on exceptionalism, measurement, and judgment. We are trained to feel that we are never enough.

When I finished school, I floated around a little, unsure of what to do with myself and with my time. I have never thought of myself as a driven person, and yet after working so hard for so long, I was both burnt out and restless. I took up gardening, needing to do something with my hands – something that brought me into the physical world. Eventually, I felt the nagging urge to try kickboxing. One Friday night, I convinced Meg to attend a class at our neighbourhood gym. We descended into the basement together, stepped into a dark, crowded studio, and hedged our way along the back of the six p.m. kickboxing class. As I have since learned, every gym has its own particular smell – a bespoke mix of leather, body odour, and cleaning products. This gym was no exception. While its unique smell calls up visceral memories for me now, I hardly remarked it on that first day. This small neighbourhood gym didn't have a boxing ring the way most boxing gyms do, so we were spared the intimidation of a big square pedestal. All the better. For us, making our way through the young, confident group as they chatted, stretched, and wrapped their hands was daunting enough.

The first time you join a class like this, they usually teach you the tenets of stance and footwork, and the basic punches – a jab, a cross, and maybe a hook if you're picking things up. You might learn the basics of a roundhouse kick. Meg and I were given the preamble and then thrown into the mix, shadowboxing in line with the others. We did our best to keep up as the coach offered instructions and other students went through the motions around us. I felt laughably awkward trying to navigate my suddenly alien limbs for an audience. The exertion came with a price, of course. After years of inactivity, this one hour of training cost me days of recovery. The next morning, I was so stiff and sore that my now former husband, Leif, had to roll me out of bed. For the rest of the week, I'd wake up feeling like I had been in an accident. But when the next Friday came around, I returned to the gym. That was more than four years ago.

Meg had helped me get through the door on that first day but didn't keep attending the class. I was on my own. I stayed on at that first gym, with my first coach and training partners, for many months and continued to return periodically in the years that followed. As I became more interested in pushing my limits and exploring the psychology of fighting for myself, martial arts became an increasingly important lens through which I began to reconsider the world around me and my place within it. For the first year I kept my new interest quiet because I recognized that people would hear 'kickboxing' and assume it was some kind of casual no-contact cardio class. A great workout, to be sure, but I wasn't there just to exercise. I wanted to learn to fight but I saw myself through others' eyes and knew how far their imagination of me could go: about as far as a boxercise class. So I first covered and then quietly documented my bruises. In the privacy of my own home, I took notice of the way my body was changing. While I didn't fully realize it, I was hoping to redefine my body in terms of more than fat or muscle. I was trying to build a new identity from the ground up.

IMMERSION

When Leif and I moved to Vancouver from Saskatchewan, I learned firsthand the difference between the obvious cold of the prairies and the 'wet cold' of the West Coast. Throughout graduate school, baths became my go-to to keep myself calm and to bring up my body temperature after a day in the rain. Bath-heavy phases also tended to signal that I was stressed.

Once I started kickboxing, my relationship to both baths and the body that soaked in them shifted. At that time, the neighbourhood gym didn't use mats on the floor the way they do (and every other gym I've been to since does) now. We trained barefoot on hardwood. Everyone else seemed to make it work just fine, but for me this was a painful adjustment.

After the first few sessions of shifting and pivoting on the hardwood, what *had* been my feet became almost unrecognizable. While my shins developed bruises and (very) slowly started to toughen up from kicking Thai pads, my feet became raw and blistered. Over the next months, I'd conduct increasingly elaborate experiments with Band-Aids, liquid Band-Aid, medical tape, and sports tape. My feet were disgusting. One day before kickboxing class, I sat on the edge of the tub with my foot up on my lap as I tended to a massive blood blister on the ball of my left foot. As I leaned in close, eyes trained on the bubble, the blister burst – and in the process, squirted a stream of blood straight into my eye. I retched as I threw my whole face under the bathtub faucet in an attempt to wash it all away. Still gagging, I towelled off my now-sopping head, cleaned the wound, and wrapped it up in time to make it to kickboxing class. As was my habit, I showed up half-mummified, cracking jokes to deflect the fact that my feet weren't even tough enough to stand the floor we were training on. I felt transparent: if I can't handle the floor, I clearly can't survive the actual sport.

Repetition is key to learning a skill. Kickboxing is no exception. Punching, kicking, and blocking motions are not necessarily intuitive, and they depart from my body's familiar movements. I repeated them over, and over, and over again, hoping to trick my mind and body into learning and internalizing new movement patterns. Now, taking myself through these repetitions is meditative. But that muscle memory had to be earned, and my body took time to adapt. Repetitive motion, like pivoting my foot for kicking drills, would deepen the slow-healing blisters in my feet. As the craters began to form some-times three wounds deep, there were days when I teared up pressing my feet to the gas pedal on the drive home from the gym. I tried to appear normal in front of others as I walked to my car, but back on my own, I crumpled a little. My feet burned. Those nights, as I often did on training days, I filled the tub with lavender-scented Epsom salts and ran a bath. On days when my feet bled or stung too much to dip in the water, I'd keep them dangled out the side of the tub. When I wanted to get out, I'd yell, and Leif would reach in and gently lift me to my feet. Shaking his head in disbelief at the blistered mess, he'd joke, 'Those are not the feet I married.'

The feet were the most obvious markers of what I was working through. They took the brunt of the work and their changes were painful, visible, and almost immediate. The bruises were equally tangible, so I began to photograph them occasionally, along with the blisters. As I asked my body to do new things, it became marked in all kinds of ways, many of which weren't tangible. Trying to func-tion in both a completely new physicality and a new world view was a daily trauma to my ego. Growing is hard. Knowing if it's actually worth the pain is also a bit of a crapshoot. Why would anyone put themselves through pain and suffering if they don't *have* to? Those first many months, especially, kickboxing training was a recurring exercise in humility, frustration, and failure. Walking in as someone without any relevant background and no exercise regimen to speak of, I was starting from scratch. More often than not, it didn't make me feel strong, powerful, or beautiful. Quite the opposite. As we trained in front of the mirror, I was as dismayed by the flawed body I saw reflected back as I was disappointed with its awkward movements and inability to master the techniques I saw so easily deployed around me. I held on to the idea that this would not always be the case.

In the meantime, my first coach was hard on us. As he pushed, I began to lean into the challenge because it felt familiar and alien at once. Toughness is a skill like any other. It has to be practised. With his teaching, I was slowly learning to accept and even embrace discomfort rather than shrinking from it. I had just fought to be certified an expert in my career, only to enter this new space where mastery was so far off as to seem impossible. Learning a new skill, especially as an adult, can be demoralizing and exhausting. The days when I broke under the pressure made me question who I was, what I was capable of, and who I should be. All the while, I appeared to others to adore kickboxing the way a person pursues someone who hurts them. It seemed like a bad fit.

Seeing me marked up, or beaten down, those close to me often encouraged me to slow down; they didn't understand why I was training at all. Combat sports really didn't fit my profile. I don't come across as angry, a requirement some assume is necessary for a violent sport. In fact, I can be easygoing and non-confrontational to the point of passivity. When I get upset, my default is typically to turn it all inward; I go off on my own, think it through, and sort it out myself. I had never been particularly concerned with fitness, either. I didn't check any of the obvious boxes for what would lead someone to want to fight. But while I couldn't fully articulate it at the time, I had fallen in love with the belief that I could still grow and change.

No matter how discouraged I felt, the payoffs of each small success were massive. My learning curve was steep. Every day brought something new. And every time I stuck it out, showed up, tried harder, fixed one small mistake (just to unearth five others), I came to expect more from myself. There was an immediate feedback and struggle that felt different from the second-guessing of academic work. Here, in the early stages, at least, I either knew something or I didn't. (Most of the time, I didn't.) There is no 'fake it till you make it' for a clumsy new kickboxer. Because I couldn't have pretended to be an expert even if I wanted to, there was no place for my ego. I was free to embrace my role as a beginner.

Some time after finishing my PhD, I was awarded a postdoctoral grant – two years of funding in order to conduct my own research and writing project. The postdoc is a position that floats somewhere after the degree but before the elusive white whale of a stable tenure-track job. I would work from within a department that hosted my research project by allowing me access to office space, library resources, and if I got really lucky, people to talk to. My funding was tied to an affiliation with the University of California, Santa Cruz. Leif and I had to make the hard choice for me to leave, yet again. The plan was that I would go back and forth whenever possible, sometimes for a semester at a time. But this postdoc turned out to be the last of a string of work-imposed separations. Throughout our fourteen years together, we had frequently spent months, even years, physically apart. For the first decade, he toured with bands and pursued his musical career. I was away for a year during my master's degree, another year and a half for fellowships in New York, and months of fellowships peppered throughout. As I neared the end of my years of graduate school, both my husband and our parents (and friends, and acquaintances) seemed to be doing a lot of reproductive math on my behalf. Everyone had waited through my years of school, and the clock was ticking. The people around me were planning for the baby that was meant to follow. But I wasn't so sure. I went back and forth between Vancouver and Santa Cruz, and eventually, Leif and I separated. The person – the life –I had known drove me back to California one last time, and we said goodbye.

Lost, I dove headlong into training. From my very first days in Santa Cruz, I had been made to feel welcome at a local MMA gym then called Kaijin, now Allied MMA. Some things just click. When I returned to California this time, quietly unwound, the gym held me together. The physical exercise, the problem solving, the distraction from my daily life, and the catharsis of hitting things (and people) and getting hit in return gave me an invaluable outlet. But in the wrong hands, surrounded by the wrong people, that work wouldn't have had the same effect. I was emotional, volatile, and vulnerable. I was lucky to find soft landing with a coach and a community who took me in; they both challenged and nurtured me. My new coach, Radetsky, taught kickboxing five nights a week, often double classes back to back. After my very first day in the gym, I never missed a class, and we developed a rapport quickly. Radetsky trained Kyokushin Karate in Japan for many years, and later training in kickboxing and Brazilian Jiu-Jitsu as well. He was extremely knowledgeable, kind, and multi-talented, and his passion for martial arts was immediately apparent. I observed as he kept a mental note of every student's tendencies and injuries and went around the class to quietly tailor moves and combinations to accommodate a weak knee, work around a student's eye condition, or demonstrate switching stances to avoid using a sprained wrist. If you showed up, he would help you find a way to make it work. As a result, the classes were fairly diverse, with a range of ages and levels of experience training together.

After years as a scrappy graduate student, I am essentially a stray cat – if you feed me, I will follow you almost anywhere. My new training partners invited me for post-training lunches, barbecues, home-cooked meals, even Thanksgiving dinners, and I jumped at the invitations. I sat alone with my research all day, and then allowed myself to be folded into this other world every evening and weekend. Like Tomoko, my very first training partner back in Vancouver, my teammates – Elaina, Rebecca, Natasha, Reem, Katia, Andie, Carla, Ale, and Mia, among others – showed me what women can do in martial arts, and how fun and loving that relationship can be. We are each other's toughest opponents and loudest cheerleaders.

Over the years, and across geographical distances, these people have become another family. Sam Paschel, an encyclopedic autodidact who gets more done in an hour than most people accomplish in a day, holds the centre. Radetsky and Paschel – the Sams – are former college-age roommates and old friends from their Santa Cruz bouncer and BJJ gym days, and they make a good team. The Sams have taught me, inspired me, and served as my 'seconds' both in actual fights and in daily life. With them, I started watching fights in earnest for the first time. I would sit in Radetsky's living room surrounded by a group of martial artists – BJJ, karate, and kickboxing practitioners and coaches – and study both what was happening onscreen and the reactions of those around me. I tried to see what they saw, and my much more experienced new friends patiently fielded my questions and walked me through what was going on. Beyond physical techniques, they were helping me to study fighting and its psychology from the inside out, and the outside in. This is how the next stage of my education began.

When my postdoc ended, I returned to Vancouver, and to my teaching job. In the fall of 2019, I was preparing for a fight. Eager to get more training in, I decided to try out a new gym, Diaz Combat

Sports. I first met Ryan Diaz when I was doing my trial class at his gym. He is a former professional MMA fighter who trains a number of high-level amateur and professional fighters. I showed up to try a noon class on a weekday, and he checked in with me afterward to see if I had any questions. I asked him about my options for female training partners and inquired about the gender dynamics at the gym. He explained the gym's programming, which includes daily women-only open gym and Muay Thai classes. He offered me a tour of the spaces, and we talked through my training goals and preferences. And then we ended up watching our way down a rabbit hole of YouTube fight footage at the front desk. Diaz has, since that first day, always been liberal with his help, whether it's to give feedback on sparring, to answer a question about an obscure technique, to point out a problem I'm having with a kick, or to let me pick his brain about the workings of the gym itself.

The DCS Muay Thai program is run by pro fighters and professional trainers, many of whom were lured over from Tiger Muay Thai in Thailand, including Kru Lamsongkram Chuwattana, a multi-time Thai stadium world champion, and a teacher whose traditional method I am worlds away from mastering. I quickly fell into the rhythm of the school, attending classes once or twice a day, as my teaching schedule allowed. Being back in Vancouver, alone, was a bit of shock to my system after the social nature of my life in California. On Sundays, when DCS was closed, I started attending another gym, Eastside Boxing Club, frequenting their 'Female Fighters' class – an advanced class for those who identify as women and want the opportunity to spar and train together in a space of our own. What drew me in initially, however, was that the two main coaches working with the female fight team, Jaime Ward-Yassin and Evelyn Calado, are both former Golden Gloves and national-level boxers. Ward-Yassin also competed professionally. Up to this point, I had never had a female coach. And now I had two. Because I didn't know the other women on the fight team, I got to know them in the ring first. It's a heck of a way to make a first impression. It was often not until after we'd sparred once or twice that we actually engaged (without our fists) and struck up a conversation.

★

I was working at a university and a college, teaching English literature, and regularly bouncing back and forth between Vancouver and California to keep up my research, visit friends, train, and compete, when, in the winter of 2019, I came across Facebook messages from an anonymous stalker. The stream of messages was located in my filtered mail, so I hadn't noticed them right away. These included photographs of me pulled from the internet, with commentary, as well as a litany of insults, threats, and vague accusations. I initially dismissed the messages almost out of hand – what woman hasn't received random threatening messages from strange men, I reasoned; I am practically overdue.

I eventually discovered that the person harassing me is one of my former students. I have since been bombarded with dozens of his messages and threats by way of all different forms and platforms, from emails to me and my employers, social media comments on public pages for my school and accounts belonging to my friends and family, to a series of copycat accounts created in my name and image. Some of the emails I received included photographs he took while I was teaching at the front of the class. These might be sent with commentary, zooming in on, isolating, and evaluating certain body parts. Some photos were clearly from a previous school semester, but others were pulled from my gym's social media accounts and websites. He had found images and footage from some of my fights online. Apart from the obvious themes when attacking a woman (appearance, check; sexuality, check), his emails began to comment on my brutality and my need for violence. He couldn't reconcile this aggressive figure in the photographs with how 'gentle' I am in class. To an outsider, and particularly one for whom women are allowed to be only one-dimensional, those things can't genuinely coexist. Women are soft or they are hard. There can be no other layers, no complications, no contradictions.

One day, I received a photograph that had to have been taken the week before. In it, I was pictured sitting alone on campus. The photograph was taken from a stereotypically voyeuristic vantage point, from underneath a staircase. This took the idea of being watched from something that had happened in the past to something that was actively occurring in the present. I started to feel waves of panic as I walked into the auditorium to teach my freshman classics lectures. I'd make my way down the aisle and stairs to the front of the room, clip on the lapel microphone, and then lift my gaze to the dark space that was suddenly filled not with students but with potentially volatile and threatening strangers.

When people around me found out I was being threatened, they were relieved to note that I know how to punch. Make no mistake – as studies on self-defence show, confidence, skill, and physicality can, and often do, save lives. At the same time, nothing is guaranteed. I am conscious of the limits of my skill and my size. The person who sends those messages is angry and afraid. He can't face me and instead does violence from the shadows. If he were to actually physically attack, he would not follow the rules and ethics of a face-to-face sporting match. Cowards don't want a fair fight. To this day, every time I think I've closed the book on that chapter, the stalker reappears. Like other unpleasant realities, I have come to live with the idea of this false relationship floating around me. It is connected to me but also separate. It affects me, but it's not *mine*.

He, like what he represents, is out of my control. In this, and in all other areas – from my career to my relationships and my training – I have support networks in place to help me. But, ultimately, I am responsible for myself. That would be a much scarier prospect if I hadn't had all of this practise learning to push my own boundaries. Through these years of training, I have moved my limits far beyond what I ever would have thought was possible. More than the physical strength, this ability to surprise myself, continually, is central to what fighting offers.

CHAPTER TWO
★
HISTORIES AND FUTURES

On April 1, 1987, Marian 'Tyger' Trimiar stopped eating. A 1979 Women's World lightweight champion and one of the first women to apply for a New York State boxing licence – she put in an application in 1974, which was denied, and then again in 1978, when it was finally granted – Trimiar, along with two other female boxers, embarked on what would (for Trimiar, the longest holdout) be a one-month hunger strike to raise awareness about women in boxing. The boxers were publicly advocating for better pay, better working conditions, and equal treatment for female professional boxers. They were willing to put their own bodies on the line for their cause. Their demands included major network coverage of women's boxing matches, equal pay with their male counterparts, and promotion of boxing as a tool for self-esteem and self-defence for girls and women. For these women, the task of raising the profile of one woman is inseparable from the effort to lift up all women in the sport, both present and future. The echoes of that idea are still clear today. In interviews after high-profile boxing matches such as Katie Taylor versus Delfine Persoon and Cecilia Braekhus versus Jessica McCaskill, the fighters (win or lose) use a significant portion of their post-fight airtime to drive home the same idea. They are ambassadors for women in the sport. This is a heavy responsibility, and an unfair burden to shoulder – especially while sweaty, tired, and smeared in blood – but it's one that many female fighters have taken on themselves. After all, if they don't do it, who will? In Trimiar's words, 'It's my heart, it's my love … Unless women get more recognition, we will be fighting just as a novelty for the rest of our lives. There will be no future.'

As Trimiar was fighting for her New York boxing licence, so was Jackie Tonawanda. When Tonawanda's application was also denied, she fought back on multiple fronts, suing the state for discrimination and then signing up for a physical fight to make her case for equality. Tonawanda – a boxer, not a kickboxer – agreed to a mixed-rules kickboxing match against a man. After some back and forth, she was eventually matched up with a kickboxer named Larry Rodania. The year before, Beth Bussey, 1974 international women's karate champion and first-degree black belt, took on Joe Hess, the world's heavyweight karate champion, in a competition to demonstrate technical skill. Bussey was winning the match on points when Hess switched to full-contact and knocked her out. When Tonawanda took her turn – notably fighting at much less of a weight and size disadvantage than Bussey, however – she suffered a hard hit from Rodania to the left side of her face in the first round. In the second, she knocked the man out.

These two are only a part of a surprisingly robust history of female fighters competing against men throughout history, often as a way for women to make a case for their right to be treated as equals within the ring. Women around the world have long fought for respect and recognition in their chosen careers. We don't know a lot about most of these women, because they were often fighting under the radar, competing in times and places where their very presence in the ring was illegal or taboo. But there are some stories, and some records. Bessie Williams and Josephine Green competed in a prize-fight for '$20 a side and the title of the colored lady championship' in 1882. Decades later, in 1957, Barbara Buttrick and Phyllis Kugler were granted the first boxing licences for women in the state of Texas. Buttrick, a British fighter who had to move away from her homeland to pursue her fighting career, was the first female boxer to have a fight broadcast on national television, in 1954. She later went on to found the Women's International Boxing Federation. Another groundbreaker, Eva Shain, became the first female judge in professional boxing, in 1975. And in 1993, a teenaged Dallas Malloy sued US boxing (U.S. Amateur Inc.) to allow women to compete in amateur boxing. When women's boxing finally debuted as an Olympic event in 2012, Nicola Adams of Great Britain, Katie Taylor of Ireland, and

Claressa Shields of the US become the first gold medal winners. Four years later, Shields made it two gold medals back to back, the first boxer of any gender to do so. In 2019, Zeina Nassar, a German boxer, was instrumental in getting the International Boxing Association to amend its guidelines, making it finally possible for fighters to compete in hijab. And this is just a handful of boxers. There is no shortage of female trailblazers in combat sports and martial arts.

This is an issue in itself. Blazing a trail for women in combat sports seems to be a Sisyphean task; it's the sadistic uphill rock-pushing CrossFit circuit that never ends. Women keep fighting to break down barriers, and popular history responds by forgetting their names. In a 1985 special NBC *Sportsworld* report on 'Women Who Fight,' the male reporter interviews a handful of tight-lipped women who *don't* fight (they are 'unanimously' against female boxing) and then some women who actually box (they are, not surprisingly, for it). To establish some context, the reporter digs deep – all the way back to the 1700s. 'From the origins of the sport,' the Voice of God narration explains gleefully, 'only men watched only men, and they fought, and they bet, and the women weren't invited!' He segues with 'So the women invited themselves' as a way to explain the new crop of 1980s women trying to get recognition in the sport, which ultimately plays to the tune of 'these women just want a chance.' While Male Voice is likely correct that women invited themselves, he is wrong about everything else. It's a common mistake.

Hand-to-hand combat in any form dates back at least to ancient Greece and Rome. The first traces of women's wrestling appear on bronze Etruscan statuettes in 330 BC, where women are depicted wrestling with men. What we now call boxing was first recorded and regulated in the early 1700s in England, though their 'boxing' included varying rule sets that might allow anything from bare-knuckle punches to eye gouging, the use of weapons, and more. As L.A. Jennings explains in *She's a Knockout: A History of Women in Fighting Sports*, nothing about the practice was as tidy as it might seem from where many of us sit today. While pugilism was predominantly prac-tised by men in this time, they were neither the only fighters nor the most famous. Even 150 years after her career ended, Elizabeth Wilkin-son Stokes was considered one of Britain's top boxers, full stop.

Stokes, the 'European Championess,' appears on the public record in London in 1722, when she challenged Hannah Hyfield to a boxing match. The challenge was published in the newspaper, as fight challenges were at that time. As the *London Journal* announced, despite the popularity of boxing in general, 'till last Week we never heard of Women being engaged in that Way, when two of the Feminine Gender appeared for the first Time on the Theatre of War at Hockley in the Hole, and maintained the Battle with great Valour for a long Time' – a reported twenty-two minutes non-stop – 'to the no small Satisfaction of the spectators.' Despite the newspaper's incredulity, Stokes and Hyfield were by no means the first women to set foot in the ring. With the increased popularity of print culture, however, they are among the first female 'Bruisers' on existing record. Following a win against Hyfield, Stokes continued competing both one-on-one and in mixed-gender doubles competitions (in this way like a very violent tennis match) alongside her husband, James Stokes, in front of audiences that would have included some women. But the 'Championess' wasn't alone. Women didn't fight only for titles, or stage their battles only in the boxing ring, for that matter – just as girls and women of all ages don't always reserve their fisticuffs for sanctioned rule sets and organized gym settings, even today. (Just take a survey of high school teachers).

A September 1805 issue of the *Times* recounts a fight between 'Miss B***r, sister to the renowned "Champion of England."' This wasn't a title fight. Her opponent was a woman with whom she had argued previously. They were fighting over a personal matter and choosing to sort out their conflict in the ring. This was, in other words, a good old-fashioned duel. As Jennings points out, 'perhaps the most fascinating part of the story is the final line, which states that "Miss B. was seconded by her mother."' I am also struck by the paper's editorializing claim that a fight like this was itself 'proof of the heroism of British Amazons, clearly evincing that the courageous blood which flowed through veins of our ancient countrywomen is not entirely extinct in the fair sex of the present day.' Not only is women's fighting celebrated here; it is imbued with nationalistic value. Not all accounts of female pugilism from that time are so positive, however. Media and public opinion oscillated in their response to the sight of women fighting. Nevertheless, the facts are that women fought, and fought well; that they often fought in what we would now consider extreme rule sets and conditions; and that the wider public knew about it.

It wasn't until later in the nineteenth century that the idea of women practising pugilism fell out of favour and Stokes, along with the other women who set foot into the ring (or shuffled their skirts and threw hands in the marketplace), got written out of the historical narrative. As historian Christopher Thrasher argues, despite being famous in her time and foundational to the early narratives of boxing in eighteenth-century England, Stokes was 'purposely ignored' within the sport's history 'when her narrative no longer supported newly dominant notions of gender hierarchy.' Overlooked fighters like Stokes are more the rule than the exception. And their absence has had lasting consequences for all of us. Countless female fighters have been pushed out of spaces and cultural histories that didn't know how to acknowledge their contribution without fearing that men were 'losing' something by sharing those spaces with them. This determined erasure slows women down, rewrites them into the margins, or actively enforces rule sets, restrictions, and social taboos so that many women never get to meet their full potential – but it never manages to shut us out completely.

NEW WOMEN

The fitness and martial arts movement found its stride in the early 1900s, in part as a result of a widespread social shift from rural to urban centres in the West, which brought about new ideas of personal mobility and the young, independent working woman. As urban populations became denser, more women worked outside the home, became politically active, and looked for ways to negotiate their place within spaces that counted them out. Self-defence training, and specifically martial arts and combat sports such as boxing and Japanese Jiu-Jitsu, became increasingly popular with women.

In her book *Her Own Hero: The Origins of the Women's Self-Defense Movement*, historian Wendy L. Rouse notes that the fitness movement was born of anxieties about a shift from physical labour to sedentary indoor work and its effects on the spirit and body. However, the push to regain some lost essential nature by taking up sport and wellness was (like so many things) driven partly by racist ideology. Though 'sport, health, and wellness' all sound positive (the second two in particular), the fitness movement was hem-deep in the mud of classism and eugenicist thinking. As always, no one 'women's' history is uncomplicated or equilateral across the board.

Bodies, we are repeatedly reminded, are always political. As Rouse explains, the fitness movement embodied a desire to strengthen 'white' stock through exercise at a time when immigrant birthrates were climbing. At the same time, more women, including more single women, were working in cities. No longer nestled away in the supposedly protected space of the home, they had to navigate street harassment and violence in these urban spaces. The culprits, so-called 'mashers' – men who threatened, catcalled, and sexually harassed women in public – and even more severe threats, like murderers and rapists, were publicly reimagined as the dark Other, the racialized male. These women were put on the alert as they moved through the public sphere without invested (middle-class, white) men at hand to protect them.

This new generation of women at the turn of the twentieth century had to be able to take care of themselves while continuing their avowed social responsibility to the nation and to patriarchy. City dwellers or not, they were expected to become good, upstanding citizens. For most, that meant fulfilling their duty as mothers. Middle-class white women were granted limited and conditional entry into the public and male-dominated arenas of sport, fitness, and martial arts as a way to stay fit – thereby producing a stronger 'race.' The idea that they were keeping themselves sanctified and unmolested against a racialized threat made their training socially palatable, but the reality was more complicated. Although the 'city' was presented as the site of violence, Rouse notes, these 'mashers' were in fact largely middle- and upper-class white men, not the racialized men scapegoated with all social evil. Meanwhile, women often experienced the greatest damage at the hands of the men in their homes and inner circles. The real violence here was the supposed patronage and protection of the men close to them. But that was a problem not easily solved by taking an exercise class. And even if it were, that was not a class an abusive husband would delight in his wife taking. Self-defence against domestic abuse was a threat to the patriarchal status quo. So, instead, many women went along with the narrative that their would-be attackers were all out there in the city, as opposed to within their own homes.

As they tried to keep fit, a number of women took advantage of the opportunity to choose 'male' avenues like boxing, the new fitness 'craze.' Boxing is, essentially, the art of trying to hit without getting hit back. Boxers use footwork, head movement, speed, and strategy to beat their opponent with only two weapons: the right fist and the left fist – or, more specifically, the knuckles on the index and middle fingers of each hand. While boxing used to take place in long, drawn-out fights that could run for hours, in the last couple hundred years, the sport has been whittled down to a limited number of timed rounds. Boxers train for speed, endurance, power, and skill through skipping rope and footwork drills. They practise shadowboxing and hitting heavy bags or pads. They work on sparring, a kind of practice-fighting of varying intensity, against a teammate or unofficial opponent. In the early twentieth century, most 'Boxing Girls,' as they were called, learned a lighter, fitness-based version that didn't necessarily involve the same gruelling training – and certainly not the hard sparring – that male boxers practised, though light sparring was an essential component.

Although the idea that women were learning to fight back against strangers played on the surface, the real anxieties about women's physical and social empowerment were reflected in the media, including cartoons in which hapless husbands appeared beaten up, their wives standing triumphant above them. In one, a defeated young husband cowers on the floor at the feet of his angry-looking wife, gasping, 'You didn't tell me you could box!'

The idea of a woman in the home who can box is one thing, but to imagine that a woman would want to take her recreational activity public is another. Those who chose to compete in any professional way were crossing a clear if invisible social and class-dividing line. At the same time, as Rouse is careful to point out, although fitness and martial arts became fashionable for middle-class Victorian and Edwardian women, they were by no means the only women learning to fight. Rather, as is so often the case, they thought they had discovered something new, because it was new to *them*. Working-class women and women of colour weren't counted into the fitness classes, but many would have been learning these moves and techniques informally from a young age; the need to protect themselves from men was a fact of life.

Culturally, the new female martial artist was synonymous with the figure of the New Woman, a character that signalled women's independence as well as some fear or disdain for men, depending on who was describing her. As Sarah Grand claimed in the 1894 essay that coined the term, the idea that women would focus on developing themselves, rather than depending on a man, 'must appear to [men] to be a thing as monstrous as it is unaccountable.' The discussion around the New Woman of 1894 exposed the seeds of gender anxiety that are still strangely traceable today. For a woman to take any kind of fitness, and especially martial arts, to an extreme, was transgressive and therefore politically suspect.

Around this time, Japanese Jiu-Jitsu made a controversial entrance in both the United Kingdom and the United States, often showing up the 'manly' science of Western boxing. Until people like US president Theodore Roosevelt took it up, Jiu-Jitsu (often used interchangeably with 'Judo' at the time) was denigrated as 'feminine.' So women took it up.

Jiu-Jitsu was brought from Japan to the West by male and female martial artists who taught seminars and opened schools. Initially taken up as a trend in self-defence parties for society women, the discipline quickly found practical application.

On November 18, 1910, later dubbed 'Black Friday,' a delegation of approximately three hundred women, many of them members of the Women's Social and Political Union (WSPU), went to the British parliament, demanding to be heard by the prime minister. They wanted the right to vote. Instead of receiving an audience with the PM, the women were assaulted, harassed, and groped by men drawn in to oppose them, and more than a hundred of the women were arrested. For a situation like this, the women might have armoured themselves by wearing cardboard under their clothes. After this incident, the suffragettes took increasingly militant measures to protect themselves, such as hiding wooden staffs under their skirts to be used as weapons, filling bouquets of flowers with barbed wire (a sharp surprise for police trying to overtake them as they blocked their speaker up on the stage), or wearing veils to disguise their leader in a crowd, in a shell game to keep the police from apprehending her.

Japanese Jiu-Jitsu is a martial art built on the use of leverage, positioning, pressure, and balance. Jiu-Jitsu practitioners shift their weight onto certain points of contact with their opponent in order to throw or immobilize them. By using an opponent's weight and momentum against them, Japanese Jiu-Jitsu enables a smaller, weaker person to overpower and even throw a much larger, stronger one. Its applicability for women was clear: it provided the skills to disengage from, escape, and even throw men – including police – who tried to detain or attack them. Martial arts training both mirrored and enabled their political project. One of the women working with the suffragettes was Edith Garrud – a famously unassuming-looking woman of four-foot-eleven who performed martial arts exhibitions dressed in a red gown. One of the world's first Western female martial arts instructors, Garrud trained in Japanese Jiu-Jitsu and was a strategic organizer. She had started training suffragettes in self-defence a couple of years earlier in her martial arts studio located inside a dance school. As the WSPU ramped up its protest efforts, it focused on physical training and strategy. 'Not all of the women who trained in boxing and jiu-jitsu' in the early 1900s 'had explicit political motives,' explains Rouse, but 'women's self-defence figuratively and literally disrupted the existing power structure. By physically embodying the political, these women stretched the limits of the definition of the "New Woman."'

One of the early English-language Jiu-Jitsu manuals is the 1906 gem *The Fine Art of Jujutsu*, by Emily Watts ('Mrs. Roger Watts'). Using the still relatively new technology of photography, the book demonstrates the moves 'with 141 Action Photographs by G. W. Beldam.' Watts appears visually within the book, outdoors on the grass, joyfully throwing both male and female training partners around like sacks of potatoes. She also adopts an interesting rhetorical perspective with her narration. Unlike most 'how-to' martial arts manuals I've come across – even those contemporary to hers – Watts brings herself into the student/reader's imagination. She starts systematically. 'The most simple throw is the Ashiharai (a) or ankle throw,' the instruction begins. And then she steps in. 'You will start by throwing me,' she announces. 'Take hold of my coat collar with your right hand high up on my chest' … and so it goes. She positions herself (both visually and linguistically) as both teacher and training partner. She continues, 'let my imaginary pupil dispel from *his or her* mind the idea that painful falls are a necessary adjunct to the practice of Jujutsu. Everything depends on the teacher and if you will trust me I will take you to the end of the book without any mishap and hardly a bruise.' (My emphasis.) Nevertheless, she concedes, 'I cannot absolutely promise to keep you entirely free from these because you will sometimes give them to yourself until you become adept.' Watts takes pains to reassure the novice not only that she is looking out for them but that they won't get hurt or – significantly for the women – visibly bruised in the process. From that preamble on, Watts is in it with us.

It wasn't unusual for female instructors to be enlisted to teach other women. While this was a practical concern for suffragettes, for instance, who were often training under the radar, removing men from the training equation also creates a different dynamic. Seeing the moves modelled by a woman, someone who seems physically comparable to you, not only shows how the techniques might work for your body type; it also has the effect of simply demonstrating that these moves are *possible* for you. Watts was somewhat exceptional, especially for her time, in that she guided a mixed audience, both in her book and in her studio. By bringing in her own body for demonstration, she made the book accessible to her contemporary female readers. At the same time, she performed a model for men that normalized training with – and learning from – women.

A RESURGENCE

With the advent of second-wave feminism in the 1960s came a new wave of popularity for women's martial arts. Here, too, it was largely packaged as a form of self-defence. While often treating it as a diversion, the media paid some attention to this growing movement, albeit with mixed results. Each new wave of feminism seems to think they invented self-defence; popular discourse appears unaware of the work so many women have put in generations before.

In 1970, journalist Diana Gerrity participated in a self-defence course for an *Atlantic* article entitled 'Miss Superfist.' 'It comes as a small shock to realize that the side of your hand is a lethal weapon,' she writes. 'You've served tea, pounded typewriters, scribbled poetry, and powdered babies with it, made love, scrubbed linoleum, and run computers; now it can break a neck.' Note the juxtaposition here of what a woman's hands can and should do. The multiplicity of female roles and identities, the 'shock' of combining these with violence, is foregrounded here as a kind of paradox. In using the second-person perspective, Gerrity seems to encourage female readers to look down at their own hands and see those possibilities. When Gerrity puts this potential within women's grasp, it also sets up a contrast. Here, women are allowed to be multifaceted in a way that men are not. The idea of a man using his hands for violence doesn't shock anyone at all but rather is presented as 'natural.' Some creative packaging is still necessary to sell self-defence and martial arts training for women.

FEMALE BOXERS RETURN TO THE RING

While women continued to train in self-defence and martial arts throughout the nineteenth and twentieth centuries, women's boxing underwent a public resurgence in the 1990s. One of the first high-profile professional female boxing fights from that time is a match between Christy 'The Coal Miner's Daughter' Martin and Deirdre 'Dangerous' Gogarty, which appeared on an undercard for the Mike Tyson versus Frank Bruno fight.

This match drew grudging respect from critics and audience members. It was a breakthrough moment in boxing history: the space of the ring was remade. But we often don't know history is about to happen until the moment that it does. Audience members and viewers watching the card from home, individuals who had never seen Martin fight before, and who prided themselves on being boxing fans, heard a women's match announced and made cynical plans to go get a beer or change the channel.

But then Gogarty, in a sleeveless white top and white shorts with green trim, and Martin, in her signature pale pink tank top and satin boxing shorts, started to fight. Not only did the women immediately silence naysayers with a relentless pace that shocked even the professional commentators, but they fought with that ultimate combination: technique and heart. Between the commentators and the post-fight interview, all of the classic buzzwords for praising boxers were brought into play, and often in ungendered, unqualified ways. The men acknowledged the difference in pacing between women's two-minute rounds and men's three-minute rounds but described the women's intensity as 'amazing' by any measure. Gogarty was repeatedly extended a classic boxing compliment – she was noted for her 'chin' as she took hard hits from Martin, who was known for her knockout power. (Over the course of her career, Martin KO'd half of her opponents.) Both fighters were commended for their skill. As one commentator mused early in the fight, in a compliment that seems somewhat backhanded in retrospect despite being unqualified in the moment: 'Their technique is excellent. They have mastered not just the basics but some of the subtle nuances of the game.' The other announcer, a professional fighter himself, made a shift in language partway through the fight. As the women gained his respect, he began to include them in the 'we' of pro boxers as he talked about himself and his experiences. He went so far as to say they were not being paid enough for what they'd just done, and that he would have liked to have one of these women as his training partner. He said this not as a joke but as a sign of acceptance. But beyond the pace, technique, and gameness of the fighters, what really tipped the scales to make this fight famous, solidifying Martin's place in boxing history, was the *blood*.

In the early rounds, Gogarty found repeated success landing her right hook to Martin's face, and Martin's nose started to bleed. Partway through the fourth round, Gogarty connected again, higher on Martin's nose. The already bloody appendage started to gush. Between rounds, when the ring doctor approached Martin and her team (who were working industriously to slow the blood) to see if she could continue, she told him, 'I'm all right.' To the delight of the announcers, she flashed a big, wide smile to reinforce her claim.

Posturing for the ring doctor is important. The doctor is the person who decides whether you get to continue or not, and if they have reason to worry, they might stop the fight. Instead of simply insisting on her desire to continue, Martin disarmed with charm. It's not exactly common to see a bleeding fighter cracking a smile on the bench in the middle of a fight. Martin and Gogarty fought through the rest of the full six rounds. Martin bled all the while and was ultimately granted the win by unanimous decision. The announcers weren't the only ones bowled over by the women's toughness. The fighters' mix of skill, resilience, and intensity went a long way toward changing popular opinion about women's boxing. But this grit, in the memory of audience members and critics alike, takes the form of Martin's bright red blood, splattered across clothes and canvas in dramatic fashion. This is a 'non-title fight but they're fighting like they've got a championship at stake,' one announcer observed. And, indeed, they did. These women knew that every time they stepped into the ring, they were fighting for much more than just one win.

While battles like those between Martin and Gogarty made waves because of their visibility, capitalizing on the TV showcase of a big fight card, other struggles have been more frequently overlooked. In the latter part of the twentieth century, women's boxing was not getting much, if any, serious attention or financial support. Those with time and means to pursue the sport, and who were finding support for their efforts, were largely white, middle-class women. The idea of women fighting professionally has always been fraught. But for women of colour, this is exponentially truer. Trimiar and Tonawanda toiled for years for the right to hold professional boxing licences, for instance. When their initial applications were denied, Tonawanda filed her lawsuit and Trimiar took her case to the Human Rights Commission in New York. The effort to overturn the ruling barring women from boxing was eventually joined by another boxer, Cathy 'Cat' Davis. As Jennings explains, Davis was positioned as a point of contrast to the Black, 'Amazonian' Trimiar and Tonawanda. Thin, blonde, and white, Davis was frequently described as beautiful, apparently more like a ballet dancer than a fighter. She was featured, however controversially, as the first female boxer to appear on the cover of *The Ring* (or of any other major sports magazine) and, for almost twenty years, the only woman to have been featured on one of these covers. This is not to suggest that Davis's appearance takes anything away from her boxing ability, of course. She was fighting to develop a women's boxing federation in her own right, and her easy marketability no doubt helped to raise the profile of the cause. But the emphasis on her looks highlights just a fraction of the gender and racial politics at play long before fighters even make it to the ring.

Four years after Tonawanda and Trimiar's initial application, the ban on women's boxing was lifted. When the three women filed into the office and stood together to receive their licences, it was Davis who physically received hers first. Many called her the 'first woman' to have a licence in the state, and she was central in press photograph. Davis was apparently less 'intimidating,' and therefore an easier sell, than the Black women beside her. To complicate matters further, Jennings points out that at least one critic went so far as to hail Davis as the 'Great White Hope'; in the era of Muhammad Ali, perhaps the women's division would allow white fight fans to lick their wounds and imagine supremacy in the ring. As is still the case today, Black women are stuck fighting battles that started well before and extend far beyond them.

ON THE MAT

Decades after Japanese masters brought their martial art to the United Kingdom, it was introduced in Brazil and adapted into what became (at least in one version of the story) Brazilian Jiu-Jitsu. This form of Jiu-Jitsu used leverage to stand in for strength, adapting it for a potentially weaker frame. That wasn't particularly new – in Japan, the practice was egalitarian, and smaller women had already been training in Japanese Jiu-Jitsu for generations – but this iteration of Jiu-Jitsu focused less on the stand-up element and more on what would happen *after* the throw.

BJJ depends on the closest of physical proximity. Like Japanese Jiu-Jitsu, it allows a smaller, weaker fighter to defend themselves against – and even to dominate – a bigger, stronger assailant. BJJ accounts for what to do even if you are taken to the ground or attacked from behind, positions that are simply against the rules in most striking sports, despite being the likeliest forms of attack in daily life. Chances are I can't knock out a man with the massive power of my 120-to-125-pound frame. What I can potentially do, though, is negotiate myself into a position where I can cut off his air supply. In addition to the throws of Japanese Jiu-Jitsu, there is the option to negotiate with, and even immobilize your opponent, on the ground. I don't *necessarily* need to be powerful; if I understand principles of leverage and weight distribution, I can use his own weight and power against him.

Mixed Martial Arts (MMA) combines disciplines such as Jiu-Jitsu, boxing, kickboxing, and more. Those with a solid grappling background (from wrestling or Jiu-Jitsu, for example) tend to do well in MMA, as there is always the option to take the fight to the mat and off the feet. But MMA fighters also need a solid enough striking base, and kickboxing is essential to this equation. Kickboxing is not, as some might assume, just boxing with kicks. The term is a bit of a catch-all for a number of disciplines, including Japanese and Dutch kickboxing, and Muay Thai, 'the art of eight limbs.' If boxing allows a refined focus on two 'limbs,' Muay Thai adds two legs for kicking calves, thighs, the body, and the head; two knees for throwing strikes to the body or head; and two elbows for slicing strikes to the face and head. It also relies heavily on the clinch, where fighters hold each other, use their weight, and try to control their opponent on the feet. (Most kickboxing follows K1 rules, which take out the elbows and the ability to sweep your opponent's leg out from under them.) Kickboxers can block (or 'check') kicks from their opponents by lifting and meeting the kicker's sharp shins with their own. Whereas Muay Thai has a rule and point set built around an ethos of holding your ground and trading strikes, Dutch style encourages more evasion and movement, making it look a little more like boxing. Depending on the rule set, kickboxers can also sweep or trip their opponent when they lift a leg up to kick. The multitude of tools available to a fighter opens them up to an equal multitude of possible threats. While boxers can dip their head down very low to evade a punch, for instance, the same movement would be extremely dangerous for a kickboxer. The lower you bring your head, the closer and more vulnerable it is to getting kicked or kneed. Kickboxers and boxers therefore train their movement patterns differently, and they have to shift priorities in order to attend to different possible attacks (both their own and their opponent's).

None of these disciplines is practised quite the same way in MMA as it would be on its own. When they're put together, each has to be adapted in some way. Just as the boxer had better not dip their head down in kickboxing, a kickboxer might think twice before really committing themselves to a kick in MMA. Throwing a hard kick often means pivoting, turning your hip, and shifting your weight into the strike in order to get power. If you turn your hip in front of a grappler, however, they can use the weight imbalance to jump you and take you down to the ground. A hybrid, MMA is a sport of its own.

MMA fighters combine diverse specialties in order to make their own version of MMA. Yuka 'Vale Tudo Queen' Tsuji was a dominant figure in the first decade of twenty-first-century women's MMA, as was Jiu-Jitsu and sambo practitioner Megumi Fuji. A number of renowned kickboxers have made the transition to MMA, as well. Women have made their way through the ranks of the sport since the 1990s, including competing in groundbreaking all-women's divisions like Japan's Smackgirl (started in 2001 and later renamed Jewels) and Invicta Fighting Championships. Women had their first main event fight in Strikeforce in 2009, and in 2012, US Olympic medallist and judoka Ronda Rousey became the first woman signed to the popular Ultimate Fighting Championship (UFC), quickly joined by Liz Carmouche, the first openly LGBTQIA2S+ fighter in the organization. An ever-expanding audience took notice.

Women practising combat sports like MMA is nothing new, however. Contemporary MMA has as much in common with eighteenth-century pugilism as 'boxing' does – maybe more. When Elizabeth Wilkinson Stokes and her peers were climbing up into public arenas in the 1700s, looking to fight, boxing wasn't the relatively sanitized affair it is now. Each pair of opponents could negotiate its own requirements and rule sets, but these could include punches as well as kicks, hair pulling and biting, eye gouging – and sometimes even the use of weapons. They were fighting with 'no holds barred.' Though they might be some of the first names to appear in printed record, there's no way they were the first women to hold their own in the ring. And that was three hundred years ago.

As we wrestle with questions of gender and identity in relation to women's fighting, one constant is the long-standing relationship between fight training and social action. Physical activism, like that demonstrated in the 1900s, still stands, albeit in different forms. Perhaps the idea of fighting resonates most deeply in those for whom just entering the gym is already a battle. For contemporary elite boxer and coach Miosha Wagoner, there's a 'warrior mentality' inherent to fight training. Boxing, she says, 'helps you see who you are. It breaks you down and forces you to face your fears. If you're not doing something right, boxing makes you feel that. You get punched in the face.' Beyond individual growth, however, Wagoner also sees the social value for this kind of training. 'It empowers you to see your strength and the things that you can do.' A Navajo and Chickasaw woman, Wagoner is also a boxing trainer at Haskell Indian Nations University in Kansas, with degrees in American Indian Studies and Conflict Management and Dispute Resolution. She trains other Indigenous fighters by the same principles and through the same lens she views activism – as a way to 'find strength from within conflict.'

In the gym, you get a glimpse of what you are capable of outside it. This does not have to stand as solely an individual endeavour. Self-empowerment doesn't have to be selfish. For many, learning to fight means learning how to stand up, speak, protest, and push for what is right.

CHAPTER THREE

★

SELF-DEFENCE

Long before I first spar in kickboxing, I get a small taste of what physical fighting is like. I am new to the sport – only a few months into training at my first gym – and despite his commitment to instructing me in theory and technique, my coach has openly expressed his skepticism that I have what it takes to ever fight. (This assesment doesn't faze me much because at this point I have no plans to actually compete). Worse than my advanced age, I appear to be lacking something even more elusive than physical skill or athleticism. I am, in his words, 'the least aggressive person he has ever met.' On one sunny Sunday afternoon, only two students show up to class. It's just me and a man named Dave. Dave is strong and athletic, and has been training for years. He attends both the kickboxing and Jiu-Jitsu classes every week. We have trained together since I first started. He is welcoming, patient, friendly, and good natured. Dave is the kind of affable guy who seems to get along with everyone. On impulse, or because he wants the answer to an unasked question, my coach decides to give me a bit of a test scenario to see how I'll do in a fight. I am unskilled, inexperienced, tentative despite my desire to succeed, and have never really negotiated any kind of kickboxing movement beyond standing in one spot and shadowboxing or hitting pads. So, he decides, I am going to see what fighting is actually like.

Within reason, of course. My coach sets the rules: Dave is not allowed to strike me at all, so I'm in no danger of being hurt. Instead, my big, strong, male opponent has one job: to grab me and take me to the ground as many times and as quickly as he can. My one job: do anything I can to stop him.

The outcome is predictable. I am easily overpowered, don't actually know how to throw strikes at a moving target (so many moving parts!), and don't know how to create space for myself. He tries to grab me. I try to fight. I don't know how. Dave hovers in front of me and takes me down once, twice, and then on repeat. When the class time runs out, we stretch, laugh together, visit, and go our separate ways. As I leave the gym, though, nothing feels the same. It's as if the world is just as it was, only slightly off kilter. It takes me days to mull over what I have just experienced. Maybe this approach is similar to what people get out of self-defence seminars. My sense, though, is that those are meant to lead to a kind of revelation: 'This is how you fight back.' In our exercise, I got the struggle without the feeling of empowerment. I had no faith in my still-awkward tools, and I showed myself to be neither capable nor confident enough to use them. If I was supposed to have applicable skills by that point, I didn't, and I knew it.

What stands out to me both then and now is the trust I hand over within that space; we're in a dark but windowed studio in a quiet gym. It's just me and two strange men. One of them is trying to attack me, and the other is watching. Yet when my coach sets out the terms, I don't question it. A student by nature and profession, I do what I'm told, despite how counterintuitive it seems for me, as a woman, to enter willingly into this scenario. *How did I get here?*

They both refer to it afterward as the moment their perception of me changed, however slightly. 'There was something in your eyes,' they say, describing how I struggled somewhat angrily to hold my ground. But what they identified is something I already know is there. I grew up with brothers; I didn't necessarily know how to fight back when attacked or antagonized, but I learned almost by instinct how to infuriate someone by laughing in their face and taunting, 'Do it again' – even if I said it with tears streaming from my eyes. I couldn't win, but I could take some of the satisfaction out of the beating. But these guys don't know me yet, not really, and so the fact that I got a little bit mean instead of folding up and conceding seem to be a welcome surprise.

I wasn't in any real danger, I wasn't hurt, and I didn't feel legitimately threatened in any cold, rational way. I had wanted to get a better idea of what fighting would be like. At the same time, though,

I felt deeply troubled. Something had woken up inside me that I had refused to acknowledge on a visceral level.

I spend the next couple of days emotionally suspended across multiple timelines. The struggle brings me back to moments I had forgotten on any level other than a dull, general memory. Part of me is eighteen again, at a friend's party, when I suddenly find myself pushed into a bedroom by a football-playing schoolmate I barely know. As I struggle underneath the bigger man and try to escape from beneath his weight, his friends come rushing in to break it up. Other memories keep touching me, even ones that seem small and inconsequential, or ones I didn't have the language to braid together – times men I was dating blocked doorways when we were arguing so that I couldn't leave, cars I was pinned against, the feeling of a big, strong grip around my arm to keep me from running away. I had forgotten almost all of it. But my body hadn't. The exercise itself was physically harmless, and yet I live with all those hands on me for days after.

ME TOO

Only about a month into kickboxing training at my first gym, I'd gotten comfortable enough, socially, to linger a little as I packed up. One day, I even stayed and sat around to visit with other students after class instead of hurrying shyly away. As we packed up our gear, one of the male students casually inquired: 'So what happened to you?' I was confused. 'When women come in and learn to fight, it's usually because they've been attacked or something,' he said. At the time, I was appalled at the stereotype. It's reductive, I thought, and demeaning to recast women's hard work and ambition in the gym as reactive self-defence. I don't need a *reason* to want to learn how to hit things. I can do this because I *want* to, not because of some guy.

But after my experience with that first full-contact exercise, I had to second-guess myself a little bit. I thought nothing had ever happened to me, when, actually, lots of things had happened. And beyond that, the threat of worse things is always there. Despite being intellectually aware of what was and was not acceptable behaviour, and knowing what made me personally uncomfortable, I still hadn't admitted to myself that a lot of these 'small' gestures, or even outright attacks, counted. There is always the potential for something worse, I thought (and still often do, in spite of myself); I have been incredibly fortunate. On some level I accepted the conditioning that taught me to think anything I had experienced simply didn't matter. I wasn't thinking about self-defence because I didn't really believe these were legitimate threats from which I needed defending. But if I didn't know where the line was for men familiar to me – not strangers, but often acquaintances or boyfriends – how could I articulate that they had crossed it?

VICTIM

In a 2015 study of professional and elite female Muay Thai and MMA fighters, researchers Mark Mierzwinski and Catherine Phipps tried to get a sense of why these women have chosen to participate in 'hard' and largely male-dominated martial arts. The women explained that these combat sports give them 'opportunities to: (1) enjoy the feeling and significance of being physically violent; (2) feel pleasurable emotions that were difficult to achieve in other realms of social life; (3) be physically tested, physically suffer and test their mental ability when pushed to their physical limits; and (4) test their mental and physical defences against "realistic" forms of violence.' The women also value these activities for the chance to 'challenge certain conventions of femininity.' The fighters are, nevertheless, 'balancing' a gender-challenging activity with normative gender identities. It is worth noting that the subjects were predominantly cisgender women, whose presentation as hegemonically feminine outside of the gym context was considered important as a way to negotiate, or counterbalance, their fighting. 'Hard' martial arts training, the study concluded, gave these women a safe space to reverse gender roles and practise taking on more power. It created a controlled simulation in which they could experiment with different roles. Within these simulations, they no longer stood in the role of 'victim,' and were therefore no longer in need of a male protector.

Does that power extend outside the gym? One of the things this dynamic is supposed to provide is the ability for women to become their *own* protectors. It is a way for women to remove themselves from the 'victim' role prescribed for them in the male/female binary model. This argument suggests that, in a quietly radical move, women learning to fight is meant in some way to take down that system entirely. I have to admit, I didn't think of it in those terms until recently.

SELF-DEFENCE

Growing up, I was taught how to hold my keys between my fingers to keep them accessible in case I needed a weapon or a quick exit into the house; not to wear headphones (or later, earbuds) in public; and *never* to walk alone at night. But somehow, that most fundamental lesson just didn't fully stick. I love walking alone in the dark, and I do it all the time.

Still, as I walk, I am reminded of danger. I was taught to always move like I had a purpose. Appearing lost or unguarded would make me more of a target. But in all those years, apart from the abstract key-as-weapon in my hand nestled in my pocket, the idea of 'self-defence' never really entered my mind. I didn't prepare any further than the idea of simply trying not to look too abject. As a young woman, I always knew 'target' was my default. No matter what role I might want to pretend to play, I was typecast. Nevertheless, I walked. On the nights when I thought better of it and kept myself at home instead, I stewed.

Self-defence is a general term for some form of physical training combined with psychological, verbal, and boundary-setting exercises. Due in part to its active, physical component, some of the women involved in the second wave feminist movement in the 1990s, 'self-defencers' like academic Martha McCaughey, struggled to reconcile their feminist beliefs with their physical training. What initially stymied McCaughey and others was not so much the impetus to learn practical self-defence – it was clear that women needed to learn to protect themselves. What she wrestled with, as a good liberal feminist whose ideological platforms were built, in part, on a foundation of women's inherent and celebrated difference from men, was a new aptitude for what she had believed was 'masculine' violent action. Even beyond discovering her own ability to be violent,

McCaughey was shocked by how much she *enjoyed* it. Her interviews with her self-defence training classmates and instructors show that the majority of the women didn't feel that their femininity was compromised by opening themselves up to violence and physical training; rather, they claimed to feel like 'better' women when they fought. They weren't becoming 'better' by behaving more like men. Rather, '[s]elf-defense transforms the way it feels to inhabit a female body,' McCaughey explains. 'It changes what it means to be a woman.' They didn't see the so-called 'masculine' qualities of aggression or violence as antithetical to their female identities at all. Rather, these were, for them, feminine strengths that had been buried and were being excavated, one punch, kick, or choke at a time. They had found what they felt to be their true selves, buried beneath.

This feminist approach to physical training was not new, even then. The fitness and suffragette movements of the early 1900s point to the complicated and ongoing relationship between women, martial arts, and power. People all over the world still negotiate with questions of how to defend themselves, and how to hold their own within social and political spaces that would have them play the role of victim. While the party line has long been that women are vulnerable and men are physically stronger, that women should be protected and men should know how to guard both themselves and those around them, those lines are in fact not as clearly drawn by gender, race, or class as some might assume. There is still debate over whether self-defence actually *works* for women and others who are perceived as weak or vulnerable. The common idea that they will be emboldened by their training and take reckless risks – that too much confidence will lead them into trouble – is clearly driven by an agenda. And yet many women still accept this supposedly built-in limitation.

If men's fighting grows out of the idea of the duel, as is so often suggested, then the equivalent for female self-defence is the fear of rape. Men duel for honour. Sometimes to the death. For women, or others who have power imposed on them through sexual violence, rape is considered by many to be the death of virtue. But by that logic, the idea of some intact virtue is, in essence, still a duel between men. Women and targeted groups are aiming for freedom, mobility, and survival. The difference in what's on the line remains fairly stark.

It's not simply 'Can I win and uphold my family's honour?' but rather *'Can I not die?'*

FUTURE POSSIBLE

In 2017, #MeToo swept into popular culture, catalyzed in part by allegations against former film producer and now convicted sex offender Harvey Weinstein. With it, the conversation around boundaries, consent, and even micro (and more overt) aggressions expanded. It was a watershed moment, and long overdue. But I started kickboxing the year before that, which, discursively, was a lifetime away. Despite being both a feminist and a word person by profession, I had not found my way to the necessary language to categorize these kinds of experiences. It was already there, and I knew the words, but their meaning is still only sinking in, even now.

There has been a marked increase in self-defence classes since about 2015, even before #MeToo. There are clear reasons for this proliferation of seminars for women and LGBTQIA2S+ folks, with classes where Muslim women learn to thwart attacks targeting them for wearing a hijab, for instance. Xenophobia and white supremacist ideas seem to be increasingly normalized with each passing day. With a greater sense of general threat has come a wider acknowledgement of women's self-defence needs within previously male-dominated spaces. One-off classes can be a promotional tool to get women's wallets through the door (with a hope it will lead to gym memberships), but most of the best outreach programs are offered for free and teach practical, applicable skills. At the same time, they create a point of access through what tends to be a safe and welcoming space, opening an otherwise intimidating environment to people who might not normally feel welcome.

According to Jocelyn A. Hollander's 2010 study of a self-defence course on an unnamed university campus, women enrolled for a few reasons. First, the class came highly recommended by friends; the necessary permission and encouragement often comes from other women. Second, they wanted to invest in the potential of what Hazel Rose Markus and Paula Nurius call 'future possible selves.' They might be imagining some version of themselves in the future, 'someone who is assertive, self-confident, self-reliant, and able to move freely in the world.' As Hollander notes, they see the selves they could become, as well as 'the selves [they] are afraid of becoming.' Significantly, this re-imagining involves a hopeful step toward what Hollander calls 'a new conceptualization of gender.' The third-most common reason was a fear of possible violence. However, the main reasons women give for taking self-defence have to do with some form of community and their own place, their own sense of identity, within it.

But the process of re-imagining oneself isn't easy. It does not take place in a vacuum. Many of us are indoctrinated with the idea that we should be polite. I heard a story (on a podcast, I think) about a trans woman who found herself repeatedly bumped into or knocked while walking down the street. When she presented as a man, other men moved around her; that's what she was used to. Now they no longer did. With a lifetime of peripatetic training in the art of taking up space, she wasn't moving out of the way, and neither were the men around her, who had also learned, however unconsciously, to navigate the same way. Intrigued by this idea of the unconscious deference expected of certain walkers, I started to experiment. I went through, and often still step into, stubborn phases of weeks, or months, where I consciously fought the urge to move my body out of men's way. It's a game of (walking) chicken. Either they make the course correction, or we collide. Any guesses on what happens? (Like so many things, this exercise is on hold for COVID-19, but the need for it feels even stronger, as I frequently find myself having to dive into the street to single-handedly maintain social distance.) The idea that women are passive or compliant is a cliché. Women speak their minds, contribute to society, hold positions of power, and move through the world all the time. And yet even in the physical minutiae – the gendered embodiment performed by simply walking down a crowded sidewalk, for instance – my body is repeatedly jostled out of place by hard, oblivious shoulders.

Hollander followed up with the self-defence study subjects a year later to determine whether those who took the class had in fact realized the new potential selves so many of them had hoped to become. Researchers have long established that self-defence training for women and minorities brings, among other positive outcomes, 'improvements in self-esteem, self-efficacy, assertiveness, and fighting skills, as well as reduced fear.' But the results of Hollander's follow-up suggest that the value of this kind of training goes even further. The women who studied self-defence reported fewer sexual assaults than their non-self-defence counterparts, as well as proportionately fewer attempts.

This study shows that such training 'both changes women's responses to assault *and* changes women's behavioural or inter-actional patterns,' making the women 'better able to discern the warning signs of assault, clearer about their own desires in an inter-action, and more willing to speak and act on their own behalf, all elements that may reduce the odds of attempted or completed sexual assault.' By learning to establish clear boundaries from the outset, the women who have studied self-defence seem to be more confident in general, have more mobility and freedom, and inhabit the world in a way that allows them to feel less afraid. At the very least, they have the skills to anticipate and de-escalate potentially troublesome situations earlier than their untrained counterparts. Their confidence doesn't make them reckless; it makes them better able to read and navigate their surroundings.

These participants do not suddenly become superwomen or hardened fighters. Each brings different physical abilities and histories. Self-defence training isn't magic. What the students have in common, however, is that their eyes are open, and they are willing to use their voice as a tool. One former student recounted an instance where a man grabbed her and began to harass her at a bar: 'I turned around … I looked him in the eye and said, "We don't know each other. Don't touch me." This is huge for me,' she says. 'I didn't used to look men in the eye, and most often when I say things, it's too quiet for people to hear.' This is a common refrain among self-defence advocates. Regardless of general physical ability, let alone combat skills, the sense of confidence – even displayed as subtly as a vocalized 'no' or direct eye contact – makes a difference. The same mental calculations that fighters make apply here, and the stakes have the potential to be even higher.

As studies and anecdotal accounts agree, even if you can learn all the moves in one day, or in one series of seminars, that doesn't mean you will be able to execute them in a high-stress situation. Training is a process, and even consensual fights get messy. But the key here is that just because it isn't guaranteed to work, that doesn't mean it is guaranteed to fail, either. Ryan Diaz echoes a common and in many ways fundamental belief of self-defence training: you are likelier to get away if you *try* than if you don't. 'What's the first rule of fighting?' he prods. 'You have to go out there *believing* you can win.'

BOUNDARIES

When it comes to martial arts, including self-defence, many of the principles of technique actually seem quite counterintuitive. Our bodies want us to close our eyes to protect the delicate orbs when something is coming at them, for instance, but that's the worst thing you can do when someone strikes at you. It just makes you more vulnerable, with no way to protect yourself. Despite this work to reprogram my earlier coding, I still don't have a full sense of what 'fighting' is like for a lot of other people, when conflicts are immediate, unregulated, and not for sport.

In promotional material for the earnestly named Women Empowered program, connected to the 'Gracie University' BJJ system, Eve Torres Gracie makes a case for the program's necessity: 'In a perfect world, women wouldn't need self-defence because men wouldn't perpetrate these crimes ... but the world is far from perfect.' Even today, the narrative remains about men. Sadly, Torres Gracie isn't wrong. It should go without saying (but also bears repeating) that the men who attack women are the problem, not the women. Boys and men should be raised to understand the implications of violence and to value consent; as a society, we have to hold men to higher standards of behaviour and accountability. But that significant evolution in education and regulation doesn't happen overnight, and I've still got to live in this world. So I keep watching the promotional clip: The first lesson, Torres Gracie instructs, well before any fight or attack breaks out, is that 'the most important self-defence tool that all women possess is the ability to set boundaries: verbal, physical, and psychological.' She continues: 'The challenge is that most women won't establish boundaries that they don't feel capable of enforcing.' The key, she notes elsewhere, is to establish boundaries ahead of time, not only as a signal to the other person but also as a testing ground *for yourself*. This is about confidence in your own judgment and ability. Not sure if you should have your guard up, or be prepared to use violence if necessary? If you set a boundary and the other person disregards it, then you have your answer. This lesson extends into all areas of life. For me, unpacking and internalizing the idea of proactive boundary setting is going to take some work and some time.

Consider the physical aspect of boundary setting. Rule-based combat sport training is often interwoven with tactical life skills and practical self-defence training that extend beyond the arena. It's against the rules to kick someone in the groin in sport combat, for instance, and yet that also happens to be a fairly effective move if you are being attacked by a man. A violent attacker is not going to stop choking you when you tap – you'll have to actually choke them or break a limb. They won't be wearing padded gloves, and no attacker will simply lower their hands and walk away when the sportsmanlike two, three, or five minutes are up.

The very first lesson of kickboxing, from day one, begins with the most basic and important thing: learn your footwork. Learn how to be quick and navigate well on your feet. This readiness is essential for most martial arts competition, but it also applies in real life. When you have good footwork, you use it to establish boundaries and maintain your safe distance. 'How do you fight in a street fight?' one of the male students in my class asked the rough-and-tumble kickboxing coach one day. 'You don't,' the coach replied. 'You run.'

STRIKING DISTANCE

Footwork and body awareness are key. Faced with a potential threat, instead of standing square in front of the person, you can start to subtly angle yourself so that your lead hand is forward. For right-handed people, that would be the left side of the body (for lefties, or 'southpaws,' this stance is reversed). In the orthodox stance, the left side is angled forward and our power side (the right) is back. The further back it is, the less you'll have to wind up if you do have to strike. You are already coiled and ready. This angling also makes you a narrower target. You arrange your posture without the obvious threat of 'putting up your dukes.'

This subtle shift into fighting stance lite echoes my coach's philosophy of footwork. The stance is a solid, strong way to stand that allows for quick movement. It also helps establish boundaries. You can reach your front (closer) arm out to 'post' (i.e., use your extended hand and arm to create distance). This front arm works as a kind of measuring stick. In kickboxing, when I extend my front (left) arm out fully to just a few inches away from my opponent, I know two things: I'm at the perfect distance to step in and throw a jab or a straight right hand, and I'm at the ideal distance to throw a kick. If I reach my arm out and touch them, or can't extend it all the way, then I know they are already much closer than I'd like them to be, which makes it harder for me to get away.

The real trick, however, is not only to recognize your own striking distance but to measure your opponent's as well. Someone who is six feet tall likely has a much longer reach than I do. If I'm at *my* striking distance, then I'm also well within theirs. That puts me at a disadvantage. If I don't want to get hit, I need to be further back, out of their range. But this also means that if I want to attack, I will have to be that much faster and more mobile in order to bridge the extra distance. Sticking your arm out as a measuring tool might seem like a conspicuous way to *instigate* a fight rather than avoiding it, but like so many other things, this sense of distance can become ingrained with practise. Just as some people can eyeball another person's weight or height, people who do this kind of training develop that sense of distance without having to literally hold out their arm. Arm's length becomes an internalized and legible measurement. In that case, sticking a posting arm out toward the other person could be used intentionally as a sign to them, to physically communicate that *they* had better back up. You can perform the boundary for them just by reaching it out.

This approach is great … unless you're dealing with a virtual threat. Experiencing something like an online stalker points to the almost laughable limits of arm measurement as self-defence. I can't figure out how to position myself in relation to my potential opponent if I can't find him.

When faced with harassment from my former student, I waved off repeated offers from campus security. The head of security was kind and patient and eager to support me, as were my employers. But a virtual threat is a tricky thing. Once it became clear that the stalker was either currently on campus or had an accomplice, the school assigned a campus security detail that would check the hallways around my classrooms, pace nearby during my office hours, and keep my daily schedule on file. One morning, I walked through the halls of my department with my earbuds playing something loud and fun to get me cheered up and ready to face the day. An introvert in a job that requires extrovert energy, sometimes I need a little extra push so I can go into my lecture with my head on right. It was still early in the morning, so the campus was secluded and quiet as I ducked into my office and closed the frosted glass door behind me. The music played in my ears. I hung up my coat and, without turning on the lights, managed to finally forget myself for a glorious moment. I started dancing.

My moment of levity was quickly cut short, as I noticed a shadow that kept moving slowly, back and forth, in front of my office door. No knock, just someone standing right up close against the door, shifting away, and then returning. I froze. I watched and waited, unmoving, for about a minute. They stopped, too, but I could hear breathing. Stalemate. Eventually, I heard a buzzing and beeping sound, and someone speaking my office number into a radio. I poked my head out and the security guard startled – which startled me – and we both had to take a moment. I told them who I was, and they explained that they had heard a commotion in my office. They had come to protect me from my dancing self (I could have used them at some bars in the early 2000s). I had been trying to forget my predicament, but in doing so, I was immediately reminded of it. Another day, I was followed so assiduously by the security guard assigned to me that I started to have a panic attack; I found myself actively trying to lose my tail as I made my way to my car in the campus parkade. Rationally, I knew that having a fifty-something man in a uniform follow behind me was meant both to keep me safe and to show me (and the stalker) that I was being looked out for. Evading him was counterproductive. He was there to help. But it didn't feel that way. Not having a present, visible opponent was unsettling, but strangely, having a male security guard trailing me made me feel remarkably like I *did*. The man sent to protect me functioned as an unintentional surrogate for the man who was threatening to hurt me.

Over the next weeks, I saw versions of my opponent standing in the doorway of the auditorium, auditing my lecture (I almost gave one of them a shout-out from the podium, but what would I even say?). The security guards became a perverse body double for the stalker, a physically manifested and almost always male reminder of the invisible, still anonymous, and as-yet unlocated threat. Someone truly was watching me, there was no question of that. And I could measure *them* with my arm. I could hear the buzz of their radio and the rhythmic pace of their shoes, in step with mine, as they followed me up the hall and down the stairs.

KEEP YOUR HANDS UP AND PROTECT YOURSELF AT ALL TIMES

With the idea of self-defence on my mind, I am intrigued when my good friend and training partner Sam explains to me the lessons he is passing down to his son. Although he and *his* father, Sam Sr. (let's call him Mr. Paschel), might differ philosophically in any number of areas, and although Sam Jr. has amassed decades more martial arts experience since his childhood, when it comes to self-defence, he still refers back to the basic principles handed down to him from his dad. As he walks me through them, some of the Pittsburgh Paschel family lessons seem so foreign as to sound almost cartoonish. I was raised in quiet residential neighbourhoods of various small prairie cities. In my sheltered experience, the idea of kids fighting was relatively unimaginable. Apart from witnessing a few scuffles on the grounds of my high school, I experienced fighting with strangers only as an element of fiction. My brothers didn't fight anyone but each other, and the idea of getting into a real fight was never even an issue – or even much a conversation, as far as we can remember – in our home.

Although the idea of dads teaching their sons to be tough is ubiquitous in popular culture (and despite having read *a lot* of martial arts–related books by male authors who seem to pleasure themselves to thoughts of the essential nature of their own scrapping), I haven't had any interest in trying to validate the cliché. The dudes have solid coverage. And yet, when I went looking for insight on self-defence, I found myself polling people of different genders and various backgrounds. Seeing how some men are raised to think about violence, in particular, highlighted the differences between their relationship to it and mine. For one gender, the role of fighting is so inflated and over-represented as to seem natural, whereas for others it is often oversimplified, defined as one-sided, or erased entirely.

The main principles of self-defence, as taught to Sam, are as follows: Hit first. Hit hard. Take the heart.

What this means is that if you're going to have to deal with a group of hostile people, identify which one is in some way the leader, the one to which the others look for direction, the heart of the group – and attack *that* person. As quickly becomes clear from Sam's narration, many fighting lessons speak as much to the model of masculinity and the environment in which the elder Mr. Paschel grew up as anything else. He came from a blue-collar neighbourhood in Pittsburgh where there was real clout in showing who was toughest. Street fights were a fairly regular practice. Sam Jr. grew up in a much more sedate neighbourhood. But parents tend to pass down the lessons that served them in their own lives, sometimes regardless of how applicable those approaches are to their children's own, often quite different, lived experiences. These lessons point to a very real condition of existence, especially for men, who move through the world in a way that is certainly foreign to mine; I'm eternally a potential victim of violence, while being a 'man' often seems to mean seeing men as potential opponents.

When fighters step into the ring, the referee takes both competitors' gloved hands or wrists in their own and advises both competitors to 'keep your hands up and protect yourself at all times.' If it reaches a point where one fighter is no longer 'defending themselves intelligently,' the referee is within their rights to call the fight. But there's no referee in daily life. Which brings me to a central Pittsburgh Fight

Club lesson: *Keep your hands up*. This lesson is punched and kicked into boxers and kickboxers through repeated training and often negative reinforcement – and the same principle can apply in a non-sport setting. Mr. Paschel taught his son how to find excuses to touch his face while talking to the other (potentially combative) person. Touch your hair, keep your hands visible near your face, scratch your ear or your nose. The idea here is that the visibility of your hands attempts to subconsciously diffuse a situation – they are in sight, and therefore not a threat. But perhaps more pragmatically, these hands are mobile and conveniently located, ready to protect your head if someone strikes. Body subtly angled, hands near the face; you've gotten into your fighting stance without anyone realizing you've done it.

No street fighter, I nevertheless file this technique away and filter it through my own lens. To be constantly at the ready suggests we are always in a potential fight. That's an exhausting way to live, and yet it is a painful reality for many, including women, LGBTQIA2S+ folks, and people of colour. While many of us have been imbued with the awareness that we are always in danger of being attacked, there must be some balance between being constantly afraid of being hit and preparing for the possibility, even in subtle ways. There is, of course, the reductive stereotype that casts men as natural warriors and women as inherently passive nurturers. But for every deluded male warrior, there is also a person who has had to protect themself from one. Perhaps being a 'better' woman, as in McCaughey's estimation, means being one who, in whatever small way she can manage, isn't simply subject to the whims of some protector.

IN NAME

Dealing with harassment, I eventually had to take on the status of 'victim' in order to protect myself and those around me. Sometimes people ask why I resisted going to the police for as long as I did. I stalled through a month of nearly incessant online threats and harassment, day and night. Initially, I put it off, hoping the situation wasn't serious. As socially confrontational as an ostrich, I stuck my head in the sand and hoped whoever it was would simply get bored and stop. I didn't consider the police a reasonable option, and didn't want to participate in a legal process that could have a lasting and negative impact on someone's life – even if he was behaving like an asshole. But when I think about this question in terms of victimhood, I'm sure my reasons weren't purely political. My resistance was also due to my selfish aversion to the role into which his threats would cast me as soon as they became official.

Because I was being harassed at work as well as privately, my situation created a domino effect that extended to everyone around me. As I prepared with my university's head of security to make my report to the police, she offered to accompany me as my advocate and primed me on how to be taken seriously. As she explained, it is important for me *not* to act like everything was okay, not to make my usual deflecting jokes, not to downplay the severity of the situation or hide its effect on me. For a 'victim' to be taken seriously – we victims are told – we have to demonstrate fear. We have to call attention to our own vulnerability. This is, of course, the exact opposite of what a fighter is trained to do. For years now, I had been literally and psychologically beating myself up trying to become strong, undaunted, and independent. Now suddenly the terms of the battle were being reversed. I feared what would happen if I truly internalized the word *victim*.

The day of my initial in-person interview with the police officers assigned to my case, I made myself physically sick gearing up to be vulnerable and open with total strangers. (Not my strong suit. If I had an emotional-fight nickname, it would be Alison 'Boundaries' Dean. But there I go again, deflecting with humour.) The four-hour window of time in which the officers said they were coming to meet with me passed with excruciating slowness. Finally, after the window closed, I called in to learn they simply weren't coming. I was devastated. When I was left on my own, now *as* a victim, it all felt even worse.

ONE-SIDED

For most of my life the space of self-defence was tied most clearly to questions of mobility. I am a grown-ass woman, I tell myself, and I resent being told what I can and cannot do. I feel trapped within the double-bind of responsibility – either I restrict my options and hours, staying home at night and refusing to travel alone, *or* I take myself out into the world accompanied by the nagging feeling that if I get attacked it's my own damn fault. Sometimes, my refusal takes the form of rebellion. It means going out, whether for a walk in my neighbourhood or meandering around a foreign city for hours and stepping into a Muay Thai gym alone, halfway across the world, where the instruction is a confusing mix of Thai and French. If I waited for others, my life would pass me by. Many of my best adventures have been alone.

Self-defence wasn't what I had in mind when I started training in combat sports. One of the muscles I strengthen daily in training is humility – I know how vulnerable I still am to others who are stronger, faster, or heavier than I am. As a result, perhaps, I haven't taken the connection between the gym and the street very seriously. As friends have pointed out, however, it doesn't take two people to make a fight. Only one person has to want to fight for it to happen.

Although self-defence and martial arts are in no way synonymous, the overlap between them – particularly in terms of the way the two are often gendered – is instructive. If physical combat and fighting are considered self-evident for 'men,' the conversation becomes complicated and often contradictory when anyone who doesn't fit that category trains for martial arts or basic daily survival. I think of my own training as combat and sport – a physical and psychological arena in which to sort through my identity as a person, among other things.

It wasn't until I started to receive the stalker's threatening messages that the lines started to blur for me in any real way. When he started focusing on photographs of me kickboxing and boxing, fixating on how *he* would fit into that equation, he paradoxically reinforced the legitimacy of my fighting, while also turning it into something else. I had gone in wanting to learn a skill, but his threats recast my combat training as self-defence, retroactively. He wanted to switch the categories of my work, without my having a say in the matter. But then, after all, it only takes one person to make it a fight.

Which brings me to the primary (and arguably the most fascinating) of the informal Pittsburgh fight lessons: if it seems like the other person is about to attack and you can't get away, 'hit first, hit hard.' In sparring and competition, my coaches constantly yell at me to 'be first, be first.' Instigating the action signals aggression and has a psychological effect on your opponent (and in many cases makes it harder for them to attack you the way they'd like). It has the added benefit of showing the judges that you are controlling the action. In a real-life self-defence setting, however, 'be first' feels counterintuitive. If schoolyard arguments have taught us anything, it is that 'they hit me first!' is a significant point. Doesn't hitting first *start* the fight rather than avoid it?

Having the presence of mind to 'be first' also recalls the idea of boundaries as something that must be proactively established, and then – once established – trusted and enforced. If the boundaries have been breached, even in ways less overt than a punch in the face, then you have two choices. Stand your ground or not. This idea makes me *deeply* uncomfortable, perhaps because I would rather put things off and react; that has a certain defensibility to it. Being first seems like the hardest part. This is probably why it is one of the more important lessons that self-defence offers more overtly and martial arts training more abstractly. If my impulses are any indication, this paradigm shift could be instructive for a lot of women.

What I am mining from this lesson is that it comes down to giving yourself permission to trust your gut, or intuition, for what it is: the first, most necessary, and most universally viable tool. It takes practise and confidence to trust your own reading of a situation, but that work doesn't necessarily need to take place within a gym. The next step – the hard step – is to honour it, whether in a moment of physical conflict or in other areas of life. If the big idea with boundaries is 'don't draw a line you aren't willing to enforce,' then self-defence is about teaching how to draw that line, and then giving those people who are socially cast in the role of potential targets the tools we need to actually enforce it. Learning not to 'look like' a target can only take us so far. Many will *always* see some of us that way, no matter how we posture and regardless of how purposefully we stride.

Strangely, this idea does come back around to the idea that when your line is crossed, you must believe in yourself and hold to your convictions. Be first. Take the heart.

CHAPTER FOUR
★
LOOK THE PART

When Thomas Page McBee wrote his autobiography, *Amateur: A True Story About What Makes a Man*, he took the exploration of masculinity as his project. Like many others before and since, McBee presumed that at the heart of masculinity is fighting. Having never trained nor fought before, McBee, a trans man, decided to sign up for a boxing match to gain insight into this privileged 'masculine' space. His now low voice commanded attention in a way his previous register hadn't. He presented as male, and this identity was not questioned by the people around him. Still, he retained the lived experience of the body and identity that had moved through the world only years before.

He observed the men around him in the gym, noting the codes of behaviour. McBee's goal was to become a conscious member of the community of which he was now a part. Painfully aware of how the flawed, toxic aspects of masculinity have failed men and women, McBee claims that, when he began his transition, 'I thought I could still be "better," even if I traded being "like a guy" for becoming one. What I wasn't prepared for, when I began injecting testosterone, was the way the filter of my body changed the meaning of the way I spoke, the way I dated, the way I touched and was touched.'

MY BOXING IS EVERYTHING

Writers love boxing. The list of authors fascinated with pugilism includes Joyce Carol Oates, Jonathan Swift, Alexander Pope, Lord Byron, Ezra Pound, Ernest Hemingway, and Norman Mailer. Many liken the process of writing a book to a boxer's fight. The fight itself is just the tip of the iceberg, so to speak; maybe only 10 percent of the whole package is visible to others. To put it another way, imagine the sight of a duck gliding along the surface of a lake with apparent ease, and compare that to what's hidden from view – legs paddling furiously beneath, just to keep afloat.

Author, MMA fighter, and combat sports journalist Josh Rosenblatt proposes a similar connection between writing and fighting, with an emphasis on solitude. 'Fighters have their trainers and cornermen and opponents, and writers have their editors and publishers and subjects, but in the end both are out there on their own, wrestling with themselves every time. Ask any trainer and they'll say a fighter's greatest obstacle isn't his opponent but his own fear' – now, I would be remiss if I didn't interrupt to point out Rosenblatt is defaulting to the masculine for fighter here. Nevertheless – 'The same is true for writers,' he says. 'The terror of physical destruction and the terror of the blank page are the same thing.'

What most writers seem drawn to is the romance of it all; if they see themselves reflected back in the boxer, then no wonder they are inclined to see the boxer as a kind of heroic solitary genius, up there with the greats. The decor of boxing gyms invites this kind of self-aggrandizement, their walls papered with images of men turned into icons through titles, just like those famous authors on so many bookshelves.

One such icon is Ernest Hemingway, a writer known for his decisive prose and masculine bravado. And almost any amount of time spent delving into 'Papa' also means hearing about his passion for pugilism. Hemingway was known to challenge visitors to spar with him and went so far as to build a boxing ring in his backyard in Key West, like a burly spider in its roped web. Sam and I had a running joke about pretending to be Ernest Hemingway, putting on fisherman sweaters, drinking, and getting into fights. The scenario seemed ridiculous, of course, but I was also drawn to the idea of playing with this caricature of manly men. As we are unable to do anything halfway, our joke snowballed into Hemingweek, now an annual event.

For one week, the Sams and I, along with our friends, try to embody Papa Hemingway by writing, drinking, fighting, and generally seeking to feel alive. This is an exercise in Hemingway pastiche. Although our playful imitation feels faithful to the spirit of the man's persona, there's no way to do 'Hemingway' – *especially* for those of us who identify as women, and feminists – other than ironically, or at least tongue in cheek. I poke fun at this brand of machismo while also trying the swagger on for size. There's something about this approach to writing and fighting that seems both typical and alien to me. I want to better understand.

If we accept that you can write about punching … then is the inverse true? Can you punch about writing?

In preparation for the inaugural Hemingweek, I take a deep dive into his boxing stories, his photographs, and the self-driven mythology around his boxing. Ever the teacher, I compile and assign a day-by-day to-do list, style guide, and reading and writing curriculum for participants. (Hey, if you want a theme week to be successful, you have to put in the work.) This process of immersion and intellectual role playing is familiar to me, although it is typically less playful. A Modernist by training, I spent a long year of my life reading through the major texts of that period in preparation for my doctoral field exams, including more early-twentieth-century male authors than I had ever wanted to study. Throughout the process, I found the need to impose literary cleanses: weeks where I'd read only women, just to get those dudes and their ways of thinking out of my head.

The key here is that there is no room for complacency in Hemingweek. This is an engagement with a deeply gendered way of life, but one that we strip for parts. Challenge your boundaries, use your body, throw your weight around, be alive. We complete the daily reading, work on our creative writing assignments and share the results, and take on physical challenges, including daily quotas of push-ups, cold ocean dips, and exercises with instructions such as 'Ask someone to punch you as hard as they can. Write about how it felt.' As a group of fight-friendly people, we are largely playing to our own strengths with these tasks. But no one makes it all the way through the week. The reading and writing requirements alone take time and discipline, and participants have varying levels of success keeping up while also balancing their own busy lives. But really it's the drinking that proves unsustainable, and we are shadows of our former selves by mid-week. Hem always gets the last laugh.

As I have learned, however, taking cold-water swims, writing about punching, and attempting to poison my liver for a week doesn't provide me with any revelatory insight into Hemingway's boxing. I think we can all agree drinking and fighting are an ill-advised combo *at best*. Reading his writing about boxing doesn't quite answer it all, either. Hemingway is an aficionado; he loves and romanticizes things like bullfighting, even if he can't necessarily do them the way he sees them done. Who doesn't romanticize the things they love, whether they're particularly good at them or not? Some element of this aficionado's attitude was also likely true for Hemingway and fighting. What I have decided is that both the fighting and the writing say something important about the man and his brand of masculinity. They are about posturing, performing, and seeking. They show a hunger to make things clear, and clean, and simple in their brutality. The desire to own them. Writing about boxing is another way *to* box, albeit from outside the ring. It's an opportunity to analyze and linger in the activity that you love. (I'm definitely projecting onto Hem at this point. But I've done my rounds dressed in fisherman sweaters and wool pants, so I must know. I've sat at a typewriter and bled. It's my time to talk.)

Writing, like studying, is another way to feel like you're learning something from the inside out.

Before Hemingway could lure visitors into his home boxing ring, he was a man in his twenties who just wanted to fight. Famed heavyweight boxer Jack Dempsey was one of the many who apparently crossed paths with young Hemingway as he trained. Whereas Hemingway wrote passionately about boxing and his own prowess, others, like Dempsey, saw something else. 'There were a lot of Americans in Paris and I sparred with a couple, just to be obliging,' the Champ said. 'But there was one fellow I wouldn't mix it with. That was Ernest Hemingway. He was about twenty-five or so and in good shape, and I was getting so I could read people, or anyway men, pretty well. I had this sense that Hemingway, who really thought he could box, would come out of the corner like a madman. To stop him, I would have to hurt him badly, I didn't want to do that to Hemingway. That's why I never sparred with him.' Hemingway's frequent sparring partner and fellow writer Morley Callaghan offered another sobering account of his training partner, saying, 'we were two amateur boxers. The difference between us was that [Hemingway] had given time and imagination to boxing; I had actually worked out a lot with good fast college boxers.' I have never seen Mr. Hemingway box, of course. But I will say this: the confidence of mediocre men is a fucking super-power. I have met many versions of this guy. Hell, I've sparred with the dude myself.

For Hemingway, the romance of the activity was as much about *the idea* as its actual execution. Diligent, regimented study and training is not the same thing as passion and enthusiasm, no matter how much even I would sometimes like it to be. Although Hemingway famously claims, 'My writing is nothing. My boxing is everything,' his devotion is to an idea as much as anything else. Maybe he couldn't put his ego aside enough to study and train to perfect his technique. Maybe he wasn't actually that skilled. Maybe he just really liked the simplicity of getting in there and *fighting*. (I sympathize!) But because he talked his boxing up so much and claimed it as such a big part of his identity, posterity is going to fault him for anything less than a skill set solid enough to hold up all of that swagger.

Sometimes talking or writing a big game can pass for being good. But, as they say, you can't fake it in the ring.

MEN'S ROOM

The association of boxing with masculinity is not simply historical; if the men and media of the early 1900s United States have their say (and they did), we're meant to believe there is something downright *American* about it. When other martial arts like Japanese Jiu-jitsu came on the scene in the US of the early 1900s, for instance, boxing actively sold itself as indicative of patriotic (patriarchal) power. Jiu-Jitsu was exoticized, racialized (labelled 'sneaky' rather than 'honour-able,' for instance), and feminized. The more familiar and commonly valued sports of wrestling and boxing were promoted as disciplines based on natural, athletic response and brute force – and therefore masculine, American. None of this slick movement that would allow a woman to overpower a big, strong man.

In Thailand, the country's national sport, Muay Thai, is similarly held up as the pride of the country; and this pride is historically masculine. In contrast to the evasive dancing of a lot of present-day boxing, Muay Thai competitors stand and face each other, and they fight. They kick, and they kick, and they kick. Here, if a fighter is moving forward, they are likely winning. Simple evasion misses the point (and doesn't do you any favours with the judges, who are taking aggression and damage into account when tallying points). Women practise and compete in Muay Thai in Thailand, but they are set apart within the most fundamental aspects of the space itself: they are either barred from competing in certain stadiums or must pass under the bottom rope of the ring. Both restrictions are in place because the ropes are sanctified and must not be contaminated by women. Many female fighters, Thai or not, explain their adherence to this rule as a necessary part of participating in Muay Thai culture. Like anyone observing a time-honoured tradition, they set their own sense of self aside in order to be part of a greater cultural history, one that they value and admire. By positioning themselves as a blip in a longer but important lineage, as a new addition to a deeper history, some women make peace with these symbolic concessions. While many fighters simply acknowledge this distinction and accept it as part of the package or a gesture of respect, there is nevertheless a visual reminder of difference before the fight even begins.

Up until the 1980s, prizefighting in boxing was largely held in the domain of working-class men, often immigrants or men of colour. As Lucia Trimbur outlines in *Come Out Swinging: The Changing World of Boxing in Gleason's Gym*, the boxing gym has been considered a necessary male haven against disenfranchisement due to racialized incarceration and challenges to employment (in many cases due to previous incarceration). It has historically been a place for men for whom formal education or job training is not necessarily an option. Fighting has long been a trade, a way to both provide some structure and purpose, and a possible income, for those who have few other options.

Boxing is also implicitly endorsed as a means of instilling discipline in those who are thought to need it. Get them in the gym and keep them out of trouble. There is an underside to this ethos, however. Whereas the previous fitness movement was intended to strengthen white European stock, sport has also been used as a tool of indoctrination for a different population. Canadian residential schools were sites of violent assimilation and cultural erasure. In her discussion of sport and residential schools, researcher and member of Fisher River Cree Nation Janice Forsyth notes that in these institutions, administrators used a number of methods to control Indigenous children, including 'physical training programs designed to inculcate patriotic values and instruct male and female students in appropriate masculine and feminine behaviours.' This is a colonial lineage, and a patriarchal one.

The complicated history of sport in social control does not empty it of its radical potential, however. As Jennifer Hargreaves, who researches the sociology of gender in athletics, explains, sport 'has been one channel in the decolonization process through which Aboriginal groups have tried to free themselves from the damaging psychological effects of colonial subordination.' Still, the process has not been the same for women and men. In different ways across North America, Indigenous women have inherited marginalized statuses through gender as well as 'poverty, racism, poor educational opportunities, and geographic isolation.' These factors combined have considerably 'impacted their ability and interest to get involved and stay involved in boxing' and other sports. The intersections of multiple factors, not least of which include race and accessibility, affect what different people get out of their practice, what they invest into it, and perhaps why they take it up at all. One of the dangers of foregrounding gender as the connecting point is that it can seem to flatten the playing field, as if all women's experiences are the same. But in many cases, 'fighting to fight' doesn't simply mean breaking a social taboo; it means fighting against incredible odds.

A CHIP OFF THE OLD BLOCK

When professional boxing became more recognized for women in the late 1990s and early 2000s, it's no coincidence that a lot of the women whose fights were promoted were the daughters of famous male boxers, including George Foreman, Archie Moore, Roberto Duran, and Ingemar Johansson. Their entrance into the ring was allowed because it came with a kind of lineal, patriarchal blessing. The transition to professional female fighting made a little more sense from a marketing standpoint, if nothing else. After all, fighting was in their blood. Joe Frazier versus Muhammad Ali fights I, II, and III are some of the most famous competitions in boxing history. The less famous 'Ali versus Frazier IV' fight was perhaps less of a draw because, unlike the first two, this wasn't actually Muhammad and Joe duking it out. This 2001 sequel – thirty years after Ali versus Frazier III – featured Laila 'She Bee Stingin'' Ali and Jacqueline 'Sister Smoke' Frazier-Lyde, the famous boxers' daughters.

When Muhammad Ali and Joe Frazier first faced off in 1971, the contest was dubbed the 'Fight of the Century.' Here were two undefeated heavyweight boxers meeting in the ring to determine who would take the title to which they each had a right. Beyond the politics of the ring itself was the wider political climate. Ali had been stripped of his world heavyweight champion belt in 1967 after refusing to be drafted into the armed forces in 1966. A conscientious objector to the Vietnam War, Ali also had his boxing licence and passports stripped. In the meantime, Joe Frazier, an undefeated fighter in his own right, won the heavyweight belt. When Ali was once again in a position to challenge for the title, he brutally attacked Frazier's character throughout the lead-up to the event, calling his opponent a 'tool of the white establishment' and an 'Uncle Tom.' For audience members and fans at home, this was not simply a fight among two undefeated heavyweight favourites; it was simultaneously elevated and reduced to a battle between liberal anti-war and conservative pro-war politics. Picking a fighter meant picking a side.

This polarized, politically charged history carried on in the names of the women fighting in 2001, but apart from garnering considerable attention for their bout, the contrast seemed to work against them. Where their fathers had been held up as examples of skill and substance, the women's fight maintained the inherited rivalry but appeared frivolous in comparison. Even before the fight took place, reporter Amelia Hill notes that Bert Sugar, a leading boxing historian, declared the bout 'the biggest joke since Elvis Presley fought a kangaroo in the film *Matilda*.' When Ali was promoting her very first fight, Sugar had noted that she was a 'very pretty lady.' Criticized for this comment, he responded, in an article titled 'I'd Rather Poke Out My Eye With A Sharp Stick': 'Well, considering the fact that Laila Ali had not yet fought her first fight, what the hell was there to say? That if she entered the world of boxing, heretofore a man's world, she would have to be measured by their standards' and not those of the 'PC' (politically correct) crew. 'Maybe they're fighting because they love the accessories,' he mused. 'After all, they're wearing gloves, fighting for a purse and a belt, and wearing satin shorts' – this same comment can be made about male boxers, incidentally, but Sugar seems to overlook that fact for effect here – 'Or maybe it's because they're getting in touch with their masculine side. But whatever it is – and show me a man who understands women and I'll show you a man who's in for a big surprise – it would help if they could fight. To many, this unhumble correspondent included, most of them look like women going down in quicksand for the last time, wielding frying pans. Is it asking too much that, if they wish to be boxers, at least they could look like boxers?' Elsewhere, Sugar commented that his quarrel with Ali versus Frazier IV was that these two fought so badly, and yet drew so much attention, that they would hurt the potential of women in boxing. As his other statements made clear, however, the future of women in boxing really wasn't his concern at all. He was as offended by the 'very pretty ladies' fighting as he was by the fact that, by being pretty, they didn't look like 'boxers.' But with their female accessories in hand (frying pan included), they never could, because for him, boxers were men.

In the actual match, the stadium was packed with raucous fans, and Ali and Frazier fought with ardour. Still, the commentators couldn't get over the question of skill. The *look* of the fight. The men's obsession with 'technique' is telling; like Sugar, they couldn't seem to recognize the female fighters as looking 'like boxers.' The fight itself was tough, and the women were game, but the men watching could think of nothing except how it *might* be if the women just had more 'technique.' And throughout the bout, the announcers could not separate the fighters from their fathers. Whereas Martin and Gogarty had been praised for their technique and heart five years earlier, these two women with men's names were presented as once again a kind of distraction, a 'sideshow' for real fighters. For many watching the fight, however, the heart these two fighters displayed was still a win for women in the sport.

The preoccupation with the look of skill and technique stands out to me for a few reasons: I am selfishly very attentive to technique. I want to learn by studying. Ali versus Frazier IV was in many ways a scuffle rather than a clean, technical fight, but still fascinating to watch. Ali wanted to use her long range, but Frazier kept rushing her and drawing her in; this is something that has happened to me, and yet through much of the fight I don't see Ali necessarily finding the tools to get past it. I also just love the *look* of a nice, technical fight, though it's not necessarily as dramatic as an all-out brawl. I can be swayed by the aesthetics of technique as much as anyone, even though I realize the idea that a fight is only good if it looks good is a fallacy. Some fighters have ugly technique but get the job done. The announcers' preoccupation with technique stands out to me partly because I have had the very same thought while watching any number of professional men fighting. And yet rarely, if ever, have I seen commentators so readily and relentlessly critique their stylistic choices or the lack of 'polish' as they did during Ali versus Frazier IV. 'Not a lot of technique right now,' the announcer said disparagingly. 'That hook … where'd she learn that from?'

But, perhaps unlike some male announcers, I have the benefit of having watched enough male *and* female boxers to know that female fighters don't necessarily all move the same way as their male counterparts. The 'look' of the fight often isn't the same, regardless of skill level. This is one of the main reasons I like to watch women; I especially want to see someone with a similar body type and weight distribution to mine, to see what the moves would look like *for me*. As Ali versus Frazier IV went on, some of the clunkiness fell away. Ali's hands found their way to Frazier-Lyde's face and body with a sense of placement that wasn't as apparent in earlier rounds. Ali would clearly have preferred to fight at her own long range, but Frazier-Lyde was aggressive (the announcer referred to her punches as 'mauling') and kept rushing her, tying her up, and making Ali fight her fight. All the while the announcers patronized both fighters, in the most exhaustive sense of the word. Nevertheless, the match was a brawl, and an exciting one.

The tired old idea that these women coming in and fighting would potentially 'hurt' the sport of boxing was planted well before they stepped in the ring. Like Sugar's critiques, the issue really isn't about protecting the potential of women in boxing but rather protecting the supposed sanctity of *men* in boxing. No matter what happened in the ring that night, it was going to be nearly impossible to shake that bias from many commentators' and viewers' minds. The women had to fight that much harder, not only to be allowed to own their famous family names, but also because they were in the position of representing women in boxing writ large. (The critiques of Ali's technique ring a little hollow when you consider that Christy Martin, praised, rightfully, for her technique, found herself on the losing end of a match against Ali only two years later, and Martin maintains a high opinion of Ali's skill to this day.) Not surprisingly, the fighters weren't compared to other women, or to other early career boxers. They were trading on their names to get the fight, and so the commentary compared the women to their iconic fathers, either unfavourably or by attributing any of the women's technical success to them. Not exactly a fair fight. The bias about female fighters has always been there – especially in these earlier matches – but because these fighters were so clearly aligned with iconic, male boxing history, the contradictions and assumptions were made even more apparent. Each of these women carried the weight of their father's boxing legacy in there with her. It was hard for anyone involved, including themselves, it seems, to see past that.

The Martin versus Gogarty and Ali versus Frazier IV fights received such different treatment simply because of the combined skill level of the fighters – the look of the fight – and the presumption that the famous boxers' daughters had stepped into the ring without having earned it. Nevertheless, even Martin, who was given legitimacy through her representation by Don King and the doors that opened for her, and who remains recognized as a great boxer to this day (she was elected to the Boxing Hall of Fame in 2019) dealt with constant adversity. Martin, who goes by Christy Salters-Martin now, walked into her first gym after she made an impression fighting in the (pre-MMA) Toughman Contest and professional boxing cards, with no fight training or martial arts experience. Despite being sent there by an interested promoter, when she arrived, she was told that she didn't belong. The main coach, James Martin, the man who would go on to be her career-long coach and her husband of twenty years, went so far as to consider having some of the guys in the gym rough her up – even break some of her bones – in order to put her in her place. When he saw how she fought and got a sense of her potential as a competitor, however, he latched onto her, thinking she would make him rich. And she did. As Allison Glock reports, in 2010, after two decades of marriage and chronic physical, emotional, and psychological abuse by James – during which he isolated her from her friends and family, put her under constant surveillance, and controlled her money – Christy decided to leave him.

So he stabbed her.

Christy's husband and coach stabbed her multiple times with a buck knife, sliced open her calf, shot her in the chest with a pistol, and then hit her in the face with the butt of the gun. Amazingly, she managed to escape. Even – or especially – the man who was in her corner for every fight, the man who knew enough to *know* that she was as good a fighter as any other, would rather kill her than see anyone else possess her. In a perverse twist, when mounting his defence in court, her former husband's legal team claimed he was acting out of self-defence. Hoping to paint her as monstrous, they leaned on the woman's boxing career as evidence of her violent nature. (He was sentenced to twenty-five years in prison.)

ENTER AT YOUR OWN RISK

Just as there is a danger to lingering too long in the art and literature – the created worlds – of men, I worry about how much I skirt along the margins of masculine spaces, thinking I couldn't possibly fall in. I want to borrow, take, and transform. But it would be complacent to think I can excavate the parts I want from a male-dominated culture without being affected in more ways than I imagine. To what extent does what you do become what you *are*, for better and worse?

How do we reimagine these spaces in order to avoid replicating the same toxic traps?

The physical spaces of martial arts gyms – the old-school and long-standing boxing gyms in particular – often retain the impression of a male space partly through their familiarly gritty decor. The stereotypical *Rocky* gyms – no-frills spaces with old posters and advertisements papering the walls, duct tape, speed ropes, and a bricolage of old equipment – have the smell of sweat and history lingering under the layers of visual history. The look of the bare-bones MMA dojo or the old boxing gym works as a reference in itself. But the other way this masculine status quo is maintained is, in part, through the culture of performed toughness that works hand in hand with fighting. This combination of visual and performative signals becomes most obvious when something disrupts it. Boxer Mischa Merz opened her own gym, Mischa's Boxing Central, in 2013. She chose to paint the door of the otherwise orthodox-looking boxing gym a nice solid pink. The colour leads to 'some interesting consequences,' she says. 'Sometimes people ask if men are allowed inside. Sometimes they don't even notice the colour ... I suspect, though, that without even realizing it, the pink door can act as a kind of filter. Men who walk in wanting to learn how to fight are mostly pretty comfortable with their masculinity.' The men who can't bear to deal with a woman as a coach or a training partner 'are the kind of men I never see in my gym, the ones for whom masculinity is a costume – one that's oversized and menacing.' It's a small detail, but it sets the tone for the gym and those who enter it; the pink greeting becomes a kind of gatekeeper, weeding out macho or misogynistic men who refuse to enter. The decor isn't everything, of course: women holding visible positions of authority, diverse programming options, attention to language and pronouns, sliding scale payment options, and accessible and inclusive facilities – the image and architecture of a space sends messages and sets the tone for who joins, and what happens within.

For some, however, the gym still has distinct value as a masculine space. In this case, even if other genders are present and participating, their role is to conform to the codes of the space, and to maintain the status quo. Stay in the background, don't make too much noise.

Positioning MMA fighting as synonymous with masculinity, Jonathan Gottschall's *The Professor in the Cage: Why Men Fight and Why We Like to Watch* is determined to maintain the homogeneity of these spaces, whether real or imagined. Gottschall mentions women only as a foil for men as he situates MMA fighting within a deep dive into the history of the human race and man's relationship to conflict in pivotal moments of civilization. And I do mean *man's* relationship, bless his heart. Calling on science, anthropology, and carefully selected historical accounts, Gottschall builds a case for fundamental differences between men and women – but only obliquely, as yet again, women really aren't the point. Gottschall, a husband and father of daughters, employs the women under his roof as tropes to show the distinction between the masculine space of the MMA gym and the feminized space of the (his) home. Fighting is male. Fighters are men. No need to distract from the dominant narrative.

Perhaps not surprisingly, when this man imagines fighting, he consciously self-selects in terms of his choice of gym. Dude does not simply want to train; he is seeking the exact opposite of a pink door. He is drawn to an MMA gym with a big window, so he can place his own masculinity on full display.

CATEGORY CRISIS

The co-ed nature of spaces like MMA gyms generally allows for a fluidity in training partners. In official competition, however, gender lines are drawn. This binary assumption is more complicated than it might appear, and the fault lines show most clearly when we pay attention to who is left out. In one of her many interviews after being pressured to come out as a trans woman in 2013, MMA fighter Fallon Fox explained that she decided to try her hand at MMA after watching videos of female fighters. Seeing the other women in action, Fox admired the combination of 'toughness and femininity' of female MMA fighters – the very mix that women are still taking to social media to demonstrate today. This coexistence is part of what drew her in. In this case, the duality is not just in the space of the gym, but specifically within the women themselves. It offered a point of entry for Fox that felt right for her now more fully realized identity. Her sense of the sport's potential to create options for women to step outside constricting gender expectations is telling. Unfortunately, the politics around the sport did not receive the fighter with the same open-mindedness that she had attributed to it. Instead, entering the sport as a queer, Black, trans woman, Fox found her options continuously limited by the prejudices and assumptions of the community.

Whereas the UFC's Liz Carmouche openly voiced her support for Fox and declared that (if they found themselves in the same organization and weight class), she would be happy to fight her, one of the more vocal opponents of trans women fighting in the female division was the organization's other early female signee, Ronda Rousey. Rousey claimed publicly that Fox should not be competing against women. Weighing in on Fox's status as a fighter, UFC fighter Matt Mitrione attacked her with careless slurs, claiming Fox has 'mental issues' for wanting to go in there and 'beat up women.' His reasoning is revealing. Fox is 'chromosomally a man,' Mitrione claimed. 'He [Mitrione refuses to acknowledge Fox's pronouns] had a gender change, not a sex change. He's still a man. He was a man for thirty-one years … Six years of taking performance de-hancing drugs you think is going to change all that?' Whereas Rousey and Mitrione object to Fox's inclusion in a female division for the same basic and flawed reasoning (the idea that she isn't a 'natural' woman and therefore has an unfair advantage over 'women'), Mitrione's tirade – for which he was subsequently suspended from the UFC – shows another layer. The only reason Mitrione can imagine or comprehend a trans woman choosing to fight against other women is through the lens of male-on-female violence. The idea that someone who identifies as a woman wants to compete against other women is inconceivable for him. Mitrione can't see past his ingrained understanding of male-on-female violence as natural to someone who was raised as a man, in a man's body. But what does that say about Mitrione's concept of masculinity?

In addition to the policing of biology and sex, weight classes are another way women's bodies have been regulated in MMA. For years, the UFC refused to open a 145-pound women's division; fighters like Cris Cyborg (Cristiane Justino) who were naturally taller and heavier than a 130-pound division would normally allow, had to nearly destroy themselves to make an extreme weight cut, or else lose the opportunity to fight. Consider Rousey as a foil in some ways for Cyborg. Where the pretty-faced blonde Rousey was distinguished as the second female on the cover of *The Ring* magazine, Cyborg – a dominant fighter in her own right – was mocked for her 'unfeminine' appearance. With a dramatically and controversially cut musculature, Cyborg was repeatedly mocked by the top voices in the UFC, including the organization's president, Dana White. In a public press conference, White joked that she looks 'transsexual' and resembles [male MMA fighter] 'Wanderlei Silva in a dress and heels.' He then got out of his chair and imitated her walk. MMA pundits Joe Rogan and Tony Hinchcliffe joked on Rogan's popular podcast that Cyborg 'is the only woman who cuts weight by cutting off her dick.' Rogan made a similar claim about Fox, who he said is just 'a man without a dick.' If women's faces are a preoccupation in fighting, then men's penises are, perhaps not surprisingly, the other male obsession. Rousey won a lot of fights, as did Cyborg; Cyborg was an intimidating prospect for almost anyone she fought – and continues to be, although the UFC eventually chose not to renew her contract. She moved over to Bellator MMA and became the champ there instead.

To complicate matters further, consider the case of Amanda Nunes. 'The Lioness' is the first openly gay UFC Champion – and only the third UFC fighter ever to hold two division titles (Bantamweight and Featherweight) simultaneously. Nunes also has the distinction of having defeated both Rousey and Cyborg. Whereas White made fun of Cyborg, he defends and supports Nunes. The organization puts her forward as a perfect example of their 'We Are All Fighters' campaign, celebrating her role in bringing greater visibility to LGBTQIA2S+ fighters. The fact that the distinctions of the first openly gay fighter (Carmouche) and the first openly gay Champion (Nunes) in the UFC are both held by women hints at uneven expectations or allowances for men and women in terms of sexuality and gender performance.

In 2017, four years after the controversy around Fox, Nong Rose Barnjaroensuk made history when she became the first transgender Muay Thai fighter to compete at Rajadamnern, Thailand's oldest stadium. (She is not, however, Thailand's first transgender female

Muay Thai fighter; she was famously preceded in the 1990s by Parinya Charoenphol, or 'Nong Toom.') In an exception to the stadium's strict dress code, Nong Rose is allowed to fight wearing a sports bra rather than compete bare chested. She also appears to have been granted exceptions from cutting her hair short, as the other stadium fighters must. Unlike Fox, however, if Nong Rose wants to fight, it will be a man standing opposite her, not another woman. Her presence in this space marks a remarkable shift, and an opening. It also points to the closed doors barring the entry of any other female fighters, and the complicated position that Nong Rose is assigned in fighting as a trans woman. Both the concessions and the limitations surrounding her fight highlight her status as an exception, in more ways than one.

Whereas fellow fighters like Rousey and Mitrione berated Fox, refusing to accept her femininity, Nong Rose's competitor Sua Yai leaned into an objectifying and performatively flirtatious pre-fight discourse. According to a *Vice* report by Frances Watthanaya, 'During an interview, when asked to look at his opponent,' Nong Rose's competitor responded by saying, 'I can't look at her, she is so beautiful that I will fall in love.' When the reporter 'asked him to estimate Nong Rose's bra size ... without skipping a beat Sua Yai answered 36 inches leaving [his opponent] both flattered and embarrassed.' As Watthanaya points out, Sua Yai underestimated his opponent right up until the moment the fight began. In the end, Nong Rose ultimately won both a historic landmark and the fight itself.

ON BOXING

In her 1985 treatise *On Boxing*, Joyce Carol Oates offers a poetic ode to the 'sweet science of bruising.' *On Boxing* has become literary boxing canon. Celebrating the drama and brutality of the sport, situating it as its own form of embodied poetry and theatre, Oates holds up a funhouse mirror to boxing. When men, fighters or not, look into it, they see something vital, urgent, masculine. Despite her misgivings about its brutality, Oates's devotion to boxing belies a conflicted romance with a kind of purity that comes, in part, from distance. Always an audience member, never a fighter, she is the ultimate observer. In her preface to the 1994 reissue of the book, Oates confides that boxing is a deeply personal subject for her; indeed, 'to write about boxing is to write about oneself – however elliptically and unintentionally. And to write about boxing is to be forced to contemplate not only boxing but also on the perimeters of civilization – what it is, or should be, to be "human."' This is the scope Oates attributes to her work ten years after its publication, and though that connection between boxing and life is certainly present throughout the text, this claim bears fruit in discomfiting ways today.

As reader, I'd like to give myself over to the book and see the boxing world through Oates-coloured glasses, but something keeps getting in my way. Like many men before her and since, the author has read the room and seen what she wanted to see. Her audience is male. As the lone woman present in that imaginary room, she takes her own interest, and her own privileged presence, as the exception that proves the rule. By Oates's estimation, the world of boxing is the land of men. 'Men fighting men to determine worth' is compared to 'the female experience of childbirth' – each is a biologically hard-wired truth, a space of struggle and reckoning, it seems, that accommodates one sex and excludes the other. By setting up a 'natural' distinction between boxing and childbirth, Oates offers an equation in which the 'unnatural' female who wants to fight gets lumped in with the childless woman, or the woman whose reproductive organs don't line up with this cisgender model of femininity. (If men fight men to determine their masculine worth, who do women fight in childbirth, I wonder?) 'In any case,' Oates famously states, 'raw aggression is thought to be the peculiar province of men, as nurturing is the peculiar province of women. (The female boxer violates this stereotype and cannot be taken seriously – she is parody, she is cartoon, she is monstrous. Had she an ideology, she is likely to be a feminist.)'

We can give Oates a 1985-era alibi here; it was a different time. We can also note that she uses distancing language. The way she says 'thought to be' is vague and passive, for instance. She doesn't use an active verb to own the claim for herself. Oates grammatically puts space between herself and these claims the same way I might post my arm against an opponent to keep them at a distance. But by repeating the claim uncritically, Oates gives it more life, more power. The 'female boxer' in particular gets closeted away between brackets. Oates keeps that monster contained in a cage built of punctuation and casual sexist disdain.

Women are an aberration within *On Boxing*, and yet Oates herself is a woman consumed by the sport. To be clear, I understand that the history she describes doesn't include me. When Martin and Gogarty step into the ring for that watershed boxing match in 1996, they are doing so a year after *On Boxing*'s ten-year anniversary. It would be wrong for me to read the book anachronistically and expect the author to know what has happened since. Still, Oates doesn't even leave the space open for us. For Oates, boxing *is* men, and vice versa. The sharp edges of this line serve as a good reminder for me. As a reader who is somewhat familiar with Oates's work and voice, I made the mistake of thinking of the author as a woman, when I should have been reading her as a boxing writer, which is how she clearly wants to be read. And her most-read text as a boxing writer uses the same time-worn narratives as those of her male counterparts.

As she sees it, 'women, watching a boxing match, are likely to identify with the losing, or hurt, boxer; men are likely to identify with the winning boxer.' Who would want to put themselves through that? But if we do, it is because we have been trained to see ourselves and be seen that way. I don't think it's that simple. A decade before *On Boxing*, visual critic Laura Mulvey coined the term the 'male gaze.' As Mulvey explains, women in movies, news, and advertisements (as well as in much literature and works of fine art) are most often depicted from a heterosexual male perspective. The camera lens functions as an extension of that gaze. The audience watching is therefore placed in the point of view of the man who watches, like the male boxing reporters who can't see past the idea of women as victims. What follows, then, is that the visual world is often constructed from the point of view of a certain audience – the dominant one, the powerful one, the 'male' one – and each viewer, regardless of their own gender, is forced to see the world through those eyes. They are asked to first experience it by identifying with the male – whatever translation comes later, this point of view is always necessarily internalized in order to simply see. Just as most of the world is made for right-handed people, for instance, we are taught to view the world through one dominant visual scope.

Adding to the conversation almost twenty years later, writer and critic bell hooks notes that studies of 'the gaze' are divided primarily by gender, and particularly those in feminist and visual theory by white women have historically failed to take into account the dimension of race. hooks points out that feminist theory is often guilty of overlooking the fact that experiences of Black women and white women, for example, in relation to that gaze are not reducible (in sum: #notallwomen). In her words, Mulvey's theory argues that 'placing ourselves outside that pleasure in looking ... was determined by a "split between active/male and passive/female."' But, as hooks explains, 'Black female spectators actively chose not to identify with the film's imaginary subject because such identification was disenabling.' To assume that all female viewers are passive is, in other words, to lump all into one assumed gendered and racialized experience. I bring up Mulvey and hooks in order to point out that while subject positions affect us differently, they still have an effect. We all still learn them to some extent, whether through direct association, necessary acts of translation, or a long-held resistance. Even if a viewer approaches the image with an oppositional gaze, they still find themselves having to do an enormous amount of work just to exist within a world that, visually and otherwise, devalues their point of view.

What this also means is that when someone like Oates aligns women with victims, it's not a simple or innocent move. It's insidious. Women are positioned to see ourselves as victims. And white women especially are taught to identify with the dominant view, to see ourselves as *just close enough* to that power to feel entitled to it; we are more likely to identify with, to see as natural – and seek the power of – the victor, the abuser, the male. In the process, many women are *trained to* see ourselves the way those in power see us, whether we choose to accept that view or not.

In later years, Oates explored other boxing narratives in her fiction, including creating a character who is a female boxer. Like so many others, she watched the world of sports evolve, and she shifted and changed along with it. But in *On Boxing*, a book that still influences readers today, the author wants to pass as somewhat invisible, her gender present but also downplayed as neutral ('neutral' reads as male, game, one of the guys). By positioning women this way, Oates is also constructing a place for herself. She is the exception. As a non-fighter, this is the author's way of communing with men she admires, a loophole for entering a space that might not have her otherwise. This is her entrée into the ring.

I understand this impulse. Which leads me to an uncomfortable question: Am I so put off by this book because I see parts of myself in its author?

DOGMA FIGHT

Just as boxing was the foil for Japanese Jiu-Jitsu in the early twentieth century, mid-nineties Brazilian Jiu-Jitsu had to contend with pugilism – the so-called height of 'masculinity' – in order to prove itself. At that time, whoever held the heavyweight boxing championship belt was widely considered the toughest man in the world. It stands to reason, then, that if you wanted respect, you had to challenge the biggest guy – or, by extension, the manliest, toughest martial art – in order to truly win the fight. But because the first Ultimate Fighting Championship (UFC) event in November of 1993 was an unfamiliar proposition, outside of familiar rule sets, protections, fight purses, and recognizable title contention, most boxers were uninterested in taking part. Eventually, boxer Art Jimmerson agreed to join the first competition. Jimmerson, who famously and kind of hilariously appeared in UFC 1 wearing boxing shoes and a single boxing glove on his lead (left) hand demonstrated only a vague understanding of the tournament's concept. 'They talked about it being somewhat of a reality *Mortal Kombat* game,' he said years later. '*Mortal Kombat* and *Street Fighter* were real popular back then, where they had different martial arts in one game. I thought, "Wow, a video game come to life. Man, the boxer in those games always lands his jab. Why not me?" I was excited because it would be a challenge.' UFC was trying to fill a niche in a new pay-per-view market that was, at that time, simply a mix of 'movies, porn, and Mike Tyson.' In trying to position it as 'real' fighting, the promoters inadvertently laid bare the truth that lies beneath that conceit. Even 'real' fighting, with some goal of fantastical supremacy in mind, is in some sense, a game.

While the earliest UFC fighters are unabashed in imagining themselves as playable characters (and current ones actually do appear *as* animated video game characters), this blend of fight and fantasy is a privileged one. For frequently targeted groups, like women, LGBTQIA2S+ folks, and many people of colour, self-defence bears no resemblance to the fantasy play of *Street Fighter*. I myself have never confused the two. My vulnerability is too ingrained.

Real street fighting in a more basic sense is by no means the sole purview of boys or men. Sociological studies on street fighting for young girls show that this type of fighting is performative. The taboos for young women make it harder to navigate their role in public fighting, but the purpose of street fighting for girls and young women, in particular, is about establishing boundaries. It is a strategic move designed to set the tone, publicly, for how they want to be treated. They establish themselves as aggressors – active agents – rather than potential victims. Many young people see fighting as a necessary exercise that enables them to move more freely. This isn't a game. They are not fighting to defend their 'master's' (now their coach's) style. They are fighting to create a space in which they can exist.

NEITHER/NOR

The history of fighting has been richly generated, populated, and reproduced fist over fist with men. But I refuse to subscribe to the narrative that men get to have *all* the fighting, now or across any major section of human history. This masculinity is built into their history, just as it is built into the version of boxing that most writers describe. But history is a key word here. When I pull out commentary on female fighters over the years, the stereotypes are glaring for what they reveal about those speaking, not about the women they're (not actually) discussing. The idea that women could dilute a man's sport, and therefore his essential nature, points to just how fragile that model of 'natural' masculinity would have to be. As thousands of other more confident or open-minded male coaches, training partners, and competitors have demonstrated over the last centuries and decades, that fear is misplaced.

Any masculinity that needs to be so carefully guarded is not the kind to be preserved. We clearly need to rethink how we teach and reinforce notions of masculinity for boys and men. We also need to question how the rest of us might also be carrying the same ingrained assumptions. What's concerning is not just that these ideas exist, but rather the refusal to accept that these 'male' spaces can change; that women can be women *and* fighters – as well as all kinds of other things – and there doesn't need to be anything monstrous, damaging, or intrusive about acknowledging that coexistence or exploring what it might add.

CHAPTER FIVE
★
GRIN AND BEAR IT

I signed up to fight in California, but a return to my teaching job meant I had to move before I could step into the ring. Back in Vancouver, after joining my new gym, Diaz Combat Sports (DCS), I was encouraged to attend the women's advanced Muay Thai class. There, I was warmly welcomed with friendly classmates, good sparring, and an enticement to stay for the mixed advanced Muay Thai class that immediately followed the women's class; I enjoyed that class quite a bit, but in that second hour and a half, I worked harder than I could remember ever working before. It was exhausting and thrilling to push my limits that way. After that, I started attending that later Muay Thai class almost exclusively. I'd go in early to catch the end of the 'women's only' period, which bustled with energy, laughter, and affection. I got to listen to the participants' conversations and feel like I was part of a community, even as an observer. But because I wanted to compete, I was intent on getting the hardest and most consistent sparring possible, which seemed to be the later class, the mixed group. I'd sit among the women, like a fly on the floor, as I taped up and stretched, and then I'd collect my things and move over to the other side. I couldn't figure out how to bridge all the parts of what I sought.

More often than not, I was the only woman in attendance for the mixed sparring class – a stark contrast to the demographic of the gym's other Muay Thai sessions. The beginner and intermediate classes were often at least half full of women and the women's only classes routinely packed the gym. But in the more sparring-focused class, if two women showed up to the same session on the same day, our training might go on as usual, or it might be radically changed. Instead of working with everyone, as we usually did, there were many instances, both in my Vancouver training and in other Muay Thai gyms I've visited, where suddenly we 'ladies' were *only* allowed to work with each other. I can understand, on one level, why this might make sense; there are many men who have trouble regulating their temper or power (although someone with that lack of control generally should not be in a higher-level sparring class). On a more basic level, two women might be closer in size, weight, or level of experience to each other than to our male counterparts. But this was not always the case. And where classmates routinely switch partners many times throughout the class, the effect of being assigned to a single person is one that can limit our experience and opportunities. Part of how we grow is through training with different people, and working through issues with different levels of competition. After being treated as an equal five days out of six, these more limited training days felt off-putting and deflating.

To complicate matters further, if the other woman didn't like being stuck with only *me*, and kept from her usual freedom to move through multiple training partners, then it would be a long training session. The few times I've lost my temper in training have come when I was tethered to a partner who didn't want anything to do with me. Perhaps she wanted to hit me hard and not be hit just as hard back (she's used to training with men who don't retaliate in kind); or, as likely, someone saw me as an unknown and therefore dismissed me as a partner who would need to be taught and would simply slow her down. Suddenly, instead of training, I'd find myself stuck in a tense but tacit interpersonal negotiation, one I'd rather not have to deal with. If I came off too soft, or deferential, I would be underestimated, bossed around, and patronized. If I was too hard, I seemed confrontational, and things could get tense.

These are dynamics I am so used to managing with men as to make them almost second nature. But these male-female dynamics also take different forms. If I start sparring with a man for the first time and he won't do anything but tap me gently with his glove, or worse, shadowbox in front of me, I respond with a quick, stiff jab to the face. That tends to get the message across clearly, and we move forward. The last time I did that, one of the coaches noticed the shock on my new training partner's face. 'Oh, yeah, she's a killer,' he laughed, and then it was clear that my partner was not to simply patronize me for one round until he could get a real opponent. Like him, I was there to train.

My female training partners had always been warm and welcoming, greeting other women with open arms. This was also the case with the many female training partners I eventually connected with at DCS. I learned that I relaxed most with partners who were open to working with me and to being both confident *and* vulnerable. Training together was a dialogue, as opposed to a conflict. One woman kicked so hard I was compelled to ask her to give me a lesson after class. And she did. She was confident, generous, and willing to be open about her own questions and challenges. The occasional days where we'd overlap were the ones when I felt the lightest and the most willing to ask for help, instead of fighting to show I belonged.

With sporadic new female sparring and training partners, I was reminded of how intimate training can be, and what a difference it makes working with someone whose temperament, rhythms, and cues you know well, versus those of a total stranger. On the days when something was lost in translation, I wasn't able to communicate my needs and we seemed to have trouble gauging each other. I'd never had this kind of problem with female partners before, and the tension of these questions (What does it mean to be exceptions together? How do I deal with the fact that I am losing my temper in uncharacteristic ways? How will this strange training dynamic translate to my actual fight?) was no doubt compounded by my pre-fight stress. Combined with that was the emotional challenge of trying to belong somewhere entirely new. I was so fixated on the misfires that I had trouble giving it a fair shot. I can't imagine I was the best partner.

After an unusual week with a series of these 'ladies only' training exceptions, I showed up to a small class, just me and three bigger men. The teacher looked at all of us and shook his head. 'This won't do,' he said. 'Three big men and one tiny lady.' As we stood together in a circle – in the advanced class to which he had originally invited me – he turned to me, in front of the others, and suggested that perhaps I'd be more comfortable over on the other side (in the beginner or intermediate classes), doing pad work. This wasn't really about my comfort, however. The size imbalance was clearly going to mess with the symmetry of what he had planned that day. Fortunately, one of the regular students in the class spoke up on my behalf. 'No, she belongs here,' he said. 'She's one of us.' The gym owner, too, called out from the desk, reminding my teacher that I had a fight coming up in a week. I needed the sparring. For my part, I turned to the biggest, scariest-looking guy there, a tall, tattooed man I'd never met, and pointed my finger at him. 'I'm tougher than *this fucking* guy,' I declared, only half joking. The coach finally conceded, and, of course, paired me with the large man I'd just insulted to make my point. We started a kicking partner drill together, and he smashed me with a good, solid kick. I smiled to myself. I deserved that. And it was worth it. From that point on, we got along fine.

SMILE

With gyms currently closed during this seemingly never-ending COVID-19 crisis, I have a different set of issues. Entirely alone, without anyone to yell at me, cheer me on, or knock me around, I have taken to exercising outdoors. One day, after a few rounds of non-stop shadowboxing, I eventually drop my hands, lift my gaze back to the world, and walk toward my bag, which is resting on the ground nearby. But someone has been watching. 'Smile!' an older man instructs as he makes his way toward me. I freeze. 'Why don't *you* smile,' I retort with a nervous laugh. I've gone so long without talking to another human being that my communication skills have fallen by the wayside. He caught me off guard. He comes closer and starts to tell me about fighting, and asks me if I've ever fought before. I mumble short replies and step away, returning to my shadowbox-ing. But it's just a pretense. I wait two minutes, pack up, and leave.

This is a familiar interaction. When I first started training, I knew I wanted to get better as much, and as quickly, as possible. That goal helped me to overcome my usual shyness about being in a gym. My kickboxing classes took place in a studio within a diverse neighbour-hood gym, and so it was unlike an MMA gym, for instance, where nearly everyone is interested in martial arts. While I didn't feel comfortable working out on my own within the open space of the gym, I was able to push myself to attend group classes within the imagined safety and closed doors of the class studio. Soon, however, even my new cocktail of kickboxing, Pilates, and yoga classes wasn't enough; I needed extra practise, beyond what I could learn in my (three-times-a-week) kickboxing class. I summoned my courage and booked private training sessions. As a woman in a gym, if I don't know what I'm doing (or, as it turns out, even if I do), more often than not some random guy will come up and tell me. But the way I saw it, if I was out there in the open space of the gym but someone was *already* teaching me how to train, then the rabble wouldn't have to step in. I could bypass the inevitable frustration by showing up with my own Alpha. So I budgeted my first new bit of teaching income, stopped buying clothes and eating out, and convinced my kickboxing coach to take me on for private training.

It worked. The gym was small enough that people with similar schedules recognized each other. Even as I started with baby steps to do some additional work in the gym on my own, without my coach next to me, I didn't have to deal with as many conversations as I normally would in that setting. Most of the regulars there either saw me working one on one with the kickboxing coach, or saw that I was already in the kickboxing classes, and generally abstained from offering their two cents when I was hitting the heavy bag on my own. Others might comment about me to my coach, but not directly to me. Their homosocial bonding spared me from having to be interrupted and pulled out of the comfortable shell I was working to build through focus, earbuds, and determination, so that was fine with me.

I have since learned enough of the language to be able to pass in martial arts studios and dojos more easily than in generic gyms. When I travel, I visit only MMA, boxing, and Muay Thai gyms. In these kindred spaces, the only time a stranger is likely to come up and give me unsolicited advice on technique or approach is if I attend a beginner class or visit an open workout period. Then (as much as I don't like to admit it), one way I try to get around having to talk to uninvited visitors is to go in and work only on things I feel very confident about. I'm not smooth when it comes to hitting a speed bag, for instance, so even though I desperately want to master it, I tend to avoid going near that thing unless I am feeling confident, I'm surrounded by people I train with regularly, or no one else is around. (There are always workarounds; a kind assistant coach at my boxing gym encourages me to stay after class when the gym empties. I practise on the speed bag in peace while she does her other work.) Even when working on things I can do very well, I might still be approached by some strange man who wants to explain to me how to do the thing I am already doing, or to ask my credentials to justify or explain the intensity of my training. If publicly flexing only my strengths doesn't work to keep the peace or stave off random mansplainers – and it certainly isn't helping me to fix my weaknesses – then I retreat. That, in turn, makes me angry. (In fact, the only tried and true solution I've ever found is to take a sledgehammer into the park to practise tire slams; no one, and I mean no one, bothers me when I am holding a sledgehammer.)

Training itself is not frustrating. More often than not, I walk into the gym in one attitude and leave lighter and refreshed, in a good mood; it's like I've hit reset and get to start the day over again from that point on. The times when I get interrupted this way, though, my reset has been stolen from me. It sends me back to where I was when I came in – or worse off, because I know what I've just lost.

There is a problem with this attitude. It shows that I am still learning how to be a fighter on my own terms. Without the security blanket of my coaches or teammates around me, and without anyone for me to hide behind – especially when I am feeling vulnerable or upset – I can be too apt to see myself the way strangers seem to view me, as a woman simply exercising to 'look good,' or someone play-acting at martial arts. Too often when someone tells me to smile, I laugh instead of explaining to them how patronizing that demand is. It doesn't occur to me in the moment to tell strange men to fuck off and mind their own business. I don't like the potential for uncon-trolled violence that I'm all too aware can be attached to encounters with strangers. And as contradictory as it seems, I don't *like* conflict; outside of the official rules of engagement, I have a bad habit of making myself soft and small in order to avoid it. But then I'm the one who misses out on the chance to hold my ground or to know what it feels like to refuse to shrink. Even as I am literally training to fight, too often I fall short of allowing that psychological part of my training to truly take hold.

ALLEGIANCE

I see myself as conflict averse; this is both true and not true. I co-organized a political art exhibition that opened at a community centre in Santa Cruz the week after my first fight. At the opening, which was largely populated by older women, a man, maybe in his fifties, showed up to protest the event. At first, he stood outside the picture window facing the room with a sign held up against the window. This did not garner him the level of response that he desired, so he made his way in and began to verbally challenge the women, who until that moment had been visiting pleasantly, paper plates and cups in hand. The man did what he could to take over the space with energy, force, and the way he held himself as a power within a room full of women. Organizers and participants took turns listening to him. They tried reasoning with him and ultimately asking him to leave, but he refused. At one point, he pulled out his camera and began to film everyone there, narrating his intentions as he did it. The bigger his self-righteous aggression got, the more diminutive the group seemed to become. I grew increasingly livid. As a relative outsider in the community, I didn't address him directly, but stayed close at hand and eventually held myself as a kind of warning at the border between the man and the group he was addressing. I crossed my arms and made myself tall. I took up space. I was strong in my anger, and still fresh from fighting only days before. As I stood, I suppressed a deepening impulse to grab him by the back of the arm. I'd throw in my shoulder and leverage my body weight to yank him out the door, where I would follow him out to the parking lot and deal with whatever came next.

I did none of those things, however. There was no call for me to introduce physical conflict into that space. The irony of the fact that I was daydreaming about manhandling a stranger at an event I was cohosting at – no joke – the Resource Center for Nonviolence was already thick enough. So I stood. Eventually, a young graduate student let him talk her ear off for a long time as she offered him her undivided attention and deference. Finally, after he'd talked himself in circles, she offered to walk out with him. *That's* how we got him to leave. A ritual female sacrifice was put forward to stroke his ego. For hours after, I stayed angry about this man, the way he was able to claim the space from everyone else, and what was done to placate him. What struck me as I rage-ate the large frozen yogurt buried in candy toppings I had picked up on the way home was the new feeling that had accompanied my anger. I'd been frustrated before. But for the first time, I had felt not just an abstract desire for physical aggression but an actual capacity for it. My body *knew* what steps it would take to carry it out. In that moment, I realized violence had become conceivable for me in a way it had never been before. This capacity, whether I chose to use it or not, reminded me of the love I had grown for my strong, capable body, for the things it could do for me. I wasn't small by default. I could choose to take up space. That night also showed me that if things had gotten physical, I wasn't powerless. I had options.

One of the things that fight training does is to hone important tools, like discipline, humility, and dedication. Academia has given me these same skills, to some extent, but there is an added dimension to fighting. In a predominantly masculine space, I bring my own personality, my own abilities, and my own physicality into play. I do deflect stress by making jokes. I prefer a training setting that allows me to work, and process, in a way that is true to my personality. Where I can be determined and focused, but still myself. I love training with *certain* women, just as I appreciate the different challenges that come with training with *certain* men. The two groups serve my growth in different ways, but I tend to be most at home with training partners who challenge me while also allowing me to be silly, tough, vulnerable, competitive, and determined, all at once.

The more women I watch doing the things I want to do, the more women show us how to inhabit space in their own unique ways, the more female fighters battle it out in the public eye, the more comfortable it gets for all of us. I love watching female training partners, coaches, and fighters demonstrate techniques, for instance, because their body inhabits the movements in a way that feels recognizable, and possible, for mine. When I was first learning kickboxing, we used to train in front of a mirror. I'd stand in the back row, and instead of watching myself, I'd watch the star student of the class, Tomoko, as she flowed smoothly through the moves. I tried to fashion my movements and pacing to match hers. At the same time, the co-ed nature of so much fight training, and of the MMA gym in particular, is also one of its strengths. In addition to teaching us how to fight, naturalizing a space where women and men function as equals gives us all an opportunity to work in close quarters with people who bring diverse life experiences and capabilities to the mat. I learn different ways of being as I move through different groups. I also impact the male-dominated spaces through my presence.

In the period when I was trying to find the right tone with my female Muay Thai training partners, I was simultaneously falling into a rhythm with my classmates in the Sunday morning Female Fighters class over at the boxing gym. These specific classes were only held once a week, but they were coached by two women, former national level and professional boxers. In these classes – where everyone who showed up identified as female *and* as a fighter, and where none of us was the exception because we all had been the exception – I found that balance of fun, vulnerability, and fierce yet supportive competition I had been craving since leaving my friends in California. In one of the first classes I attended, we had a hard session of bag work in which a room full of skilled, determined, no-bullshit women worked themselves ragged following the coach's instructions, all while cheering and whooping aloud to egg each other on. The buzzer rang for a one-minute break between rounds. With the sound of pummelled heavy bags suddenly silenced, music filled the room. As if on cue, the group of women burst into song. Fifteen sweat-soaked women danced along to the Lizzo track blaring from the sound system. They sang to each other, and to me, and waved their boxing glove–clad hands in the air as they danced. We revelled in our own unique mix of joy, fun, and punishingly hard work. The buzzer went off again and we snapped back to hitting the bags as hard as we could. The juxtaposition was fast enough to give you whiplash, and it was one of the truest illustrations I could imagine of what I love about martial arts, and about the power women have not just to fit into a space, but to transform it.

At martial arts competitions, most women I have come across seem genuinely happy to see others like them, who know what they are working through, and who might serve as training partners at some point in the future. The biggest difference between the dynamic of amateur women and the men that I have seen, or male fighters I've talked to, is that once the fight is done, often so is the rivalry. After a fight, more often than not, the woman I just fought will seek me out, or I will seek her out. We might sit cross-legged on the floor, side by side, comparing notes; I watch the other women around me as we size up competitors who might make a good fit for our own teammates, trade contact information across camps, add each other to social media, and congregate in groups to try to set up sparring dates where we will, no doubt, knock the stuffing out of each other. Competition is, at its best, an act of love and solidarity. In the intermission of my doctoral defence, my dad sprang up from his seat in the audience and took me by the arm as I tried to rush out to hide. 'They're asking you hard questions because they care what you think,' he told me forcefully, lovingly. This was sweet of him, even if it didn't fully comfort me at the time. In fight camp and competition with other women, however, I can see some parallel wisdom to this claim. I'm going to hit you for real, because I respect you. Because we have something to prove, both individually and together. As a small group within a much larger male space, we know that after we fight, we will still need each other. We fight for authenticity. But – like me skulking around the women-only period in the gym just to hear them ask each other about their date on Saturday, their kid's project, or to check up on how their big meeting went, or like the moment I gave my heart to a room full of dancing boxers – we also seek someplace to belong.

CHAPTER SIX
★
ANYWHERE BUT THE FACE

Despite the widespread presence of women in martial arts, competitive female fighters are often still considered an anomaly, and one that needs to be explained. When a woman wants to fight, she always hears the same two questions. One is 'Why?' And the other is 'But aren't you worried about your face?'

At one point, well into his training regimen, academic-turned-MMA-fighter Jonathan Gottschall described the thrill of showing up to work sporting a black eye. Inhabiting this rarified space with his badge of honour, described as a 'purple hammock of blood sagging under one eye,' the amateur fighter had a revelation: 'I found that somehow, in some very elemental dimension, I outranked all the other men present.' Even more, this badge of honour meant that 'now and then a woman looked at me in the way – or so I've imagined – women look at men who are dashing.' I can't speak to Gottschall's imagination, or this system of ranking to which I am, apparently, not privy.

I fought on an all-women's boxing fight card in early 2020. The event took place on a Saturday night, and a group of us from the same club, along with our female coaches, met up the next day for a celebratory brunch. It was a lovely morning, full of camaraderie and laughter and fun. We were a sight to behold, partly because half the women at the table had fresh, shiny new black eyes, bruised cheeks, or both. Clearly, we'd had some kind of a night. But no one talked about the 'dashing' glances we were getting from people who we imagined must be suddenly overcome with desire for us. Instead, one of the topics of conversation was a logistical discussion about how to live in the world for the next few days, or week, as a woman with a black eye. Women who had male partners suddenly couldn't be seen in public with them; for anyone looking, the associations of battery were too immediate. One brilliant suggestion, from my team-mate Tora, was to wear our Eastside Boxing shirts or sweaters wherever we went until our faces healed. Then strangers looked at your face, but before they would have time to worry, their gaze would pan down to the writing and their question would be answered. We had all fought hard the night before (and through the weeks and months of training before that), and every woman there was certainly as proud of their hard work, resilience, and power as Gottschall was of whatever he did to earn his banana hammock. And yet we didn't (and don't) have the luxury of feeling as though our marks from fighting caused us to outrank the men around us. Often, it's quite the opposite. Even when we feel most powerful, it puts us back in the place of having to take into account the way we look through others' eyes. And to them, we look like victims of abuse.

As seems to be the theme, this characterization is longstanding and ubiquitous. In a 1996 article in the *Vancouver Sun* titled 'Tough to Get Used to Women in Boxing Ring,' Archie McDonald throws in his two cents about women 'intruding into the male domains' of sport – the least defensible of which, he claims, is boxing. McDonald is responding, like many others, to that infamous match between Martin and Gogarty. 'When I see the wounded face of a woman boxer,' McDonald opines, 'I find it difficult to believe it has been inflicted by another woman. A battered woman is a battered woman. I get a queasy feeling in my stomach. It is a conditioned response. When I expressed my feelings to Wendy Long, our resident protector of women's sporting rights,' he continues – and there's a *lot* to unpack here already – 'she replied, "is it better that I walk around the ring in a bikini holding up a card with the number of the round on it, or that I'm out there competing fairly just like a man?"' Not surprisingly, McDonald doesn't give readers an account of how he actually replied to the real-life long-suffering token female on whom he had just foisted his opinion; he turns away from that encounter, instead, and picks back up on his monologue. 'It's just that I thought women had more noble emotions than men,' he says. 'Sensitive, caring, compassionate, humane. In the good old days women waited at home, wrung their hands and cried in front of a radio while Rocky

Graziano, son and husband, went to war with Tony Zale.' But those 'good old days' are now over, and he laments the time when 'moms left spankings to fathers and walked out when Friday night fights came on TV.' Perhaps worst of all, 'Now [women] are in the ring slugging it out, sometimes showing as much skill as men and usually more ferocity.'

I don't know what irks McDonald more here – that women are fighting with as much skill as their male counterparts, that they are undergoing some damage in the process, or that they are being hurt at the hands of other *women* instead of men. (Whatever the hierarchy between the three, it's a noxious mix, and one that is certainly not unique to this critic.) To make matters worse, for him, instead of women disappearing when boxing comes on TV, this sacred male space is being intruded upon. Men like McDonald would prefer to keep that imagined homosocial space to themselves; their joy is dampened by the idea of women who don't want to just get up and leave the room. Or the ring. If this version of masculinity hinges on its exclusive relation to violence and the power that goes with it, then it sounds like a pretty scary prospect, indeed, to have those spaces compromised and the arbitrariness of their power laid bare.

MARKED UP

While the idea of a fighting body is often stereotypically reduced to chiselled musculature, fighters don't all necessarily fit into this type. There's also a way of carrying the body, of holding one's ground; being a fighter means being comfortable holding your own space. Another common aesthetic for a lot of fighters is the seemingly requisite tattoos, as well as other visual calling cards. There are also aesthetic markers like the cauliflower ear, which is common in male fighters – particularly MMA, wrestling, and Jiu-Jitsu practitioners – but much less so in women. The condition that causes cauliflowering (broken, bumpy cartilage) is often avoid-able – there are protective ear coverings for wrestling, as well as ways to drain some of the blood when injuries are relatively fresh. Cauliflower ears, then, are sometimes an aesthetic choice. A male fighter friend of mine explained how he was pulled over one night on the way back from a gig. He's a drummer in a jazz band and was in a black suit and tie, and despite the outfit, the police officer immediately tagged him as trouble. 'You're a tough guy,' he said. The ears overruled the suit. For those in the know, the ears signal someone not to mess with (or someone *to* mess with, depending on where your head is at, I suppose).

Some visual hallmarks come with the territory. Scarring; crooked or unnaturally flattened noses from repeated impact – these are all markings of fighters, as well. Surgery scars and marks on shins and elbows are common. I have slight bumps along my shin bones from deep bruising and micro-fracturing, and that's from sparring and fighting in shin pads, not even bare-legged. When MMA or Muay Thai fighters kick their opponent without padding, and the other checks the kick, which means they lift up their leg to block the kick with their own shin, sharp bone meeting sharp bone, the skin will often burst open at the point of contact.

Scars are not simply aesthetic, though, and losing the integrity of the skin can become a real problem. When a boxer gets hit above the eye and that delicate skin around the forehead or eyebrow slices open, it leads to bleeding mid-fight. But the issue doesn't end there. Long after that cut has healed, the fighter will go into the next fight (and the fight after that) with scar tissue, like a virtual dotted line marking the points where their skin is the weakest. Scar tissue makes it easier for that spot to keep splitting open, which leads some fighters to go so far as having their brow bones shaved down somewhat, to make them less defined and therefore less of a sharp edge (to keep their *own* bones from cutting through *their own skin*). Blood from a cut can get in a fighter's eyes and obscure their vision, of course. It can also have a psychological effect on the judges and the audience. It's easy to be swayed by the sight of blood as a signal of the opponent's success.

If scars are potential liabilities within the ring, they also function like merit badges outside it. They incrementally remap the contour of the face and body to reflect a life of fighting. In 2015, Australian Muay Thai fighter John Wayne Parr had *International Kickboxer* magazine stage a photograph with all of his previous stitches drawn in (although the ones in and under his hairline were not made visible for the image). Parr has collected over three hundred stitches to his face over the course of his almost thirty-year (and counting) Muay Thai and boxing career. The result is a raccoon-mask of stitches threaded around and above and between his eyes, as well as a nasty few winding up his lower lip that would do Frankenstein's monster proud. The image folds time by showing the accumulation of damage all at once, as if incurred in one fight, rather than over a lifetime. It makes the scarring present for the viewer in a manner that is hard to ignore. That's a whole lot of stitches, but Parr narrates them in surprising detail, telling which fight, and often even which strike, caused each gash.

Whereas Parr's scars are celebrated – with some caveat about injury – the female members of the Parr family have to fight outside the ring in order to earn their right to the same kinds of markings. The Parrs, who own Boonchu Gym in Queensland, Australia, have made an appearance again recently in the discussion around cuts and scarring, but this time it is other members of the family who are speaking. On June 4, 2020, Angela Rivera-Parr, a former professional Muay Thai kickboxer, boxer, and MMA fighter, posted an online response to Thailand's (all-male) Boxing Committee's vote about whether to make elbow pads mandatory for female Muay Thai fighters. As Rivera-Parr argues, 'on behalf of myself and my daughter Jasmine' (a Muay Thai fighter in her own right): 'Women are tough, conditioned, skilled, and dangerous. Fighting is fighting, Muay Thai is the art of 8 limbs. No pads for professional fighters, Man or woman.' The Parrs, along with a number of other Muay Thai gyms and fighters in Thailand and beyond, are responding to backlash around the regulation of the aesthetics of female Muay Thai. As Muay Ying, who focuses on issues around Muay Thai, explains, the debate follows a social media post 'several months ago depicting a few good-looking women with cuts on their faces' with a 'caption [that] called for extra protection for women. This is another example of how women are objectified in Muay Thai and how beauty is prioritized BY OTHER PEOPLE over skill level or the fact that they're a fighter.' Whereas John Wayne Parr joked five years earlier in his caption to the scar photo that his 'modelling career days are over,' these markers tend to get a pass for men that is harder to come by for women. For the

Parr patriarch, the scars point to the gritty realities of an illustrious fighting career. These were earned in battle.

I train in Muay Thai, but I don't compete in the sport, which means I don't have to worry about taking one of these elbows for real any time soon. I like practising them on pads, though, and I've always appreciated the strategy of the elbow, as it was explained to me. An elbow to the face is a hard shot – bone on bone – but that's not its only function. The way many elbows are thrown has them landing across the forehead or the brow bone. Like the punches a boxer takes that open up the space above their eye, the cut along the brow or forehead produces a lot of blood. The elbow is the kind of strike that tends to draw blood that then streams into your opponent's eyes and makes them look as though they are being beaten up. Blood is persuasive to the audience, whose cheers and cries can affect everyone in the room, including the judges and the fighters themselves. I've always enjoyed the theoretical, strategic aspect of this kind of strike. But a gash from an elbow does cause scarring, as any cut will. In Thailand, especially, noticeable scarring is actually frowned upon for both men and women, though men are not openly criticized for it the way women are. Muay Thai fighter Sylvie von Duuglas-Ittu admits, 'I get a lot of shit for my cuts. People who are watching me in the ring get very excited because I keep fighting and am generally smiling afterward; gamblers and viewers love that. But they're not badges of honour here, socially; a cut is a mistake and having multiple cuts means you haven't learned from that lesson.' For female fighters, and younger ones especially, the aesthetics of fighting, even within the heart of the sport itself, don't so readily allow for them to carry these signs of battle. This bias extends beyond the look of the fighter, however. As former Spanish Muay Thai champion Desirée Rovira explains, 'Most Thai female fighters do not fight in a forward, muay khao, clinch style [where they get in tight and grapple at close range – the perfect distance for throwing elbows] in part because of the risk to the face.' Many female fighters adopt the 'fimeu' style instead, which involves more control of distance through kicking and controlling the space. For women, the cultural values around the look of scarring impact the style of fighting they adopt within the ring.

Female fighters who train and compete in 'hard' martial arts like MMA, boxing, and Muay Thai are often asked about the damage that can come from fighting; they are expected to address the question of 'risking beauty for victory.' This is often the biggest issue, for a lot of people, when they hear about women training and fighting – my friends and family included. The concern is, first and foremost, for the face. Explaining her objection to the question itself, which situates beauty as a determinant of value that women are told they must consider, von Duuglas-Ittu tallies her scars, nose breaks, and glued cuts, and concludes: 'I look differently than I did before. But, if you happen to find me attractive it's because of Muay Thai. My body looks the way it does because of how Muay Thai has shaped it. I am happy and healthy and have light in my face because of my love for Muay Thai. My face *is* changing.' These scars and breaks point to lessons and experiences. Like aging, the signs of life are marked on the body, but there can be a satisfaction to a line or a mark that has a very clearly locatable origin. On the objection to 'permanent' marks from fighting, von Duuglas-Ittu confides, 'Here's the secret that people who don't know fighting don't understand: everything about fighting is permanent. Every time I get in the ring I come out of it a different person and a better fighter … permanently.' Part of why people fight *is* to change, to grow, to push themselves. It makes sense, then, to welcome the outward signs of that journey, whether through developing musculature or scarring, or both.

The current debate about elbow pads for women points to one of the many gender double standards even at the professional levels of martial arts. Female fighters are expected to look strong, and the aesthetic aims for clearly defined musculature – weight training is often a must – but there's still an expectation to prove oneself not just as a fighter but also as a woman. In the marketing of fighters, and in female fighters' self-representation through social media, there is an implication that women must be feminine or sexy *and* tough. But the two must coexist seamlessly. Of course, there is no rule that says female fighters have to be feminist. And if they are, the model and definition of what that means is a moving target. The #DontRushChallenge that circulated on TikTok and Instagram some time ago highlighted this double-edged gendered dynamic (although any glance at some weigh-in outfits and the way a fighter like Rousey poses on the scale while stripped down, with her shoulders back, chest out, and a wry pout, suggests another way this comes into play). In the #DontRushChallenge videos, the participants play on variations of a formula: female fighters appear tough and sweaty in their gym clothes – the way most who know them as only fighters are used to seeing them. Then the camera gets obscured for a second. When they reappear, they are all decked out in their 'regular' clothes – whether that's an outfit that looks like it's meant for a night out, or full-on evening wear. My social media accounts were flooded with variations on this theme, but the similarity across most adaptations was striking. There was a consistent desire to look both super tough and stereotypically feminine, even sexy. But these things aren't mutually exclusive. Sociological studies have shown that, for women engaging in 'hard' martial arts in particularly male-dominated spaces, there tends to be a call to balance that masculinity with equal displays of hegemonic, and often heterosexual, femininity. And whether making these videos for themselves, or for an audience, there's a consistent refrain: 'I am tough *and* feminine. I can be both. (And perhaps by being both, I'm even more of each.)' These same fighters are often met with exclamations of surprise when people find out what they do – something along the lines of 'but you're so pretty' or, more pointedly, 'you're too pretty to be a fighter.' But that assumption, as ignorant and baseless as it is, also shows a lack of understanding of how the professional fight business works.

In 2012, the year Olympic boxing finally admitted women, Mary Spencer was preparing to fight on behalf of Team Canada. Spencer, a boxer of the Cape Croker Ojibwe First Nation in Ontario, was also making history as an Indigenous woman in sport. A decorated boxing champion, Olympic favourite, and humanitarian, Spencer gained a contract with CoverGirl cosmetics. As soon as she became a 'model,' this identity seemed to overshadow the actual work – the boxing – that had raised her profile in the first place. When Spencer's Olympic appearance didn't result in a medal, many news headlines sounded almost gleeful in their coverage. Being pretty, or presenting in a way that is sexualized, can play a big part in the marketing of women, just as looking tough is part of the package for marketing men. There are certainly exceptions to this rule, but the fight game does not fully remove gendering from its aesthetics.

JUNK MAIL

In one of his most persistent themes, the man who sends me threatening messages obsesses over the concept of *beauty*. As it turns out, the class in which we met was a first-year college English literature course I taught called 'Monster Theory,' or, alternatively, 'The Monster's Body.' We studied monstrosity as a theoretical concept and a metaphor for difference, cultural bias and fear, and anxiety about social and political change. When it comes to monsters, there is just no getting around the aesthetic: the body always represents so much more than itself. In a bit of unintentional humour, many months later, the stalker's messages start referring to me as the 'Bride of Frankenstein' – a character from an old film I showed in the course. With his limited imagination, he decides I must be wildly insecure about my own appearance. This monstrous reference is clearly intended to sting. For him, my dual roles as both teacher and fighter are mystifying. I must be there to try to punish men, or fuck them, or both. (Because *he* is obsessed with appearance and sexuality, he must tell himself that I am, too.) At the same time, his messages try to convince me (read: himself) that he could beat me in a fight. Throughout this narrative, his anger takes shape in a specific, if consistent, fixation: the fantasy of destroying my face. As a surrogate for this literal violence, he collects photographs of me, crops my face, and scrawls messy red text across them instead. Virtual scars.

In the 1935 film *Bride of Frankenstein*, the monstrous 'Bride' is actually quite beautiful. She has tall, dark, dramatic hair with a white streak cutting through it like lightning. Although she bears the same stitching as her clunky Boris Karloff counterpart – a visual reminder that she is something unnatural – the filmmakers were careful not to let these stitch marks obscure her features. Once again, there's a prohibition against scarring up a woman's face. Monsters are apparently no exception. In the big twist near the end of the film, we discover that the Bride is played by the same actress as the character who depicted *Frankenstein* author Mary Shelley in the opening scene. The woman is doubled. The female author *is* the monster.

Just as Mary Shelley crossed conventional societal lines and inserted herself into the male spaces of authorship back in 1818, 'monstrous' female fighters are crossing lines into a self-declared masculine space. Like Shelley, they are refusing to accept the space on its own terms, and instead are turning it into something else.

Bride of Frankenstein? I've been called worse. I'll take it.

CHAPTER SEVEN
★
MENTAL TOUGHNESS

'Thug' Rose Namajunas is one of the top-ranked competitors (and the former champion) in the UFC's Women's Straw-weight Division. She is perhaps as well known for her unconventional approach to a professional fighter's lifestyle and personality as she is for her MMA skill. Namajunas is reportedly a homebody; she tends to talk about love and kindness, and mostly keeps to herself. More importantly, she is unusually candid about her feelings, concerns, and insecurities. She has even been known to cry out of frustration (scandal!) in hard sparring sessions. Upon losing her title belt to Jessica Andrade in 2019, Namajunas caused an uproar by saying she was happy to have the pressure off her shoulders. In her post-fight interview, she admitted to not being entirely solid about her choice to keep fighting, and so in that moment, anyway, losing was a kind of relief.

Like Namajunas, Bellator MMA's Rory 'Red King' MacDonald, an elite and accomplished martial artist, has expressed misgivings about fighting. When interviewed after successfully defending his Bellator Welterweight Championship, MacDonald stood on the canvas of the octagon in which he had just fought, and admitted – with the gold championship belt strapped around his waist – that he was questioning the very nature of his life's work. A professional MMA fighter since he was sixteen years old, MacDonald claims to have found himself increasingly conflicted between his religious beliefs and his career. In the interview, MacDonald declares that he is not sure he still has a 'killer inside.' As he explains, it 'takes a certain spirit to come in here and put a man through pain … I just don't know if I have that same drive to hurt people anymore.'

While they have both since returned to fighting with arguably the same ardour as before, Namajunas and MacDonald opened themselves up to criticism by publicly admitting their ambivalence about the combat sports in which they excel. MacDonald's detractors have openly worried about his ability to do whatever it takes to win. Those who criticize Namajunas tend to jump straight to a harsher psychological evaluation; they accuse her of being emotionally unstable because of her tears and admissions of uncertainty. Despite the fact that she has risen to some of the highest ranks possible for a fighter, her emotionality is regarded as a fundamental weakness.

By whatever different – and gendered – standard they are judged, both Namajunas and MacDonald have been accused of not being mentally fit for fighting because they expressed some form of doubt. By displaying nuanced feelings, and by admitting that title belts are, at times, uneasy burdens, the fighters have run afoul of the single-minded, unquestioning, somewhat elusive, slippery concept of 'mental toughness' that is prized in MMA fighting. And, as the two fighters continue to compete, this raises questions. How are emotion, empathy, and vulnerability connected to the drive, focus, and aggression required of a fighter? And how do we tend to read and communicate these traits differently across gendered norms?

Mental toughness, like bravery, or faith, is one of those things that no one really sees when things are going their way. It counts most when they are not. Faith – whether in a deity, in one's coaches, or most significantly here, in oneself – is only truly important when it comes up against the potential for doubt.

YOU'RE ONLY EVER FIGHTING YOURSELF

In the second week of the COVID-19 social distancing shutdown in Vancouver, Radetsky starts making instructional videos – daily assignments – and texting them to Paschel and me as part of our ongoing group text. Our shared relationship in text, like in life, is a seamless mix of silly puns, intimate discussions, and a near-obsessive stream of martial arts technique, analysis, and appreciation. Throughout the social distancing period, Radetsky records videos detailing daily assignments, his toddler Dari climbing on him or mimicking his movements in the background as he demonstrates and explains the technique. He sends these instructions every morning. Over the course of the day, we each work on the technique or drill, film it, and then share our homework with the others, who respond with encouragement, feedback, and tips. It's a way to train together while apart.

I am almost religious about completing these assignments. In complete isolation, this is one way to be connected. Perhaps more importantly, it's a way for me to feel that I am growing and training during a period when I otherwise feel very lost. One day, a month into distancing, Coach switches randomly from offering a specific technique to a different kind of assignment. Our task, he explains, is to stage a five-round fight. Two minutes per round for women, three for men – we are observing actual competition times. We each make a game plan, and then follow our strategy, adapting it from one round to the next as our 'corner' (still just me) sees fit. The idea is to simulate a fight, and to imagine how it will work and how we might need to anticipate and make changes to the plan throughout, depending on what does and doesn't succeed with our (imaginary) opponent. We are to film the assignment and deconstruct it for the tape.

As I listen to Radetsky's instructions, my stomach falls. I'm shaking my head. *Nope.* I frown the word as I bow my head and wag a finger in the air. That sounds like a terrible idea, and I have no desire to do it. What that means, of course, is that I'm intimidated. While I shadowbox regularly, I don't feel I have the necessary imagination or insight into planning, cornering, and fighting (there's a reason I don't write fiction! I study the world around me – I don't know how to make one up). I'm nagged with old insecurities about my ability to control my technique and movement. I can barely handle *my* side of the fight, let alone both.

The day passes – I don't do it. Another day goes by, and the task weighs on me. I avoid it.

Some months ago, a coach from our community, Jeff, offered to do some work with me as I was preparing for a fight. We did pad work and drills as well as some guided shadowboxing. In addition to – or rather, as a part of – being a long-time martial arts coach, Jeff is an avid documentarian. An archivist at heart, he has been filming and photographing fights and training sessions for decades. In an attempt to illustrate the importance of shadowboxing, he took out his laptop and (speaking in hushed tones) showed me digitized video footage of his beloved former students, fighters I now know as coaches and local Santa Cruz legends. I sat cross-legged on the mat as he propped the computer on a folding chair and we clicked through his files. In one, a young kickboxer, Aaron, my first boxing coach, was training in the middle of an old gym space while others looked on and called out words of support. Jeff was manning the camera and cornering Aaron at the same time. Aaron was fighting a tough match – he slipped and cut angles against his opponent; he blocked kicks and counters with attacks of his own; he circled around him, clutched and kneed him, threw punches and narrowly escaped being hit with strikes himself. His teammates yelled advice or analysis to him as the fight went on. The fighters worked through an intense but technical battle. It amazed me because I could see the push and pull of the struggle, the moments when the advantage shifted from one to the other, the instances where one set up a pattern and then exploited it. But I was not actually watching two men. Aaron was all by himself. It was the first time (and one of very few times since) where shadowboxing didn't just look to me like someone flowing through moves on their own. I was watching a battle between a young kickboxer and one tough-ass Invisible Man. But the mirage wasn't in my mind – it was in Aaron's.

When the fighter understands the game and can feel the rhythm of the moves in mind and body, they can play both parts, inhabit both sides of the ring. It's like when you've known someone for so long that you can already anticipate what they will say or do in any situation.

For the same reason, shadowboxing is widely agreed to be an essential tool for fighters. Simulated battle is as old as martial arts itself. It has been around since at least the ancient Greek and Roman empires. In many Asian cultures, martial arts choreography is literally an art form (in Japan 'kata' is a foundational part of martial arts training). While this form of simulated fighting has been around for ages, George Dixon is credited with inventing the now ubiquitous practice of shadowboxing. Dixon, a fighter from Nova Scotia, Canada, was the first Black world champion (in boxing or otherwise, apparently) and the first boxer to ever win two world championship titles, claiming his second in 1891. Dixon was something of an autodidact and supplemented his training using his own patented combination of footwork, hand weights, and a tidy little invention now known as the heavy bag. (He went as far as to outline these processes in his 1893 pamphlet 'A Lesson in Boxing.') Despite the difficulty of social conditions, his diminutive size in a time when boxing didn't adhere to weight classes (when he started he was five-foot-three and about eighty-seven pounds), and the constant presence of blatant racism working against him as a Black man in the nineteenth and twentieth centuries, Dixon trained and competed relentlessly. Winning the world bantamweight title in boxing in 1892, he paved the way for world heavyweight champion Jack Johnson and many others. Dixon's training innovations are a product of his work ethic and the hurdles he faced. He credited his technical skills especially to his simulation training, his shadow-boxing. Whether borne of necessity or strategy or both, shadow-boxing is as much a mental exercise as it is a physical one.

Sport and behavioural psychologists have long claimed the benefits of visualization exercises. Shadowboxing is that and more – it's a form of embodied visualization, taking the theory to the furthest logical extent. Fighters are often encouraged to practise part of their training in front of a mirror. Working with a mirror gives the fighter a chance to see the flaws in their technique or holes in their defence. We eventually learn how to locate the gaps in our opponent's defence by identifying our own, and vice versa. The mirror also gives the fighter a visual antagonist to face off against, a reliable adversary who also happens to be perfectly matched in weight and height. Practising without a mirror, the fighter is challenged differently. Sometimes, they will start with a pylon or an object on the ground as a stand-in, and eventually their opponent will simply be in their mind as they practise shifting and angling in relation to their shadow's movement. It's at once an exercise in imagination and in suspended disbelief.

I know why it's valuable, and even necessary to do this five-round shadow fighting exercise. But the idea of going through with it fills me with anxiety and self-doubt. I'm suddenly shy. I feel exposed.

Later that week, the words 'mental toughness' start poking at me like an annoying mantra, and I know I can't put it off any longer. I'm embarrassed about having hidden from the training I said I wanted.

I know from experience that the things that scare me this way are the things I need the most. Knowing that doesn't make it any easier, though. I work through the morning and early afternoon, as usual. Mid-afternoon, I go out to the park for my daily training break. I claim a few metres of space to jump rope and shadowbox in Stanley Park, now Vancouver's communal living room. I film that day's kickboxing homework assignment. And then I work toward a school deadline until it's time for my next break. That evening, I tell myself grudgingly, it is time for my fight.

I have set up puzzle mats in the middle of my apartment with the idea that they will make it easier to transition my indoor training from MMA and boxing gyms to Zoom classes, yoga videos, and Instagram live sessions. I dress my bulbous, rainbow-coloured, stuffed llamacorn (yes: a llama unicorn) and my tiny beloved childhood stuffed raccoon in T-shirts emblazoned with my gym's logo and set up a chair for them at the edge of the mat next to a water bottle. These are my corners. This has to be the most uncool fight setup possible, the fact of which is both appropriate and inconsequential. I am supposed to be able to rise above all of it, I tell myself. But who am I kidding – I need the support. I consider wearing boxing gloves to try to make this simulation feel different from my usual shadowboxing, but when I pull one onto my hand as I stand in the middle of my living room, I feel ridiculous, like a kid playing dress-up, and toss them aside. Muttering to myself again, I compromise by wrapping my hands instead. In terms of protection, wrapping is entirely unnecessary. My hands and wrist don't need to be bolstered against the air, after all, and I haven't made any form of physical contact with people *or* objects for weeks – thus the reliance on the admittedly green coaching staff of Lego the Llamacorn and Rakki Raccoon – but I'm trying to meet my imagination halfway.

Fortunately, the act of wrapping my hands is mnemonic. It's a moment of ritual and devotion and a satisfying slowing. I linger in the process of winding and smoothing the cloth as I draw the lines around my wrist and hands, around and across, around and over again. After thousands of repetitions, wrapping has taught me to shift into another mode. Today, the sacramental gesture is not lost. It helps me to get where I need to be.

I open my phone to the notepad app and try to sketch out a plan. I set up the camera and try to do a round to practise and get a feel for the space and the assignment. It goes terribly. I am sliding around on the sleek new flooring, like Bambi on ice. I'm hesitant and self-conscious. I want so badly to see the opponent in front of me, but there's no Invisible Woman offering to take me on. I'm on a mat in the middle of my own apartment, and – like every other day – there's only me.

After an underwhelming warm-up round, I figure I've come this far and decide to begin in earnest. I look for something to spray on my feet as I prepare to work on brand new mats. Hairspray, strangely, helps to give some tackiness to the bottoms of the feet, to gain more grip. In the absence of hairspray, which I don't seem to own, I get a non-toxic kitchen cleaner and spray the bottoms of my feet to keep them from slipping on the smooth mats. I set my phone's timer and open the camera and press record. The fight begins. Most championship fights tend to have a slower first round or two. This isn't intended simply to conserve energy, although it might do that, too. Each opponent needs to get a read on the other's rhythm and tendencies, try out different moves to see how the other responds. I throw jabs to see how far my opponent's hand moves to parry it, for instance. If they move their hand down too much when I jab at them, I happily take note. Later, I will fake a jab and take advantage of the opening created by that too-big movement to hit them with a hook instead. This is the kind of reconnaissance work early rounds are often meant for, especially in sports like boxing that, depending on the rule set, can go a whopping ten rounds, or MMA championship fights, whose five five-minute rounds stretch out to twenty-five minutes of battle. That is a really long time to be in a fight. These early minutes of the fight are the place to study, test for holes or weaknesses, get a sense of what your opponent can do, and set up expectations for them about your own rhythm and patterns that you can later undermine.

In my living room, I start with a jab. And another jab. And then … before I know it, the fight gets out of control. The game plan goes out the window. It's still the first round, and now I'm throwing right hand power punches; next, I find myself in the clinch. We're locked in conflict, both throwing knees at each other's ribs, and it's still not even two minutes in. Things have gone off the rails.

This kind of frenetic pace isn't unheard of for a fight; when there are only two-minute rounds – in most women's fights, for instance – there is no real time to waste. The short timeline dictates the style of fighting. Between each round, I take thirty seconds to respray my feet, but I'm too keyed up even to drink water. I'm impatient. I want to get it over with. Each time, I tell myself that I will focus on my game plan for that round. Each time, I go into the next round and make some improvements, but ultimately find myself knocked a little bit off course. I am trying to see two people, and to be strategic, but I'm not entirely sure who is doing what. This exercise requires that I tell myself a story and believe it, but I am still struggling with giving myself over to my imagination.

There is a famous scene in the movie *Fight Club* in which Edward Norton's character's boss, Richard Chesler, tries to fire him. Norton's unnamed protagonist starts by countering the termination with an offer to let the company keep him on the payroll without any work. This is clearly a ridiculous request, and Chesler isn't buying it. As his boss calls out to security to have him removed, Norton's character tightens his right fist, which has been dangling down along the side of his chair. As if accosted by an alien limb that winds up and swings, Norton is punched hard in the face by his own fist, knocking him onto the floor. Both he and Chesler are locked in a wide-eyed stare as Norton's arms proceed to knock himself onto a glass coffee table, then yank him up to eventually be thrown into a set of shelves. We can hear him begging for mercy – his plaintive voice an unsettling contrast to the cool control of his violent body – as Chesler simply stares on, incredulous. At the risk of giving a decades-old movie spoiler away (here's your chance to skip a few lines past if you haven't seen it), this scene does more than show the lengths to which the character's imagination (and insanity) will go. It also points to what we will later realize is the duality within the protagonist himself. He is both himself and his best friend / greatest threat, Tyler Durden. This pantomime in the office foreshadows the big reveal; this scene is more faithful to the character's true self than it seems.

I recently taught this film in a freshman English literature course as part of a unit on Robert Louis Stevenson's *The Strange Case of Dr. Jekyll and Mr. Hyde*. In their essays, a small but notable cluster of students wrote about *Fight Club* as a variation on *Jekyll and Hyde* using the Jungian theory of the 'shadow self.' (The first paper I read that brought this psychological reference into play impressed me; I love a good theoretical frame for an argument, and it's not a reference I had emphasized in my lectures. After the second and third eerily similar 'shadow self' papers came across my desk, however, I began to worry that instead of looking at an interesting interpretation, I might end up filling out a lot of paperwork about plagiarism.) The 'shadow self,' for Carl Jung, is the opposite of the persona we put forward (for ourselves and others). The shadow is 'that hidden, repressed, for the most part inferior and guilt-laden personality whose ultimate ramifications reach back into the realm of our animal ancestors and so comprise the whole historical aspect of the unconscious.' The shadow is largely perceived as negative, though it refers to the amoral aspects of our psyche that are denied when we are conscious. We may learn about our shadows, in this model, through observing the behaviours and tendencies of others, then determine how to project our assessment of what we do or don't like or value into our own self-analysis. It's only once a subject can accept and assimilate both sides (take the shadow on as part of themselves) that these can be reconciled.

This duality is something I have struggled with outside of the ring. I had a university instructor once who hesitated to let me into his undergraduate class because, as he put it, his being my teacher would mean that we couldn't date. I stared blankly and said I was fine with that exchange – I needed the credit. At the end of the term, we met to discuss my evaluation, which consisted of one enigmatic claim that has frustrated me ever since: 'Your self-doubt is at once your biggest strength and your greatest weakness,' he announced with finality. For the second time, I simply stared at him, taken aback. I inwardly wrinkled my nose as I sat dumbfounded yet still no less eager to please. ('Okay. But what does that actually *mean?*') Strangely (because really, what *does* that actually mean?), this isn't the last time someone has graced me with this assessment. So I keep it, resentfully, in my pocket. But I don't like it.

By the time the end of the fifth round of the shadowboxing match comes, I'm red-faced, sweaty, and breathing hard. As the last buzzer goes, I chastise myself – I know I've thrown at least one illegal elbow in the course of the fight. In my mind, I'm competing under K1 kickboxing rules, which do not allow elbows (unlike Muay Thai) and still, somehow, I've managed to disobey the rule set that I selected for *my own imaginary fight*. I stand shaking my head as I catch my breath. Going in, my goal was to incorporate a lot of low kicks set up with punches. The logic behind it is this: if you throw punches first, it distracts from the kick you're about to throw; a 'naked' kick on its own is easier to see coming and to defend against. My other main goal for later rounds was to try to be aggressive and control the space, and to move forward, rather than what I usually do, which is move backward (yes, I have developed the strange ability to almost punch better moving backward than forward; we can talk about my commitment issues another day). Those were my tangible goals, and I think I actually did work on those things in this exercise.

But if it weren't for video footage of the rounds, I really would not know most of what happened in that fight. My memory is largely susceptible to erasure by adrenaline. Part of what scared me about the idea of doing the fight was that, for it to actually work, I had to let it feel kind of real. And for me to go into a real fight takes some winding up. As I have learned, there's a period of moodiness required to prepare. I have to steep myself in a certain amount of aggression in advance, just to be able to walk in and flip that switch when the time comes. I look at the disarray around me. The tension still hangs in the air. I have nearly torn apart the puzzle mats as I shifted and shuffled around. At some point I even bumped up against the wall. I don't know where she was hiding, but partway through that match, the Imaginary Woman showed up to fight. And I worry that I let her dictate the pace with her game plan instead of imposing my own.

In psychological terms, shadowboxing is meant to signify a process of overcoming a negative self-image. This negative self-image holds us back and keeps us from succeeding. Now, I'm no Jungian. My mind wanders more readily to Peter Pan wringing and wrestling with his shadow in the Disney cartoon than it does to Jung or even 'Jack's smirking revenge' from *Fight Club*. Of course, I am the woman in the mirror. Is she the one holding me back? Am I the one holding *her* back?

Right now, I am the only living, breathing person in this apartment, and I'm sincerely unsure who won the fight.

LET ME IN

When women were first allowed to compete in Olympic boxing and the UFC, in 2012, it marked an important moment in combat sports. Female fighters are suddenly, among other things, potential business. But it's those of us who came to martial arts later who really benefited from that. For long-time competitors like Emily Kwok and the women who came before her, the path was unclear.

Kwok holds a number of distinctions, including being the first Canadian woman to receive her black belt in Brazilian Jiu-Jitsu, and the first to win a BJJ world championship. When she entered the BJJ circuit as a new student in the early 2000s, she'd show up to tournaments and either fight women of all different sizes and levels of experience or – in the absence of any women at all – take fights with men. As someone who had signed up, paid her fee, and likely travelled some distance in order to compete, she would be 'fortunate' to find men willing to fight her and make the day worthwhile. Otherwise, she would not have had the chance to participate at all. Regardless of however many dozens of (male) competitors were present and ready at the tournament, she would be the odd woman out. The thing about competing is that the best way to get better at it, like so many things, is to do more of it. Just as hitting pads is not the same thing as sparring, sparring in your own gym with your teammates is not the same thing as actual ring or competition experience against someone for whom winning is contingent on you losing. If a female athlete goes for months without ever finding someone who can or will fight her, it can keep her from progressing the way she would if she had access to antagonists to push and challenge her. We get better at fighting *by* fighting. At the same time, as Kwok notes, pushing herself in these kinds of environments against much bigger opponents also led to lifelong injuries that might have been avoided had she stayed within her weight class. It's not exactly a win-win situation.

Even now, the field for women can be scarce compared to the pool of competitors available to men. My first martial arts competition was a kickboxing tournament in Santa Cruz. I had never been in a fight. I had never been hit full-on by someone who really meant it. When I walked into my first gym, I'd had no intention of ever actually fighting – at least not consciously. And now here I was. This was to be my first, and what I assumed going in would be my only, *test*. After about a year and a half of consistent training, I had gotten to a point where I was too curious to ignore the next step. I really wanted to know (which is to say, what I feared finding out the most was) how I would respond under that kind of pressure. As I prepared to compete, I did so with the knowledge that there was no guarantee another woman in or even near my weight class would be available to fight. For weeks, I went through fight camp assuming, and hoping, that there would (and some days, maybe hoping a tiny bit that there wouldn't) be someone for me to face.

When I walked into weigh-ins the day of the tournament, I was told there was another woman close to my size who had registered just that morning. As I sat outside on the pavement surrounded by teammates and coaches, some of whom were also going to be competing that day, my training partner, Mia, pointed my opponent out to me as she walked by. The other woman noticed me just as I turned toward her. I smiled shyly, out of reflex, and she smiled back – but her smile had a different quality to it. When she saw me and recognition flashed across her face, she looked … pleased. The way you look at someone who has just handed you a gift. I was a doe-eyed first-time fighter coming in at 130 pounds, whereas she had competed multiple times in MMA and was walking into the fight at 140. The other females signed up (and there were only a handful more) were around 160 or 170 pounds. Not even close. We were it. Normal weight brackets and stricter governing bodies, like in boxing, require that fighters be within five pounds of each other. When you are a woman at a martial arts tournament, however, you can either take whatever opportunity there is to compete or you can simply pack up your things – after weeks or months of prep – and go home.

As my friends watched my competitor warm up for our fight, I could see their faces fall. Her skill and experience were clear from the way she hit the pads. She was also switching stances as she got ready, which meant that I would have to contend with someone who could fight either right- or left-handed and could shift between them at will. As my coaches and training partners knew, I still had a rookie tendency to freeze up like a kid at a chalkboard trying to solve a difficult mathematical equation every time I faced a southpaw opponent. How was I going to navigate someone who could switch back and forth? I sat with my back to her team and opted not to look. I didn't want to psych myself out. I watched my training partner's concerned faces instead. Reading the worry painted across them, and the way they tried to control it in my presence, was oddly calming.

Despite all the moody days and stress-filled moments in the weeks preceding the camp – and there were many – I felt really good. I was wearing my very own black cut-off Kaijin logo T-shirt. It was a gift from my training partner and friend Elaina. I put it on to show my affiliation. I was proud to be there representing my team – and afraid to disappoint them. Aware of the danger of stressing myself out, I joked, and relaxed, and I experienced nothing like the pre-fight nerves I had expected. I had been through a lot to get there. Being so close to the goal was a relief in itself. The first sign of my own heightened tension was in my warm-up pad work with my coach, Radetsky. I was all dressed and ready, geared up, hands wrapped, and had made what felt like a million trips to the bathroom to pee. After less than a minute with him holding pads and calling out strikes and combinations, I was beat. I hadn't felt that tired in months – and that scared me. I wanted to panic – how had I messed up so badly already? How was I about to go into a fight when I was completely exhausted? My coach assured me that this was normal and, in fact, just what he wanted. His hope was that I'd get my first adrenaline dump out of the way a few minutes before the fight so that when I walked in I'd catch my second wind and not become immobilized, the way I felt there with him.

Radetsky gave me a moment to collect myself, but there was one more thing I had to do to prepare. I have trouble kicking people hard – an inconvenient hurdle for a kickboxer, I'll admit. I enjoy kicking pads and heavy bags with as much power as I can muster, but I have always had difficulty committing that kind of force to actual bodies.

I'd only ever kicked people who were my training partners and coaches, my friends. In a rare moment of gruff pre-fight coaching, Radetsky instructed me to kick his leg as hard as I possibly could. I kicked it. No, he insisted, *harder*. I tried again. He got about as close as he gets to yelling as he urged me forcefully, and repeatedly, to kick him harder, and harder, and harder. Finally, I managed to follow through with a kick that was strong enough to hurt him. When he was satisfied that I could throw a kick like I meant it, Radetsky said, 'Okay. You're ready.'

IN THE MOMENT

For me, the scariest moment of any fight is the moment right before it begins, as I'm called up and step into a surreal in-between space. It's a moment where it's too late to back out, and it's too early to know what's going to happen. Autopilot, no control, just herded from place to place until all of a sudden – 'go' – someone is going to attack you unless (and likely even if) you attack them first.

Once the bell rang and my opponent and I made contact, however, any fear went away. It wasn't until I watched footage of the fight that I realized she was better than I was. She was, of course, punching me and landing hard kicks. But at the time, I didn't feel them. And I wasn't awed or impressed by anything she was doing, which no doubt worked to my advantage. I did things I had drilled hundreds of times. I even did some things I had drilled but never managed to do successfully in sparring; there's a kick catch I'd never gotten right in training, and suddenly I reached out and did that very move mid-fight. I didn't even realize I'd done it – someone pointed it out to me afterward. The gift was that I wasn't the scared, frozen deer in headlights I'd feared would show up on the mat. I fought up a level and showed up stronger in the match than I did in my daily training.

I could hear my corners clearly, and their voices were my anchor. At one point, my coach yelled 'one!' And I dutifully went in for a jab – which was intercepted by a teep from my opponent. A teep is when you kick your leg out straight forward and strike someone with the ball or bottom of your foot, like you're kicking open a closed door. She saw me coming in for the jab and, like interrupting some-one loudly when you know what they're about to say, knocked the momentum right out of me. Of all the hits I've taken in fights, this is the one that I remember most clearly. It didn't hurt so much as startle me; that reading of my intention, and interruption, was a lesson I still hold on to. In that same first round, she hit me with a hook, and I lost my footing on the slick flooring and slipped. If someone had told me I was going to get knocked on my ass in the middle of my fight, I would have assumed they had uncanny access to my deepest, darkest nightmares. And yet when it happened, I didn't care. I jumped back up to my feet, unembarrassed and eager to show it hadn't affected me, and we kept going. Soon they tapped the ten-second mark, and I knew that was when I was meant to throw down. I could hear Radetsky yelling 'go, go, go,' so I waded in and traded strikes until the bell rang.

My feet had betrayed me, but there was no time for it to have an impact on how I felt about what I was doing, or what I could do. At the end of the first round, I went back to my corner so they could give me water and instructions and I could catch my breath before going back out for the second. Radetsky had me stand facing him with my arms raised up high onto his six-foot-three shoulders. I was meant to focus on him, drink water, and breathe. 'Can you pour water on my feet?' I asked Dom, the assistant coach, who was stand-ing next to Radetsky. 'Water?' he asked, perplexed. 'So I don't slip again,' I said. 'I think water will make you slip more,' Dom mused, his outstretched hand frozen between pouring the water and with-holding it. We were mid-debate when Radetsky told us to stop. We only had one minute in between rounds and he had coaching to do. 'Deep breaths. Relax. Take it easy,' he instructed. 'Like a spring day –' I chirped brightly. 'No,' Radetsky interrupted, pointing his finger to direct my wandering focus. 'YOU don't talk. I TALK.' Coach then proceeded to explain the game plan, which no doubt included a one-two and ended with a low kick. (The left-hand jab, the right-hand straight, and the kick to the thigh can all be relatively safe-distance strikes that don't require making yourself too vulnerable; they were, and still are, well suited to my rangy style. I tend to keep a bit of a distance.) My comments and questions, even my tendency to kid around lightly, had always been tolerated, even encouraged, in training. But this wasn't practice. It was a fight. I was learning the difference, in real time.

My opponent and I fought it out for the appointed two rounds, and then went to a third for a tiebreaker. With about thirty seconds left in the last round, I thought to myself, 'Okay, now I'm tired. Is it almost over?' The fight itself is a matter of minutes, and I was used to training for at least two hours at a time. It seemed baffling that my arms and legs could get so heavy so fast. I was punching through water. Stress and adrenaline bring a different kind of exhaustion. Suddenly, they tapped the signal for the ten-second mark, and we threw punches and kicks in a flurry to battle out the last moments of the round, throwing any energy left into the mix. This was the last chance to make an impact on the judges. The bell rang, and I returned to my corner. Radetsky and Dom quickly removed my headgear and gloves and pushed me back into the middle of the ring, reminding me to shake hands with my opponent's team. We stood in the centre with the referee in between us as they called out the winner. My opponent's hand was raised, and I clapped. I congratulated her. 'This was my first kickboxing fight!' she told me as we hugged. 'Me too!' I exclaimed, blissfully. (It was only later, when she added me on Instagram, and I saw her MMA belt title and previous competition footage, that I realized what she meant by 'first' was not first fight ever, but literally – first *kickboxing only* competition. When I competed in my own 'first' boxing fight, almost two years later, I knew not all firsts are created equally, that experience of stepping in front of an opponent, regardless of discipline, makes a difference.) I shook hands with her team as she shook hands with mine, and then I turned back to my corners.

I walked over to them with the 'aw, shucks' attitude of someone who'd just *not* won their fight, but they were … elated. They picked me up and hugged me and swung me around and patted me as we made our way out of the line of competition. The Sams were overflowing with support and happiness, and their pride left me in utter disbelief. Less than an hour earlier, no one was entirely sure I could throw a kick, for real, at a stranger. Instead, I had gone into my first fight clear-eyed, light, focused, had exchanged strikes with a more experienced fighter, and had taken it to the final bell. My team surrounded me, and even strangers were coming up to compliment us on the fight. What we learned (both my team and me) was that when things got tough, I was present. I was game; I had shown up as the best version of my fighting self. At that moment I wouldn't – couldn't – have asked for anything more. My heart was full. I was hooked.

As my female Santa Cruz teammates and I started to compete more regularly, we supported each other for every fight. At one competition, after waiting through scheduling delays, my teammate Reem fed me a banana because my hands were already wrapped and taped; she dipped it in peanut butter and broke pieces for me like I was her child. For one of Mia's fights, five of us drove along to another city and proceeded to follow her around, carrying her things and catering to her needs and specific dietary requests throughout the day. We started to refer to a competition day as a 'fight birthday,' because it was the day when everyone served and supported you in the most outstanding ways.

But these acts of care are really only an extension of what is already there in fight culture itself. When you're all geared up, people need to support you in very material ways: pulling your pants up for you because your gloves make it impossible, taking your spittle-dripping mouthguard out, pouring water into your mouth for you, and then putting that thing back in; holding an ice pack against your back or chest to get your heart rate down; speaking softly and calmly to you, if needed, to make you feel safe and confident and to urge you through to the next round. For the first couple of months at my new MMA gym in Vancouver, my Muay Thai coach took my hand wraps from me almost every time, sometimes five days a week. He would reroll them, and then personally wrap my hands for me before class, signalling when to close and open my fist as he wound the cloth. Sometimes, at the end of a session, he'd disengage the Velcro on my wraps and signal for me to extend my arms. I'd comply, watching the cloth unravel between us like a mummy whose damp bandages he'd then roll into a loose wreath and place gingerly around my neck. My teacher didn't like the style of wrap I had been using before. He wanted things done 'properly,' and this was his way of teaching me. Still, the repetition of simple gestures like these from a coach who had himself been, and had since trained, the best in the world, was one that inspired my trust in him as a person, even if I didn't always understand his reasoning. These intimate gestures, the touch, the eye contact, the regulation of breath, the wrapping of hands – this isn't treatment reserved for female fighters. This is also how coaches and teammates – a competitor's 'seconds' – serve all the toughest and scariest male *and* female fighters in the world.

MENTAL TOUGHNESS

The first time I noted the expression 'mental toughness' was in my second or third kickboxing class. In the first class, I had learned the numbers and movements of the three most basic punches (one, a jab; two, a cross; three, a hook). I had also had the opportunity in that first or second class to kick a Thai pad for the first time – my very first attempts at a roundhouse kick. The roundhouse involves pivoting on the ball of one foot while lifting and swinging the other leg almost horizontally or upward, as if you were going to use the sharp bone of your shin to slice through your opponent's abdomen, from one side to the next. When training with pads, we practise a similar motion, but my partner holds a set of thick, heavy pads strapped to their forearms to catch the kick. Instead of letting it hit them, they absorb the kick with the pad, bracing their core and creating some resistance at the moment of impact, partly so the strike doesn't knock them back. The first time they met hard pads, my delicate, virgin shins went into shock. When I showed up to the next class a few days later, I tried to explain that it would be impossible for me to do the kicking part that day – my shins were bruised. And that is when my coach gave me the first of what would be many iterations of his speech on mental toughness. He held the pads and insisted that I kick them, and I lifted my leg and tried to swing it toward the pad. Through some obdurate disconnect between mind and body, my leg would lift and move toward the target, but at the last minute it would shrink back and refuse to connect. Like playing a game with polarized magnets, the leg simply would not close the last inch of distance.

Mental toughness, in one sense, means finding the mental and emotional will to push past that kind of physical aversion. The same principle applies to exhaustion, or moodiness, or fear. That day, I was supposed to simply *decide to* kick the pad anyway, even though it hurt. But I couldn't. I didn't have the tools or experience yet to switch on that kind of mental/physical override. In a scene that feels comic, that kicking exercise culminated with my frustrated coach trying to make the override happen in spite of me. As I bounced uncertainly on one leg, he grabbed the other and threw it into the pads himself, all the while repeating 'mental toughness' and lecturing me about what it takes to be a fighter. It hurt. My shins really were tender and angry, and I was dumbstruck and embarrassed, jarred by the … *violence* of the process. But in the days and weeks that followed, I was also increasingly fascinated by the promise that you could simply decide something didn't hurt – or that it might hurt, but that pain wouldn't be the most important thing. That somehow you could choose to push past it. In order to get there, though, you have to convince yourself that it is possible.

These acts of will are chemical as well as psychological. Ultra-marathoners can trick their bodies into going further, even when it seems as though muscles and limbs are completely spent. One theory for this phenomenon, as explained by the *Radiolab* podcast 'Limits,' is the theory of 'The Governor,' the idea that there's a specific part of our brain that manages the distribution of resources. As a biological self-defence mechanism, 'The Governor' is conservative; it hoards more of our energy supplies than our bodies truly need to survive, just to be safe. If you trick 'The Governor' by swishing an energy drink around in your mouth, for instance, triggering the cue that you are receiving new energy supplies, then you can access some of those emergency stores. Another way that extreme endurance athletes unintentionally 'trick' their bodies is through one of the deepest stages of exhaustion that the body experiences: hallucinations. Struggling to keep moving after days on end of cycling, exploring for their own reasons what it means to be pushed to their furthest point, ultracyclists explain the stage at which they begin to experience horrific hallucinations; as they ride, they begin to see zombies, insurgent attackers, or monsters hiding in the shadows along the side of the road. Remarkably, when a cyclist begins to see these nightmarish scenes, their support crew, who rides along beside or behind them, tends to reinforce the athlete's mirages rather than try to reason with them ('Yes, they are after you! Hurry!'). Perversely, these terrifying hallucinations allow the athletes to keep moving (after all, who would simply stop if they were being chased by zombies?). Pushed to its furthest points, the body kicks into a kind of fight-or-flight response. Either way, the athletes find a way beyond what seems 'possible' in order to keep moving. Here, ironically, we have mental toughness *through* mental breakdown.

But that hallucinatory shortcut is not necessary in an actual combat situation. One of the reasons fighters are often eased gradually into fighting is to become able to fight rather than flee. Martial artists often train first in general movement, then pad work and partner work. This is followed by a foray into light sparring, and then hard sparring. The actual fighting comes later. This step-by-step sequencing helps build up the ability to simulate the conditions of a fight as closely as possible while still being physically able to take in the information and learn from it at each stage; it helps to mitigate a paralyzing overload.

There are different schools of thinking when it comes to how to build up this kind of training, however. Muay Thai fighters spar almost every day, but lightly. In traditional Thai training, sparring is strategic and light, even playful. (Another practical reason for this: in Thailand, prizefighters compete frequently; they might fight more than once in a week. If sparring were always as hard as a fight, their bodies wouldn't be able to take it.) Brazilian Jiu-Jitsu has some parallels to this approach. Every class ends with a bout of sparring. While exhausting, Jiu-Jitsu sparring is not *necessarily* damaging, as the student always has the option to 'tap' to end the position. (Nevertheless, if we account for both ego and inexperience, BJJ does often tend to cause all kinds of injuries.)

Boxing gyms seem to have a more aggressive ethos. In general, boxing sparring tends to be harder, and therefore might take place less frequently. But in some cases, hard sparring is the norm. Mike Tyson famously knocked out many of his sparring partners. In a video profile of some of Tyson's sparring partners, the narrator actually corrects the terminology, saying it does not seem fair to call anyone who shows up to support Tyson's training a 'sparring' partner, as that's really not what they're doing. Anyone who steps into the ring with Tyson, for practice or not, is going to meet a full-on fight. Needless to say, Tyson ran through fighting partners as frequently as most of us change our socks. Tyson is an interesting character, and certainly one for whom fighting and aggression bleed well beyond the ring. When it comes to his hard training, however, he was not simply an ungrateful or unsportsmanlike jerk. He was doing what he was told. This is how his coaches wanted him to train. For them, what would work best for the fighter was to simulate a fight as closely as possible in every round and every outing, so that he would never have to ramp up to it; the heat of the fight is where he would live.

There are advantages and disadvantages to both approaches. Too little hard sparring leaves a fighter inexperienced and unable to withstand the stress and pressure of an actual fight. Too much hard sparring, however, can simply shorten the span of a fighter's life (in the ring and in general). There are only so many hits any of us can take before we just can't bounce back.

I suffered my worst loss to date in my fifth kickboxing match. I knew I wasn't quite *right* as I went into the fight. Everyone believed in me, and I was in great shape, but even with all of my hard work, something deep in my gut told me I just didn't want to be there. Between my move back to Canada, training at new gyms with strangers, and navigating the lifestyle shift, I felt like I had been fighting every day for months. I was worn out. It's hard to know how or why it happens, but sometimes you walk into fight day and for some reason(s), even after all that work to get there, you just don't have it. It happens at all levels, whether the fighter fully understands why or not. The UFC's Donald 'Cowboy' Cerrone fought Conor McGregor in what was to be Cowboy's highest-profile fight ever – and he lost in a matter of seconds. Cerrone later admitted that something in him, for some reason, just didn't want to be there. In another case, after working for years to get to nationals, an amateur fighter I interviewed chose at the last minute *not* to fight because she was so burnt out; again, after everything it took to get there, she felt she was missing something she'd need to follow through the way she knew she would have to. One common idea is that 90 percent of the growth and benefit you get out of a fight comes from the training; the day itself is only that last 10 percent. But that 10 percent can challenge or cement the things you have learned. It's not everything, but to miss the chance to fight, or to show up as someone who doesn't seem to do justice to all of your hard work – that can be painful to accept. It takes an incredible amount of work, mental preparation, and sacrifice for a fighter to go into a match. How do we account for the days when, after putting in those weeks and years of dedicated work, they just don't *have* it? Overtraining, psychological drain, the emotional toll of sacrifice and life imbalance – they all play a part. Mental toughness is not static.

The week after my fight, I returned to my regular training looking to make a change. My still-recent loss was frustrating largely because I couldn't figure out how to shift gears; I was trying to fight to get the most points, whereas my opponent was trying to knock me out. The mix of styles did not work in my favour. My problems were largely mental, emotional, and situational, but I couldn't just fix those things. In preparation for the fight, I had been training in the Female Fighters boxing class once a week and spending most of my time (five to six days a week) practising Muay Thai at an MMA gym. I could not yet spar at the boxing gym, however – to do so in boxing requires a membership with the provincial boxing commission, and to gain membership, fighters have to pass a physical examination, including blood and urine tests. I had not yet cobbled together the time or money to take that on, and so I simply attended classes. The same requirements don't apply to the MMA gym, and so I was sparring multiple times a week, almost exclusively with men. Although they were all quite a bit bigger and heavier than I am – though not all necessarily more experienced – sparring for all of us was always, as a rule, controlled and contained. After my disappointing fight, however, I decided I also needed practice dealing with a different kind of opponent.

In the ring, I have trouble against pressure fighters, people who drive forward and attack. Unfortunately, that is exactly the kind of opponent I am most likely to meet in an amateur women's fight, especially one that has short rounds. There's no time to feel things out with two-minute rounds, and the restriction encourages women to come out swinging and put it all on the line as quickly as possible. In Muay Thai sparring, no one was fighting me that way. I was getting great training, and learning important skills, but I decided it was time to round out my skill set to prepare for the kinds of fights I was actually taking.

I finally started sparring with the Female Fighters group at the boxing gym, where the coaches as a rule selected our sparring partners and nearly always matched us by weight. This greater size parity was interesting because it meant that neither fighter had to negotiate the other as carefully as they might if mismatched. I believe that matchups that cross different experience levels, genders, and weight classes teach a different but also essential skill set: how to read your partner and adapt your own pace, power, and style accordingly. By observing and working with a range of different partners within the gym, you learn control, and also – for women, especially – you learn how to read which people you should avoid. But the switch to training with partners who were all my size was an opportunity to focus on other things, and to more closely simulate official competition.

In the boxing gym, sparring was much less frequent than elsewhere, so I might get two to four rounds in per boxing session, as opposed to seven or eight in Muay Thai. As I quickly learned, these sparring sessions were not playful; the women hit hard, and as a rule we did not stop for blood. I liked it. This was as difficult as my other training, but in a way that departed from what I was used to. I have always appreciated the presence of joy in training environments, and so I was drawn to the jubilant atmosphere of this group of women who beat each other up and then hugged, and danced, and sang together between hard rounds of training. In these early sessions, I also started to re-evaluate the way I saw myself as a fighter. An evasive fighter, I had never thought of myself as a bull, for instance, but after exchanging harder strikes, I realized I liked the sight of blood. I didn't feel bad about that; it felt well earned. The flipside is, of course, that when I got hurt, no one would be stopping for me, either. When my partner bled, the coaches yelled for me to hit them again, and I knew they would do the same if I were the one on the other end of the punches.

At one point in sparring, I took a hard hit to the liver that made my body shut down. I shelled up and covered myself with my arms as Tomoko punched me into the corner. I just barely remained standing under a barrage of hard punches until the buzzer rang and I was able to double over in peace. When I stepped out of the ring and asked my coaches what to do in that situation, they laughed and voiced their empathy. When you get hit hard in the liver, your body waits half a second and then closes up shop. Every fighter seems to have a story about a time it happened to them. This isn't a 'bite down on your mouthguard and keep going' kind of thing; the answer is simply to shell up, and if you can, try to get away and make space so you can buy your body time to start working again. The short answer, in other words, is: don't get hit in the liver. But if you do, cover up, breathe, and try to survive.

I became mildly obsessed with how to avoid taking another shot like this. Tomoko was one of only two or three competitors in the gym close to my weight, and so we were frequently matched together. I was always happy for this, because she was my first training partner ever, at my very first gym, and we were delighted to be reunited after years apart. Unfortunately, our familiarity also means that she has my number; perhaps no sparring partner is as intimately familiar with my strengths and weaknesses as Tomoko. Needless to say, she easily landed another hard hook to the body the following week. This time, instead of managing to wait it out a few seconds for the buzzer, I was overwhelmed and unconsciously took a knee (this would be equivalent to tapping out). As I ducked out of the ring again, head down, I was kicking myself even as I knew that this failure would strengthen my resolve.

After seeing me doubled over for a second time, our teammate, Cat, a much younger but also much more experienced boxer, offered to help. She spent time after class working with me on my fighting stance. As a kickboxer, I stand with my body somewhat square to my opponent; it's necessary because I'm not just punching, I also need to be able to use my legs to kick and block my opponent's kicks. In kickboxing, standing at too much of an angle would put me at a disadvantage for using my legs the way I need to. It would leave my front leg begging to getting kicked out from under me. But in boxing, my square stance leaves me vulnerable to getting hit in the body. Cat helped me think about how to shift to a narrower boxing stance so less of my abdomen is available to my opponent, who really only has two targets: the head or the body. Then, she led me to the corner of the ring and had me stand up against the ropes and lift my arms up in the air. When I was in place and essentially defenceless, she instructed me to flex and breathe. Then, she punched me in the abdomen. Fifty times. (Afterward, I did the same for her.) This is how she had been taught conditioning, she explained. And she was willing to work through it with me.

As a rule, it is best to avoid getting hit in the body. But the other way to defend against getting hit hard is … to get used to it. Boxers protect from getting hurt by practising it, one, two, or fifty hard punches at a time.

ROPE-A-DOPE

When Muhammad Ali finally returned to the ring three years after having his licence revoked, he was a different fighter than the one who had left it. 'Superman plots do not get interesting until kryptonite has been shoehorned in somehow,' combat sportswriter Jack Slack explains. 'Now Muhammad Ali was older, slower, and in the mix with a far superior crop of heavyweights than three years earlier.' As Slack sees it, Ali's unconventional, dancerly fight style had served him well because he was young, strong, athletic, and uncommonly fast for a heavyweight. By the time he returned from his fighting exile, however, he could no longer rely on his athleticism to forgive technical and strategic gaps. He had to rely instead on strategy, grit, and a stubborn will.

In one of the most famous boxing matches ever recorded, Ali competed against up-and-comer George Foreman for the world title in what has been dubbed the 'Rumble in the Jungle' (1974). Faced with a younger, stronger, and very strategic opponent, the aging Ali took lessons from his first few post-hiatus fights. He realized he needed to fight differently and changed his approach. For the Rumble in the Jungle, Ali relied not on his agility and grace but instead on his ability to stifle and tire Foreman out. He clinched and squeezed the stronger fighter when he got close. Even more famously, however, Ali let himself be backed up against the ropes of the ring – a move coaches constantly warn against, as it cuts off your ability to escape and squares up your feet, which makes it harder to draw any real power into your strikes. It takes away your options and leaves you a sitting duck. But Ali put himself in that position on purpose. Forfeiting any real bravado, Ali held and shelled for protection, letting Foreman attack him. He covered and waited, letting the other fighter tire himself out while the give of the ropes held Ali up. In *The Fight*, Norman Mailer explains the logic behind this move: 'Standing on one's feet it is painful to absorb a heavy body punch even when blocked with one's arm.' Even in a defensive posture, 'the torso, the legs, and the spine take the shock. Leaning on the ropes, however, Ali can pass it along; the rope will receive the strain.' Literally using the structure of the ring to support him, Ali was able to withstand strikes that he could not take on his own. Then, when he saw an opening, or when Foreman was weakened from all that work, Ali attacked.

While perhaps not the smartest strategy (Ali still took a lot of damage by offering his body up to that many strikes), the rope-a-dope approach is infamous partly because it looks a whole lot like losing. So much of fighting for sport (where there are judges involved, in particular), is not just hitting the other person more, but *looking* as though you are winning. Winning is somewhat subjective, and rhetorical. It's partly an aesthetic. That's why Muay Thai fighters yell 'Oooy-aaay' victoriously, whether they have actually landed a good strike or not; they will also yell that when they get hit, in which case it means 'I blocked it! It didn't hurt!' It makes no difference that the judges and audience can see with their own eyes whether or not the hit landed. This isn't about pure, cold reality. Fighting, though very materially real, is also a kind of theatre. It's about creating an impression. This is also why you will see fighters who have just been clearly defeated walking around the ring pumping their fists in the air and waving their arms victoriously above them as they await the judge's decision. The question is not whether they know they lost, but rather whether the *judges* know it or can still be swayed to think otherwise. They are playing a part: the winner. To shell up against the ropes and wilfully absorb punches, then, is to risk taking a submissive stance in the service of a long-game, strategic purpose. It's an inelegant solution to being outpowered, or outmatched, and one that raises the stakes. In the Rumble in the Jungle, it paid off. Ali won. But he had to knock Foreman out to do it.

CHIN

Whereas we can all learn to override a number of psychological and physical hurdles in our lives, not every hurdle can simply be willed away. Anyone who has participated in or observed combat sports more than in passing has heard reference to what we call a fighter's 'chin.' The chin is durability, the capacity to take a hard hit (or many hard hits) and keep on going. 'Chin' can also be used synonymously with having 'heart,' but it's not the same thing.

You can condition your core or your shins, for instance, to become somewhat more durable, but the same principle does not apply to the head. Apart from strengthening the neck, there's not much you can do. Concussions are cumulative; the more you get, the more you loosen the lid of the jar, making your brain susceptible to becoming concussed more frequently and from smaller impact, or movement. Looking to better understand this phenomenon, sports reporter James MacDonald talked to Dr. Anthony Alessi, an associate clinical professor of neurology at the University of Connecticut. As Dr. Alessi plainly states, while the decision to stay in the ring can be one of determination or mental strength, the ability to physically withstand head trauma has nothing to do with will. He offers the analogy of a storm. 'Let's say there's a storm, and the concussion is the storm. It causes a rupture in your basement wall, and now you've got water flowing into your basement. That rupture in the basement wall is like rupturing the nerve cell. Now you've got all this water flowing in – which would be the calcium – and the only way to get it out is to pump it out. And that's what the nerve cell does,' he explains. 'The body diverts energy to get these pumps working. That's why knockouts occur, because the brain is saying: "Listen, I gotta shut it down here and get this thing going again." If you get another storm before you've even repaired the first one, you're going to have an overwhelming amount of calcium rushing in, and that can sometimes even result in death.' As the foundation analogy suggests, a fighter's 'chin' – their ability to take these storm-like strikes – decreases over time, as if they have a certain number of hits they can take. This is what is colloquially called getting 'chinny' or having a 'glass jaw.' If the fighter keeps going, it's not so much a question of if they will run up against that invisible limit, but when.

There is, nevertheless, a widespread appreciation for a fighter with a good 'chin.' It's a metaphor for the elusive concept of toughness. As MacDonald observes, however, the fallacy of the 'chin' highlights the connection between an idea of toughness and maleness; specifically, 'the sturdiness of one's chin has almost replaced the size of one's genitalia as an indicator of masculinity. It's as though fans are eager to credit the fighter for the fact that he possesses a granite chin, attributing it to mental strength rather than something that is entirely beyond his control.'

There is no shortage of examples of women with incredible chins – the instant-classic matchup between UFC strawweights Weili Zhang and Joanna Jedrzejczyk immediately comes to mind – which shows among other things that this idea of measuring masculinity has to be recast. In their twenty-five-minute championship fight, the two 115-pound women battled it out in a non-stop performance of skill, speed, resilience, a certain disregard for self-defence, and a lot of sheer will. Jedrzejczyk apparently landed a shocking 186 'significant' strikes, and Zhang landed 165. Many of these strikes occurred simultaneously, as they clashed and nearly matched each other's movement and speed at a frenetic and relentless pace. By the end of the fight, Zhang was badly marked up, and Jedrzejczyk's face was so swollen and misshapen that she was nearly unrecognizable. It was only a matter of minutes before memes depicting her as an alien, Pinky from *Pinky and the Brain*, or (my personal favourite) Megamind, began to circulate online. As lighter fighters, they are less likely to knock someone out immediately with one blow, the way we see in heavyweight fights. Damage is also cumulative, however – say, over 150 hard hits in less than a half an hour – and so a smaller female fighter's 'chin' might look a little different, but it is no less a factor.

There is a narrative about commitment that seems to translate through the idea of the chin. In one of the most entertaining post-fight interviews I have come across, Bellator MMA's Henry Corrales stands, expressionless, as the announcer congratulates him on his win. Corrales has just defeated Aaron Pico, and yet his face doesn't communicate the usual glee, relief, or pumped-up bravado of some-one who has just won a fight only seconds earlier. Corrales had been injured and was down in the fight when he pushed through and managed to get a technical knockout against Pico. 'Big' John McCarthy, the interviewer, wraps his hand around Corrales's neck and shoulders as he opens the interview by divulging that Pico had said, before the fight, that he knew his opponent, Corrales, had heart. Pico understood that Corrales would fight it out regardless of what he threw at him. Standing there with the microphone in his face and a massive tattoo of a caged lion calling out from his muscular chest, Corrales calmly and flatly replies, without a hint of irony: 'Yeah, he's right. At my best, I have lived a mediocre life. And I'm ready to die in this motherfucker.' Despite a demeanour almost indifferent to the fanfare around him, his words bring wild applause from the crowd.

In an interview explaining his reasons for retiring from fighting, former UFC light heavyweight champion Rashad Evans tells sports reporter Ben Fowlkes how this kind of narrative, or 'story,' works. The story professional fighters tell themselves is 'part mantra, part willful illusion, but it's also more than that. It's like having your own personal narrative that allows you to make sense of the incompre-hensible ups and downs of life.' It is, in essence, a belief system. Evans explains that he and his fellow professional teammates would 'feed on these self-sustaining myths. They'd tell themselves that they were modern-day samurai. They were out to seek a beautiful death. They believed it, too.' In the same vein, MMA fighter Sean O'Connell explains that no one wants to hear about a fighter who is measured or modest (or, more loaded: honest) with themselves and others about their prospects and limitations. 'People have such a hard time in the fight world being realistic, or even hearing other people be realistic,' he explains. But at a high level, fighting arguably does not encourage measured modesty or harsh self-reflection. Some version of blind faith is a necessary function of often unreasonable (and 'unreasonable' can be read neutrally or negatively) perseverance.

There is a long and storied history of fighters who actually try to play out the scenario Corrales and Evans describe. And they often claim to feel betrayed by corners who save them from their own wishes by throwing in the towel on their behalf. While he is most celebrated for his skill, style, and charm, Muhammad Ali is also widely considered to have suffered later in life because of the damage he had been willing to take in the ring in matches like the Rumble in the Jungle. As a fighter, he is by no means the exception. More recently, boxing heavyweight Deontay Wilder was visibly wobbling and disoriented as his opponent, Tyson Fury, continued to strike him in the head, round after round, throughout their heavyweight boxing championship rematch. Eventually, Wilder's corner tossed a white towel into the corner of the ring. Wilder responded in his post-fight interview by saying, 'I'm ready to go out on my shield … I wish my corner would've let me went out on my shield; I'm a warrior. That's what I do.' This sentiment is consistent across professional combat sports. The refusal to give up is intrinsic to fighting. Fighters like Wilder seem to believe they are displaying the much-vaunted mix of skill, mental and physical toughness, and the even more elusive 'heart.' Many of them fathers, they express a desire to make their families proud, which apparently means potentially falling on one's shield, even if defeat is inevitable. It's not *if* you lose, it's *how*. This antiquated notion of honour seems to supersede all things – including their future presence in their kids' lives.

As far as I can find, there are two women on record as having died in Western boxing matches since women were allowed into the sport in 1993. One woman, Stacy Young, was 'beaten into a coma' and subsequently died following an unregulated Toughman boxing competition in Florida in 2003. In official, sanctioned boxing, Becky Zerlentes is listed as the only woman on record to have died as a result of injuries sustained in the ring. In 2005, she was knocked out by a right hook that struck her left temple during a Colorado State Boxing Senior Female Championship match. She was tended to by ringside doctors and taken to the hospital, where she remained unconscious and died as a result of 'blunt force trauma.' Zerlentes was a thirty-four-year-old college instructor and former regional Golden Gloves champion. This bout was meant to be her last before retirement. Even for the fighter whose blow knocked her in the temple, nothing about the match or the final punch had seemed out of the ordinary.

As boxers, we are warned of these risks every time we go into the ring. Before a boxing match, the official ringside doctor takes each of us aside (with a female colleague to supervise if he's male). As we speak with him privately, he inspects us and grills us about our medical history, previous head injuries, vision, and menstrual cycles; he even grabs our nose and wiggles it to make sure it is intact going into the fight. At the end of the inspection, every fighter stepping into the ring is made to acknowledge that we understand what we are about to do. We've been training for this very moment, waiting to test our skills in the heat of a live fight. We're dressed in our uniforms and gear; we've amped ourselves up. This line of questioning is the final hurdle to get to the thing we've been anticipating for weeks and months. 'Do you understand you could be seriously injured or even killed in this fight?' he asks. 'Yes,' we each answer on our turn. 'Are you entering this competition freely?' 'Yes,' we reply. 'Knowing the risks I've just described to you, do you still want to do it?' he asks. 'Yes.'

Fighting in a sanctioned competition, which would necessarily follow an equivalent protocol, Zerlentes would likely have been asked these same questions. This might be the distinction between an amateur and a professional, or I might be projecting my own gendered baggage onto them, but I wonder whether either Zerlentes or Young (who is described in the news simply, but predictably, as a 'thirty-year-old Florida mother') would have fought to stay in the ring if they had sincerely believed their fights would turn out as they did. I find it hard to picture either woman clamouring to 'fall on her shield.'

If we compare these two cases to the fatality rates for male boxers, the 'toughness' narrative looks a little more familiar. On average, thirteen men die in sanctioned boxing matches every year. And, perversely, the ratios are even higher when the fighter's *father* is the one coaching or cornering him, which also points to a potential history of gendered socialization tied to wading in too deep or refusing to give up. This kind of dedication to an extreme form of perseverance is widely celebrated. What it also highlights, however, is that it is possible to be *too* tough for your own good.

And then there are days when, for whatever reason, a fighter knows they simply cannot go on. In 2018, Raquel Pennington suffered (but eventually recovered from) a beating at the hands of fellow UFC bantamweight Amanda Nunes. At the end of the fourth round, twenty minutes into what was meant to be a twenty-five-minute championship fight, Pennington returned to her corner and conceded, 'I'm done … I want to be done.' Patching up her bloodied face, her (male) coach replied using a combination of aphorisms and an inclusive 'we' to urge her back into the fight. 'No, no, no … Let's power through this,' he said. 'Let's believe. Change your mindset. Change your mindset. Let's just throw everything we got. We'll recover later. Throw everything we got.' Following her coach's lead, she stepped back in and was finished with a technical knockout moments later. I don't bring up Pennington to suggest that her desire to end the fight is simply a gendered phenomenon. There are plenty of male fighters who have refused to come out between rounds (just look at the trail of dejected would-be competitors that fleet-footed boxer Vasyl Lomachenko has left in his wake). These concessions are not popular – some consider it cowardly not to finish the fight, whereas others realize that avoiding unnecessary strikes to the head is pragmatic. Rather than cause controversy about her heart or resilience, however, the conversation around the Pennington/Nunes fight centred mostly on the failure of Pennington's corners to protect her; whether they thought she should be able to make it through the fight or not, the fact that she said she was done indicates that – regardless of skill or physical state – her mental focus was no longer there. She didn't have confidence in her own ability to continue without further punishment, but she did have faith in her coaches.

As former UFC and Strikeforce MMA fighter Julie Kedzie explains, fighters need to believe they can do anything, even the impossible, and they are encouraged by their coaches and teammates to think that way. 'You have to believe that you could potentially beat absolutely anyone. It might be a fantasy, but to be a fighter and put yourself through some of these things, sometimes it helps to live in a fantasy.' In Kedzie's experience, it was easier for her to believe in herself, and her own abilities, when people she trusted – her more experienced coaches and teammates, for instance – told her she could do anything. 'If they say you can do it, then maybe you can. The story they tell you about yourself starts to become your own. What they tell you becomes what you tell yourself.' There are limits to this narrative, however. 'When you get to a point where that same story just doesn't work for you, you feel it,' Kedzie says. 'A voice in your head tells you something. Like, this isn't it anymore. And you can look at those same people you've relied on and you can see they're being dishonest with you. And not because they want to be dishonest with you. They think they're helping. But you can still feel it.' This seems to have been the case for Pennington that night, and it is likely the case for many others.

I've heard a number of variations on the definition of 'mental toughness' over the years, but Kedzie's words remind me of one of my current boxing coaches, former professional boxer Jaime Ward-Yassin. Ward-Yassin uses the term a lot. When I asked her to define it, her response added a slightly different nuance to the idea than I had come across so far. For Ward-Yassin, it is in part the 'desire not to quit when things get difficult' – the more familiar use of the term – and in part, the 'ability to understand yourself and your capabilities,' and to 'own' them. There's a realism implied here, and one that may or may not come from her still relatively uncommon position as a female pro fighter. While coaches, teammates, friends, and family may know what's best for us, 'at the end of the day,' she says, 'we need to take a little bit of ownership. It's our bodies. It's our minds … when we're in the ring,' it's us 'going through the motions,' not anyone else. It is difficult for both men and women to make their needs known – especially fighters and athletes, who are rigorously trained to follow orders and instructions. Beyond the usual ingrained obedience of the athlete, we are also trying to show that we belong in that arena; while 'every fighter is trying to prove something … for women, we're trying to prove something a little different' – we are also trying to establish ourselves as athletes who are capable of holding our own in a male-dominated sport. That pre-existing challenge can often make it harder to 'own' our narrative of what we feel we truly need.

Beyond the risk of death in the ring (the most extreme example of 'toughness' pushed to its limits), there are other ways the body and mind come into conflict. Even if the consequences are not as dramatic as death or extreme injury, damage adds up. A 'shot' fighter is one who is, in some sense, past their prime; someone who can no longer stand up to the kind of competition or hits they would have taken more easily in the past. There are the physical realities and implications of this, of course, but there is also an underlying suggestion of a certain deficiency, or loss of mental toughness. The fighter is compared to a version of their past self and found wanting. Being 'shot' does not necessarily mean getting old. It's deeper and less predictable than that. For some fighters, after pushing themselves to an extreme in some spectacular competitions (in the predictable parlance, people often call this 'going to war'), they simply never seem to be able to show up in the ring or the cage with the same intensity or ferocity they had before. This suggests that maybe people only have so much 'fight' in them, just as they only have so many potential hits to the head. It also holds an air of tragedy about it, the idea that someone with so much potential can visibly break in some way. On a more formally scientific level, it wouldn't be unreasonable to make a connection between this somewhat romantic idea and post-traumatic stress disorder.

Evans and Kedzie seem to be suggesting that when a fighter no longer believes their own story – when they no longer believe they can win no matter what – then it might be time to move on. At what point is mental toughness the ability to see past one's own boundaries and move past them, and when is it the commitment to a faulty belief? Does each of us only have so much hunger or fight in us? I wonder the same thing as I refuse to reopen my old doctoral dissertation and struggle through thicker quicksand with each gruelling new academic job application season. Was that all the drive I had in me? Did I use it up? Is it supposed to be this hard, or is it a sign that something is wrong? How do you keep digging – and finding – what you need *within* you?

CHAPTER EIGHT
★
BUILT FOR IT

The first week of a new university semester is a unique kind of stress. This time around, I'm a postdoctoral fellow in California. As a peripheral member of the department and an introvert to boot, I might be best described as a familiar shadow who shuffles through the halls, attends reading group meetings, sits in the audience at talks, and spends a little too much time loitering near the food table at receptions.

Throughout the whole first week of classes, my head hurts. Headaches are nothing new for me, so I manage it as usual. I'm also nauseated and unfocused, however, which complicates matters. After a few days, I wonder: is this just the stress of pulling together a new course and preparing to lecture in front of people again, or is it something else? The previous weekend, I took part in a gym-wide sparring/BBQ open house ('Spar-B-Q'). As always, I put in as many rounds as I could and worked with anyone who was willing. Near the end of the session, I partnered with a boxer I know. As we sparred, I was reminded of how he favours hard punches like the right overhand. This particular right overhand is a punch where the striker dips their head down and steps forward on an angle, throwing their power hand above them to catch their opponent in the face. If you really commit your body weight and momentum to it, this kind of strike can knock someone out. Watch most MMA fights and you will see these swinging. We sparred a few rounds, and I did fairly well defensively but still absorbed one or two of those hard, explosive hits. Although it can be fun to do hard sparring, I was annoyed at the choice of strike for this occasion; sparring is, after all, a form of training as opposed to an actual fight. And although close in height, he and I are far from matched in weight.

Some punches do damage just by design. But sometimes it is difficult to negotiate how hard to go, and I often tend toward wanting to push my own limits to see how I can work through it. I didn't want to go lightly that day either, so I bit down and tried to use the upped stakes (for my head) as an exercise in practising self-defence. Apart from a bit of a headache, I don't think much of the knocks I have taken to the head until days later, when I'm still out of sorts and frustratedly trying to finish the plan for my first lecture. I'm unable to maintain anything beyond a superficial train of thought. I also note that this feeling isn't entirely unfamiliar. Still, when the first day of classes comes, I walk into the lecture hall loopy but smiling, hoping for the best. Fortunately, a tidy PowerPoint and a little first-day adrenaline carry me through.

By the following week I start to feel like myself again, though an uneasy awareness of that lost week sits with me. I've been warned about the hidden dangers of concussions, although it's not something I have taken very seriously. After all, there are a lot of ways I can get hurt. Obsessing about everything that can go wrong seems like a good precursor to rolling myself in bubble wrap and hiding under the bed. I struggle with many issues directly connected to the wear and tear that goes with combat sport training. But pushing my body and my limits, and facing the risks involved in doing that, has on balance made me stronger. If I had kept playing it safe, I would have missed out on growing in ways I couldn't have imagined possible. While I certainly get hit in the head sometimes in sparring, I have been both fairly careful and very lucky.

Though I am not sure what has me all out of whack that first week of the term, the material reminder that I can addle my brain to the point where it will endanger my livelihood, let alone the fundamental elements of my personality, gives me pause. Even when we strengthen our bodies, the process is borne of tearing and microfractures. I'm stronger now. But what does this kind of damage add up to? Although I know better, when I think of 'punch-drunk' fighters, my default image is some leather-faced, hard-worn scrapper who has taken a hundred too many hits over the course of a lifetime. What would too many hits do to me?

A concussion is a brain injury caused by excessive movement of the brain inside the skull after a hit or jolt to the head, neck, or body. Symptoms vary, and are somewhat hard to pin down, but can include dizziness and confusion, headache, trouble with balance, an upset stomach, sensitivity to light or noise, ringing of the ears, and blurred vision. Concussions can affect focus, emotion, and sleep as well, leading to (among other things) an inability to think clearly, irritability or increased emotionality or sadness, and either sleeplessness or oversleeping. The long-term side effects of concussions are not all obvious, or at least not to those afflicted. A possible side effect of too many concussions is chronic traumatic encephalopathy (CTE), a progressive degenerative brain disease with some similarities to Alzheimer's. The brain's degeneration can manifest in a number of ways, potentially affecting mood, emotion, behaviour, impulse control, executive function, multitasking, motor control, or speech. It can trigger rage and memory loss, and even inhibit the ability to learn new things.

Historically, the sport that has been the biggest culprit for concussions is boxing (although it is now likely being edged out by American football). Perhaps it is no surprise that boxing has always had a problem with public opinion; there have been calls for regulation and rule standardization since the 1700s. Following a brutal beating and a boxer's death in November 1982, a group of medical professionals urged banning boxing, full stop. Out of self-preservation, the sport's governing body, the International Boxing Association (AIBA, originally Association Internationale de Boxe Amateur), changed its regulations so that all amateur boxers would be required to compete in headgear. In a notable reversal, however, in 2016 the International Olympic Committee decided that male boxers were no longer required to wear headgear to compete in Olympic qualifiers or games. According to studies, the number of stoppages due to head blows causing disorientation or a perceived head injury is higher *with* headgear than without. A 2017 study for the organization notes that there were 43 percent more stoppages when competitors were fighting in the protective helmet. In other words, they found that 'headgear not only doesn't decrease the chance of concussions and lasting brain trauma in fighters; it *increases* it.'

This statistic is not as counterintuitive as it might seem. There are a number of reasons why headgear doesn't necessarily protect the brain, as the 2017 study acknowledges: with the size of the target increased, fighters might absorb more hits and find it harder to evade them; the padding around the eyes of the head guard might limit the boxer's peripheral vision; and the fact that wearing headgear can give a fighter a 'false sense of safety,' leading them to take risks they wouldn't otherwise venture. But headgear was not really intended to reduce the risk of concussions. Though the optics of its adoption spoke to a public relations issue around head injuries, its primary function is to reduce cuts to the face and head. And indeed, competing without headgear does bring a 'notable increase' in cuts. 'Notable' might be an understatement. Fighters who compete bare-headed have a 430 percent higher risk of taking cuts to the head than those guarded by padding.

Female amateurs qualifying and competing in the Olympics won't have to worry their heads about cuts, however, because headgear is still required for them. It seems the optics around female competitors still rest firmly in the public relations tactics of the 1980s. 'For now,' a disapproving Josh Rosenblatt remarks, 'women fighters will continue to fistfight the old-fashioned way: with a giant, blinding delusion fastened to their vulnerable heads.' In this context, it seems that optics and fear of cosmetic injuries are keeping women in padding. One of the big recurring concerns about women fighting is cuts to the face. Women's value is very clearly placed on the side of looks – even, some might argue, at the expense of their brains. Others defend the use of headgear, however. If a boxer gets a bad cut on the head, even in the middle of an Olympic qualifier, they risk a stoppage, their chance to compete for gold flushed away for something possibly cosmetic and potentially avoidable. A bad, bloody cut isn't as high profile a head injury as one that affects the brain, but in terms of a boxer's record and standing, it can have exactly the same effect in the moment.

But that's not why women have been left to the old rule set. According to former AIBA president Ching-Kuo Wu, the reason women are still competing in headgear is that 'there just hasn't been as much research done on the effects of headgear for women boxers as for men. 'We have to do this step by step,' Wu said in 2014. 'Once everything is proved … then we can start to have some test[s] and consider it in [the] future for women.' Wu was not wrong about the dearth of studies, but for the president of an organization that mandates (and therefore also has power over and access to) boxers all over the world – *and not only the male ones* – the logic and acceptance of the research gap here is inexcusable. For perspective: statistics, as a practice, generally agrees that a sample size of thirty or more can be a large enough sample from which to draw meaningful conclusions. AIBA could easily find thirty women represented in any number of individual countries, not to mention the entire organization.

Headgear isn't the only question mark. Beyond the padding and into the consequences themselves, according to Robert Stern, director of Boston University's CTE Center, we actually 'have no idea at all about whether there are sex-based differences in CTE, or about how prevalent CTE is among men vs. women, because we haven't seen any women's brains that have shown signs of it after athletic exposure.' To be clear, that's not because women don't suffer significant head injuries or develop CTE. The reason we haven't got records of women with the disease is that their brains have not been studied for it, as men's have. Although the brains of hundreds of deceased men ('most former pro-football players and some military veterans') have been diagnosed with CTE, as of 2019, 'only two women have ever, anywhere, been diagnosed with the disease.' Of the two, one was 'a victim of domestic violence' and the other 'a developmentally disordered individual who was a habitual headbanger. Both women were exposed, repeatedly, to hits to the head.' The examples of the two diagnoses alone are alarming. Regardless of any history with sport, neither domestic abuse nor developmental disorders are in any way new phenomena. So where are the studies?

One factor frequently put forward for the lack of CTE research in women is the fact that in many cases, women weren't formally allowed to play sports competitively until fairly recently. In 1972, the United States government passed Title IX, a section of the Education

Amendments. Also known as the Patsy T. Mink Equal Opportunity in Education Act, Title IX declared that 'no person in the United States shall, on the basis of sex, be excluded from participation in, be denied the benefits of, or be subjected to discrimination under any educational program or activity receiving Federal financial assistance.' This includes sports.

The implications for women's athletics were massive, due in part to the framework of policies and reporting that the amendment ushered into place. At the same time, the mandated equal representation led to a cut in men's low-revenue activities, like wrestling, that made both men and women suffer – all over the country, men lost their low-revenue wrestling programs because there weren't the numbers for equivalent female programs. In these lose-lose cases, the shift toward equality takes the blame, and the name Title IX leaves a sour taste in some mouths. When the perception is that, for women to move forward, men have something taken away from them, it doesn't help the case for women in sport. And the cycle continues.

In Canada, there is no single law directly equivalent to Title IX. We have the Canadian Charter of Rights and Freedoms, which makes a vaguer claim to equality, noting 'the rights and freedoms referred to in [the Charter] are guaranteed equally to male and female persons.' But these regulations apply to government action, and do not extend in the same way to extracurricular activities in schools, for instance, which are regulated by school boards.

Some legal scholars suggest that Title IX created a clearer system for administering and mandating gender-related claims. A new generation of women were able to grow up participating in sports and competing in athletics more fully. Even then, however, many Western combat sports like boxing have been slow to welcome young women. Without any female competitors or competitions in which to participate, Irish Olympic gold medallist and featherweight champion boxer Katie Taylor famously had to dress up as a boy in order to compete. 'I used to have my hair up in my headgear and I used to be known as "Kay Taylor,"' she says. 'When I took the headgear off at the end of the fight and everyone realized I was a girl, there was an uproar.' At fifteen, Taylor competed against boxer Alanna Audley in the first officially sanctioned female boxing match in Ireland. That was in

2001. While Taylor is still competing and at the top of her game, many of the women of the first Title IX generation are well into middle age now, which makes them the first real generation of lifelong (recognized) female athletes primed to be studied.

The lack of knowledge about the effect of concussions (in general, but especially for women) is especially significant for combat sports, but it points to a bigger issue related to head injuries in women more widely. Even if you can count only one generation of women actively allowed to compete in elite amateur and professional combat sports in Europe and North America, the history of women getting hit in the head is about as old as time. And women have been playing sports like soccer for ages. Yet the effects of these activities are equally unstudied. As Caroline Criado Perez notes in *Invisible Women: Data Bias in a World Designed for Men*, 'We know very little about how women respond to concussions, even though women suffer from concussions at higher rates than men and take longer to recover in comparable sports.' Soccer – a widely socially accepted sport for women – is a notorious culprit for concussions due to the increasing popularity of heading the ball. In Canada and the USA, high-profile women are now pledging their brains to science after they die, including a number of Team USA soccer players and Canadian hockey legend Hayley Wickenheiser, in an attempt to help fill that gap.

LIES, DAMNED LIES, AND STATISTICS

Criado Perez's *Invisible Women* lays out a litany of examples of how science and design overlook women as worthy of study, consistently to our detriment. I didn't realize how different men's and women's bodies actually are, and in how many ways; the knowledge is fascinating and infuriating, considering women are so often slotted into products and categories designed for men as the 'neutral' human. Sex differences are apparently more substantial than most would assume. In fact, 'researchers have found sex differences in every tissue and organ system in the human body ... the fundamental mechanical workings of the heart ... lung capacity' as well as 'in immune cells used to convey pain signals.' In sports and training, for instance, 'isometric exercises fatigue women less (which is relevant for post-injury rehabilitation) because men and women have different ratios of types of muscle fibre,' but – repeating an all-too-familiar refrain – we have 'a limited understanding of the differences' because there are 'an inadequate number of published studies.' Sex-based differences actually seem to permeate all aspects of training and recovery in often invisible ways. With that in mind – and when 'even something as simple as ice-pack application is sex-sensitive,' Criado Perez notes, 'it's clear that women should be included in sports-medicine research at the same rates as men. But they aren't … researchers continue to research men and act as if their findings apply to women.' Here is a case of women having to fit themselves into institutions, activities, and spaces designed for men. But the influence and erasure are being imposed from the outside in.

This tendency is by no means limited to sports medicine, and as with the lack of domestic-abuse-related CTE research in women, it can't simply be argued away by factors such as the relative recency of Title IX. In these examples among others, men are figured, by a scientific structure historically dominated by men, as the standard. Women, the other 51 percent, are considered a deviation; too much trouble and expense to study because our bodies are too variable, too complicated.

The standardization of combat sports training extends beyond physical strength and capabilities, and into the gear itself. Adult training equipment is built in a kind of 'one size fits all' that does not accommodate all men, let alone women. But that's where relatively new companies like Society Nine, which specializes in boxing gloves for women, come in. Or ONX, which makes unisex striking gear with internal straps for better adjustment. These brands are notable for someone like me, who is plagued with fairly small hands and willowy wrists which, on their own, can't seem to withstand the impact I'd like to put them through. The wide range of body types and physical needs – women's and men's – means the demand for different sizes and styles of equipment is growing. As more women participate in combat sports, we might be targeted as a new niche market. If the glove fits …

It's an understatement to say it's frustrating to think of how science and design have continually failed women in ways that may still be too widespread to quantify. At the same time, I am torn about these deep levels of difference. When it comes to sport and competition, I suppose I am naïve; in my gut, if nowhere else, I still resist the idea of biology putting me at a built-in disadvantage. The weakness and paternalization of women is an old narrative, and its assumptions have been proven wrong in so many fields. *I get it.* Men have an upper-body strength that averages between 40 and 60 percent higher than women's, and a 41 percent stronger grip strength than women (of almost any age differential), among other on-paper biological advantages. But on some level, I don't really care. I still don't want any part of that argument. It makes so many things predetermined that I'd like to find the space to manoeuvre and the possibility to change or overcome. The game is rigged! I do not accept your terms. (But still: What to do with all these differences?) It might be worth having a conversation about changes to the fight rules that don't just water down men's rules but rather make the sport more suitable to women's biology. I have no clear idea what that would be, though, and I still resist the idea in spite of myself.

IT'S THAT TIME

In the late 1990s, Dutch kickboxer-turned-boxer Lucia Rijker was an up-and-coming competitor with her eye on the biggest name in women's boxing, Christy Martin. Martin had about thirty wins under her belt, but Rijker looked like a good potential match for the reigning champion. With Rijker's intentions out on the table, 'the plump Martin,' as Katherine Dunn describes her, made a point of stating that she 'wouldn't fight the lean, muscular Rijker unless Rijker passes medical tests to prove she's a woman. According to Martin, Rijker could be [a transgender woman] or be pumped up on steroids, so it wouldn't be a fair fight.' In response to Martin's claims, Rijker's camp readily offered to take tests to 'prove her unalloyed femininity.' As archaic as this process sounds, it is apparently still in practice today. According to the World Boxing Association, 'testing for femininity is done by taking a smear from the mouth of the female competitor and looking for the xx chromosomes in the cells.' Not reserved to obscure public relations stunts from pro boxers, this process is applied even at the Olympic Games.

One instance where people start to come out of the woodwork claiming to be experts on the differences between male and female biology is when it comes to discussions and regulation around transgender folks or those with differences of sexual development (DSD). Is biological science always the most important factor? Is testosterone really *magic*? After Fallon Fox came out as a trans woman, even those speaking out to support her place in women's competition made sure to note that Fox has undergone hormone therapy and is therefore not at an advantage in terms of testosterone. In 2019, World Athletics introduced a guideline restricting the testosterone levels in female athletes and those with DSDs. In 2020, middle-distance runner from South Africa and two-time Olympic gold medallist Caster Semenya lost her appeal against World Athletics, whose ban would require her 'to take testosterone-reducing hormones in order to compete in races from 400 meters to a mile.' Athletes with DSD have higher levels of natural testosterone and are apparently 'overrepresented within [World Athletics] winners.' As medical researchers argue, this increased testosterone gives female DSD athletes a 'masculine edge' over their opponents. But testosterone levels alone don't speak to all eventualities and significant factors even within an individual sport. History – even the very nature of elite athletics – is filled with physical anomalies unrelated to biological gender that lend a competitive advantage. Consider decorated swimmer Michael Phelps: what if, as Mayo Clinic Drs. J. Michael Bostwick and Michal J. Joyner ask, his 'disproportionately long arms and overly lax joints preempted him from swimming races because they give him a reach and flexibility that deprive shorter-armed, more tightly jointed contestants of victory?' Or consider 'Australian champion swimmer Ian Thorpe [who] is celebrated for huge, flipperlike feet that power him through the pool.' Even though these advantageous biological anomalies are celebrated, sexual differences are taken as grounds for disqualification.

Complicating matters further, 'testosterone is the only endogeneous biochemical variant being regulated' by World Athletics, and then, 'only in women.' In other words, as Alice Dreger points out, 'If a man has a mutation that gives him a big advantage – say he makes a lot of testosterone – he can count that as a natural advantage.' More than that, for a man to have high testosterone would be celebrated as a sign of greater masculinity. Rather than levelling any kind of playing field in sport, 'what is really being levelled here is the bodies of female athletes. Thus the game being played seems to be a kind of controlling who will count as a sexually appropriate woman: submit to being made sexually "normal" through hormone treatments or you cannot compete.' This regulation undermines and has potential implications for policies like Title IX. 'How can [these organizations] claim that they support the full inclusion of women when they reimpose a medical test for their very identity?' former Olympian and policy leader Bruce Kidd asks.

After Martin's call for Rijker to prove her femininity, the question of Rijker's sex was placed on the table for public discussion. Rather than putting the question in front of Rijker herself, reporters took up the allegations with her promoter, Bob Arum. 'All I can say is, when she was fighting in Biloxi in June, we had to get a special medical clearance for her to fight because she was menstruating,' the promoter said in what Katherine Dunn quips is 'probably the first time Arum has ever used that word at a press conference. From the pink faces of the hardnosed reporters, it might be the first time they'd heard it out loud.' When more US states began issuing boxing licences to female fighters in the 1970s, there were conditions attached. In Pennsylvania, the State Athletic Commission required women to wear aluminum bras (due to a claim that being hit in the chest would lead to breast cancer). And in California, before fighting, every female boxer was required to certify that she was not on her period. As Rijker herself later explained to Dunn, while she usually takes birth control pills to avoid having her period for a fight, on the occasion of the match in Biloxi, she simply forgot to bring them along. 'I'll never do that again,' she said. 'I got so tense that I went into the shower after the fight' – a fight she won, incidentally – 'and just stood there and screamed at the top of my lungs.' While women are no longer required to prove that they are not menstruating in order to box, in many cases they still have to prove they are not pregnant by taking a pregnancy test before the fight.

I can see why Rijker would actively control her cycle. Perhaps not surprisingly, there are certain stages of their menstrual cycle where some women feel they peak in performance. As the World

Boxing Association advises, a woman can manage her cycle through the use of hormones (like birth control) in order to sync her preferred schedule to competition day, or to manage a weight cut, although the studies about the effect of menstrual cycle on physical performance are still unclear. But the idea of physical and mood shifts connected to menstruation also comes with clichés, taboos, and misconceptions projected onto women's bodies using the language of science and the pretense of 'protection.' When boxing was first under discussion for sanctioning by the World Boxing Council, in 1995, their research board sought to understand the significant distinctions between male and female competitors. In a report they prepared as a guiding document, they refer to the risk of 'internal traumatic hemorrhages in the vagina' and worry about the variable 'effects of menstruation on physical performance,' concerns that 'read less like legitimate medical issues,' Amelia Schonbek points out, 'than like questions raised by a group of men who didn't know what to make of the female body.'

In her personal reflection on 'Boxing and Bleeding,' amateur boxer Robin Percyz remarks on the irony of a sport where bleeding is encouraged, but only of a certain kind. 'At my boxing club, the carpet lining the ring is stained with visible traces of bloody bouts and sparring,' she says. 'We can point and laugh at whose blood is whose and remember the victory and triumph that resulted from those stains.' But menstruation is considered disruptive and meant to remain unspoken. 'In the boxing community, we encounter a clear and evident divide between that of "good" and "bad" blood,' she clarifies. 'It's as clear as this: Blood from the nose – GOOD! Blood from between a woman's legs – BAD and, further, DISMISSED!' Intrigued, I conducted a casual poll about this with every reasonable-seeming man I came across for a week. I asked them to rank their comfort between seeing a pool of blood from a punch and seeing a puddle of menstrual blood, and the irrational and essentially inarticulable discomfort with the menstrual blood was *unanimous*. Menstrual blood has a mystique to it, but of course we already knew that; just ask the many female Muay Thai fighters who are required to pass under the ropes of the ring rather than stepping over them, or are barred completely from competing in some of the major Thai stadiums, as their menstrual blood is thought to desanctify the ring. Whether from cuts to the face or monthly flow, women's fluids hold a terrifying power. I will remind my uterus of that the next time it tries to ditch its lining like a bitch.

After experiencing amenorrhea, perhaps as a result of considerable amounts of exercise and large fluctuations in weight due to cutting for fights, Percyz starts to miss her monthly menstruation. What the boxer describes is likely a symptom of the Female Athlete Triad. The triad, identified in the 1990s, is a medical syndrome that can affect physically active females. A combination of low energy availability and disordered eating behaviours, menstrual disturbances, and bone health, the triadic syndrome is 'initiated by inadequate energy intake to meet the exercise energy expenditure needs of an athlete, and … associated with poor reproductive and bone health.' While these factors are real, and related to biological sex, they are also tied to basic behaviours related to fuelling and providing adequate nutrition for an active body.

When the boxer's prodigal flow eventually returns, she reclaims and embraces it, exclaiming: 'My menstruation was a metaphor for power!' For this boxer, temporarily losing her period – and the reproductive implications associated with that physical disorder – was a defeminizing process.

I appreciate the ambivalence of the blood and the boxer's point that while certain kinds of bleeding are accepted, others are very specifically not. I mention the boxer's newfound love for her period because her reflection peels back one more layer of silence involved in ignoring biological realities. It points to the importance of proper nutrition for female athletes, but not to any inherent shortcoming in the makings of women who train. A working reproductive cycle (for any reason) does not itself make a woman any more than the same unmakes a fighter.

HAS IT BEEN TWO MINUTES ALREADY?

In 2014, the World Boxing Council changed the length of women's boxing matches from twelve three-minute to ten two-minute rounds, as well as cutting down on the number of condoned fights for women.

While they were reportedly unclear about the sources of their research, their reasoning included the idea that women are physically more inclined to concussions than men; amateur female fighters are more used to two-minute rounds and would have a harder time adjusting to longer fights; there is a greater risk of injury in longer fights; 'women's endurance has been proven to be less than [that of] men. Marathon running time is much different' between men and women; and the 'menstrual cycle has tremendous impact on the body of a woman, including 12 hormones which act in the body system, creating radical changes in several areas.' In 2019, the WBC claimed it's 'Science not Sexism' that dictates the shortened number of rounds for women. Ultimately, however, they acknowledged that doctors simply 'aren't sure' whether female fighters experience concussion symptoms more than their male counterparts, or whether they are simply more likely to *admit* it when they have them.

According to the WBC, the *real* sexism isn't the benevolent patronizing of women's brains but rather unequal pay. Women in all arenas – including boxing, with its the highly inflated (male) paydays – make less than their male counterparts. I mentally nod to the WBC's pivot here, but I am still, personally, unconvinced. I don't entirely know why I'm arguing for women to have more time to get hit in the head – yes, while getting equal pay, please. But I am. As many female boxers point out, the length of the rounds and the pay gap go hand in hand. As world champion boxer Alicia Ashley explains, upon talking with a number of other professional female fighters in 2015, 'One of the major things that stood out was that they weren't getting paid.' Under the shorter fight round and sets, 'promoters were saying, however unfairly, "We're not paying you because you're not doing the same work"' as the men.

Some boxing commentators hypothesize that the rate of knockouts would go up in women's fights if their rounds were extended in duration. One assumption seems to be that many men's knockouts occur in the third minute of the round, when fighters are fatiguing. But this doesn't seem to be the case for MMA organizations like Invicta, Bellator, and the UFC, where men and women alike compete in five-minute rounds. For all of the UFC's initial refusal to bring women into the promotion (and their eventual inclusion was, in many ways, a marketing choice based on the star-power potential of Rousey), the entry of women into the organization, and others like it, nevertheless had them walking into the same round length as their male counterparts, a rule set that remains consistent to this day. There's no question that women can fight five-minute rounds in MMA, and I don't see a trend of stoppages due to head injuries in minutes three to five. But I suppose since women have only been competing in mainstream MMA promotions like the UFC for less than twenty years, we will have to wait another generation to start collecting and studying their brains (and yes, I am fully aware of how macabre that sounds). In the words of Schonbek, 'If the medical community establishes that women are indeed more at risk for concussions than men, then precautions should be taken to ensure that they can box safely. Until then, let them fight. Everybody knows that they can.'

The design of the physical world is, and has long been, made with men in mind. This is a hard fact that also functions as a kind of metaphor. The fight world, too, is male by design. This space was not made for us, and yet here we are, and here we have been, despite all these hurdles. Maintaining the status quo means forever trying to twist a 'female' fighter into a pre-made shape – male by default.

CHAPTER NINE
★
CRYING IN COMBAT SPORTS

When I joined the MMA gym in California, I finally had the chance to spar. I felt comfortable because almost everyone fought with relative restraint, and I could see that the most experienced fighters moderated their level almost seamlessly based on their opponent; they could be very technical and controlled with one person, and a lot harder or more ostentatious with another. I wanted in.

But I needed a mouthguard. When it arrived, I went through the bizarre ritual of boiling it, putting it in my mouth to mould to my uniquely crooked bite, and then running it under cold water to allow the gel to set. I took the strange object, put it in its half-moon-shaped case, and packed it in my gym bag along with my gloves, shin guards, hand wraps, and water bottle. That evening, I stepped into the rotation. My mouthguard was hard to get used to; it was too big for my mouth, despite being shaped to my teeth, and it made breathing difficult. I felt awkward but fortified. Everyone knew that I hadn't sparred before, so they went easy on me. And thank goodness for that. There's a remarkable difference between kicking a pad and kicking a person. The pad, for one, does not hit back. My very first opponent was a white-haired double-PhD in her fifties. As I stood across from this older woman, I thought, 'How am I going to hit *her*?' but before I could really linger in that thought, she had already opened the round by landing a jab to my face. Oh. This strange woman was suddenly punching and kicking me, with surprising speed and strength, I might add, and that was now a totally reasonable and acceptable thing for her to be doing. I felt like I had walked onto the field of a completely new sport I didn't know how to play, and strangers were explaining the rules to me by smashing me repeatedly in the nose. That first session, as we rotated from one round to the next, I sparred against people of varying levels of experience and men and women of all different sizes. It was exhilarating, unpredictable, confusing, humbling, and overwhelming. It was fun.

As I left that first night of sparring, I got into my car all hopped up on adrenaline and pride. I was so excited. I drove two blocks and then pulled over. I was weeping. I sat in a fast-food parking lot, tears pouring out, and I had no idea why. Among other things, this was likely my first instance of what they call an adrenaline dump (body goes into overdrive … and then crashes), and it left an impression. Adrenaline can give you superpowers and just as easily it can take them away. As it turns out, I'm not alone in that. As I have also since discovered, my tears are not limited to adrenaline, either.

In a now archived 2017 Reddit post, a user (whose identity is now simply listed as 'deleted') posed a query to the community, asking a question on behalf of a coworker who had recently taken up karate. Apparently, the friend 'was sparring for the first time and she noted that she holds her breath a lot' (despite knowing better). The poster continues that the friend 'noted after sparring she felt winded due to holding her breath and then she said she started sobbing uncontrollably and felt depressed for hours. She said the physiological response wasn't tied to any real emotion that occurred while sparring (she wasn't hurt and the sparring was light) but yet she felt "down."' The poster (whose gender isn't specified) self-identifies as a neurosurgeon with approximately ten years of martial arts training but no first-hand experience with the phenomenon their friend describes. They want to know if this is a response that is 'specific to women when they're under extreme duress.'

The scenario they describe feels familiar to me, for obvious reasons, and I read the responses eagerly. The posts, many of which are from self-identified men, are often quick to point out that not only is the friend's response *not* unusual, but this phenomenon is also not exclusive to women. And as the 'Female Muay Thai' Facebook group's conversation of September 18, 2013, suggests, tears are not necessarily limited to first-time sparrers. Here, seasoned female fighters sound off on their own experience with crying in training. In the initial post, a fighter starts off with what she apologetically terms 'kind of a weird question' and then outlines an incident from the night before, when she was 'sparring a 6'4 southpaw about 230+ lbs' and 'out of no where … started crying.' (First of all, and as some of the other respondents imply – that seems like a pretty rational response to sparring a six-foot-four, 230-pound left-handed fighter; that's like trying to fight a tall, thick brick wall that's doing everything in the opposite way you do. Having been frustrated by my ineptness against tall male southpaws myself – Josh, I'm looking at you – I could almost tear up right now just thinking about it.) As she continues, 'Luckily he had experienced a female fighter crying before & kept pressing me & I worked through it & finished out the rest of the night.' As she points out, this isn't her first time sparring with him, nor was he inexperienced with fighting women or opponents of different sizes, and this was also by no means the hardest sparring session she'd had. By all accounts, this should have been a completely normal session. She describes feeling helpless and ineffectual ('Everything I threw at him either didn't connect or didn't faze him') which suggests that there was frustration involved, but nothing else seemed out of the ordinary. 'So,' she asks her group members, 'what's the deal?' Trying to keep the tone light, she rounds up to the question: 'Has anyone else ever cried during sparring & how do I prevent it from happening again? Haha … Thanks!!'

There's a remarkable difference between the responses she gets from her community of female fighters versus the more general and co-ed responses to the related Reddit query. Context, identifiable relationships, similar levels of experience, and gender are all significant factors. Nevertheless, the first response she receives is one that works in this context but wouldn't have read the same way in the self-policing, co-ed Reddit conversation: 'Ya getn ya period?!!!' the first fighter replies jokingly, before immediately confessing that they, too, have cried, both in sparring and in pad work. A number of the fighters connect the trifecta of frustration, stress, and hormones as a kind of deadly recipe for tears. As these female fighters acknowledge communally, their bodies and emotions just don't work the same way around 'that time of the month,' when in many ways they feel uncharacteristically 'delicate.' They don't say they stop training through PMS, for the record, and I don't know any woman who does, although of course some women experience symptoms that can be debilitating. In my experience, my training partners simply respond to the training somewhat differently but don't necessarily sit it out. At one point, I used to think my coach knew, with some dark, sadistic magic, when I had menstrual cramps, because that was always the day we spontaneously switched our focus to hitting each other repeatedly with hard body punches that felt like they were being delivered straight to my ovaries. We were learning to gauge and build up the power from one (barely feel it) to ten (full power, please stop). I didn't leave, opt out of the drill, or ask anyone to go easy on me. I just *secretly* wanted to die, my eyes flirting with tears. But PMS and menstrual symptoms can take different forms, not all of which can be toughed out.

Another, perhaps more universal, factor these fighters cite is the stress of fight camp, which for any fighter is a physically and emotionally gruelling time. Tears are not limited to camp, however. Often, crying comes as a response to feeling overwhelmed or frustrated (and, as one commenter notes understandably, it 'seems to get worse if people ask me if I'm ok!'). This frustration is less about the opponent than it is about the fighters' expectations for themselves and their own performance. As with anger, sometimes the physiological response is tears, as frustrating as it is for those of us who work that way. The pressure to improve, to correct mistakes, and to work harder under greater strain becomes more acute as a fighter gets closer to testing themselves in competition.

Based on the female fighters' responses, it would seem that crying is completely normal, and a possibly socialized and sometimes hormonal response to frustration. But the co-ed Reddit conversation complicates that idea, as does von Duuglas-Ittu's article 'There is Crying in Muay Thai: Emotional Training' – one of the few sources that directly tackles this question (rather than taking it up as a social media discussion, for instance). In her article, von Duuglas-Ittu talks about the urge she has been feeling lately to burst into tears. While there are a number of reasons to cry in training, this one, she says, 'isn't a response to anything directly but more the general need for release after feeling quite pressured and bottled up by being ineffective in any varying degree for the past hour, minutes, days, weeks, years, whatever ... ' At the same time, despite her already considerable experience as a fighter, von Duuglas-Ittu ultimately concludes this feeling is something she hopes to 'grow out of.'

The hegemonic masculinity of a sport like Muay Thai arguably lends an advantage to men over women; whereas many men have been trained since childhood to hide their emotions and to refuse to admit that they are hurt – skills necessary for a fighter of any gender – women are not typically given the same lifelong conditioning. This theory is echoed in sociological studies on martial arts like MMA that point to the history of competitive Western sports education as connected to military training for young men.

In another, more recent Reddit conversation (2019), a poster – a self-identified seventeen-year-old male with the handle 'OddishVapor' – poses an open question about his experience sparring in boxing. 'I just sparred for the first time today,' he begins. He walks readers through his growing sense of defeat as he is repeatedly punished and clearly outskilled in the matchup. 'I started getting teary eyed,' he recounts. 'I was hurting but I dont think it was from the pain. Anytime anyone would talk to me I would become teary eyed and try to hide it. They told me I had a lot of heart and took the punches like a champ, but even that still got me teary eyed ... I still dont know why I'm so emotional about it ... Call me a bitch if you want, but that was my first time taking hits that hard even with headgear on and. At least I'll be coming back to the gym and I wont back down from this.'

As in the women's Facebook conversation, OddishVapor expresses a sense of his frustration leading up to his tears, as well as a growing loss of control as others tried to acknowledge his feelings or check in on him. And as in the Reddit post from 2017, the answers are sympathetic ('you're not a bitch!' other men reassure); the top-rated responses are empathetic, encouraging, and predominantly ... scientific. Most respondents (often self-identifying as male) have physiological and biological explanations for what many of them admit is a familiar response to fighting. Many of them answer his question by saying they have cried in training themselves – or have really wanted to. 'Happens to the best of us' is a typical response. Most follow that up by explaining the science behind it (the shock to the system from an adrenaline dump, for instance). And a number of them criticize OddishVapor's gym for letting the newbie spar that hard only a month into his training. Many even rightly stress the importance of clear and open communication with his sparring partners, in order to let them know what he is and is not comfortable with in terms of level and intensity. Interestingly, this didn't come up in the same way when the women were discussing a similar phenomenon; the women tended instead to volley between, on one hand, deflecting the potential embarrassment of the poster by using humour, and on the other offering practical advice by suggesting specific techniques for improving your game against a certain kind of opponent. The women use humour to insulate their peer from any potential insecurity the same way the (mostly) men use science to protect the young boxer. As the young man has already self-consciously anticipated, there is an uncomfortable connection between crying and being a 'bitch.' It seems that no matter how understandable and often even inevitable most people realize crying is, no one really wants to be associated with tears – a visible marker of weakness, and one that is casually gendered – especially in this space.

WHAT HAPPENS IN TRAINING STAYS IN TRAINING

In a promotional faux pas known as 'Crygate,' UFC fighter Daniel Cormier's opponent tried to shame the former UFC Champ Champ for crying. (A 'Champ Champ' is, charmingly, someone who holds championship belts simultaneously in two weight classes; Cormier's were light heavyweight and heavyweight). Cormier isn't exactly known for his stoicism – like a *lot* of male and female fighters, he can often be seen weeping openly post-fight, especially, but by no means exclusively, after a loss. 'Crygate' is different, however, because it speaks not only to emotional codes of conduct, but to codes about training, and rules about *talking about* training.

In 2013, Patrick Cummins, an undefeated two-time all-American wrestler and 2004 NCAA Division I heavyweight runner-up, is pulled in as a last-minute replacement to compete against Cormier in the

UFC. Cormier's star is on the rise, and he is set to make a highly antici-pated debut in a new weight class (light heavyweight), when his orig-inal opponent, Rashad Evans, is injured and has to withdraw from the fight. Pulled out of relative obscurity (he was apparently working the drive-thru window at a coffee shop when he got the call) and given an opportunity to fight in the UFC, Cummins has to make a name for himself, and fast. His response is to essentially step in front of a mic and announce: 'I made Daniel Cormier cry.' As Jonathan Gottschall very thoroughly explains, much of fighting – for men, anyway – is about good, old-fashioned, patriarchal honour. Through-out the history of time, he explains, men have died over words, because reputation is life. So for Cummins to walk out and say he reduced a grown man to tears, which suggests not only Cormier's weakness ('call me a bitch if you want,' OddishVapor says) but also his own bragging dominance? Fighting words, indeed.

As this smear to his honour circulates, Cormier decides to set the record straight. While Cormier freely admits to having cried, that is not, as it turns out, the real issue. More important than *that* he cried is *why* it happened. In 2004, when Cormier, a wrestler, was training for the Olympic Games, his coach brought in other wrestlers to spar with him. Cummins was one of those sparring partners. While any training camp is stressful, Olympic training is likely worse. Cormier was also in the wake of extensive personal tragedies, the most recent of which was the death of his daughter the year before. One day in training, Cummins 'dumped' Cormier 'on his head.' But this exercise wasn't just a regular sparring match to Cormier; in order to approach the practice with the necessary intensity, he explains, each round *was* an Olympic competition to him. When he lost to Cummins and got up to take a rematch, Cormier's coach told him, 'No, the Olympics are over for you. You lost.' Frustrated, upset, and overwhelmed by the situation, he reacted the way he would if he'd really just lost his shot at a medal. In order for the simulation to work, he had to make it real. If the match is real, so are the emotional and psychological consequences. He cried.

When it came time for the actual Olympics, Cormier nearly died due to kidney failure from excessive weight cutting, which prevented him from competing. Before he could even make it to the mat, his

Olympics were truly over. Making weight is a whole other variable – a mental hurdle that is also intimately physical. Failure to meet weight is often derided as a lack of seriousness. Some see it as a sign of cracks in the fighter's mental discipline, something a breakdown during training like the one with Cummins might prefigure. Whether an athlete is able to will themselves through a weight cut or not (hard to override your kidneys, for instance), Cormier's failure to qualify for the Olympics does not take away from anything he has accomplished before or since. What it arguably highlights, instead, is the precarity and humanity involved in struggle, ambition, and an ultimately often frustrating attempt to control the world – starting with ourselves.

On top of, but not divorced from, questions of self-mastery and control, the Cormier/Cummins tension highlights the intimacy involved in martial arts training. The crying is irrelevant, Cormier explains. It happens. Everyone has a limit. But to *speak of it*, particularly out of context, is offside. 'Those things stay in the wrestling room,' he explains reprovingly. 'We don't talk about training. That's wrestler code 101. [Cummins] knows that. He knew the things that I was going through at that time. To put himself in the situation, he went and dug up some things that he should … never have dug up. Those things stay back in 2004.'

I have experienced few social situations more personally revealing than making oneself repeatedly vulnerable to teammates and sparring partners in the attempt to master one's physical and emotional weaknesses. I've never been particularly interested in the idea of 'honour among men,' but the intricacies of 'honour among fighters' – wrestler (or boxer, or martial artist) code 101 – now, that is intriguing.

When I interview coaches and fighters, I ask them about these social codes. Sometimes the codes come to mind right away, but for many, the 'unwritten rules' are so ingrained as to become invisible and therefore hard to articulate. One of the questions I ask is about emotion, and I move from there to asking specifically about crying. One of my boxing coaches, Jaime Ward-Yassin, a former professional boxer and a vocal advocate for women in martial arts, is quick to volunteer her thoughts on emotion in fighting. Before I can even broach the question, she cuts straight to talking about the ubiquity and inevitability of strong feelings. Trained by men throughout her entire career, she explains that it is something that was always acknowledged as a part of training (both for her coaches, who she describes as being emotional people themselves, and for the fighters – male and female – that she has since trained and cornered over the years). According to Ward-Yassin, crying is inevitable, and even important. She often encourages it, albeit not in the open; if a fighter of any gender has lost a tough match, or is having a hard time in training, she will make the space for them to go off and 'have a good cry.' This could mean letting them quietly step out of the gym, or even guarding the bathroom door to create a safe, quiet space for them to sort through their feelings alone. (The *alone* part is key here.) The way she describes it, crying is a cathartic and necessary process. In this sense, it sounds kind of like vomiting; sure, nobody wants to do it, and you won't enjoy it or feel very cool as it happens, but your body has got to get that shit out. Tears, here, are abject yet inevitable.

Describing her own pre-fight process, Ward-Yassin acknowledges that not only were there tears, but that her coaches actively sought that breaking point for her. At one point in every camp, it seemed, her coaches would push her to the point where she cried. Afterward, they'd acknowledge it had been intentional. Rather than something to be ashamed of, or something to be avoided, crying was used by Ward-Yassin's coaches as a kind of metric; they'd press her to the point of tears in the stage of pre-fight training at which they felt she was peaking. It wasn't an accidental stumble, or one she could, like a lot of us, try to will her way out of repeating. It was a strategic part of the process. Nevertheless, she says, not all fighters are going to respond to that kind of pressure quite the same way. While she supports the tough love approach, she admits to addressing her male and female fighters differently in general, although the difference of approach seems to come from a sense of social conditioning (what works for the fighters based on how they were raised and how they are used to being treated), rather than an aversion to their tears.

By this line of thinking, tears can be considered an important tool in helping to teach the fighter what it looks and feels like to go through and then overcome adversity. It is an old fighting aphorism that fighters should have to go through fire in training in order to be able to withstand struggle more easily in a fight. Quoting her coach, Ward-Yassin ties this philosophy up in one sentence: 'Cry in the gym so you can laugh in the ring.'

CHAPTER TEN
★
LINEAGE

After I started training at Kaijin in Santa Cruz, I was surprised to start noticing its branded T-shirts and stickers all over town. There were clearly card-carrying gym members circulating all around me at any given time. This made the community seem huge, but it also suggested a sense of pride that seemed outsized for an MMA gym in a fairly small town. From where I sat in my uniform of blue jeans and plain black T-shirt, the way people walked around with their opinions and affiliations displayed on their cars and shirts – wearing their hearts on their sleeves, so to speak – was fascinating. It was hard for me to imagine being committed enough to a group identity to make that kind of statement.

This branding has a deeper and more widespread meaning than I realized. The Santa Cruz Skateboards logos are not (or have not always been) benign 'I am here' tourist branding or the local go-to T-shirt choice. The logo corresponds with the territory, and parts of California are notoriously pieced together in an alternative map of otherwise invisible surfing and skateboard turf boundaries. Likewise, there are invisible camps between martial arts, and particularly Brazilian Jiu-Jitsu, communities. The BJJ gi, a pyjama-like tunic that ties with a cloth belt, is visually coded with all kinds of significant territorial markers. From rank and experience (belt colour) to affiliation (logos and sewn-on patches), the gi can signal not only intention and belonging within an activity but also one's place within a particular community.

Even more overtly than my own field of academia, fight culture is preoccupied with concepts like hierarchy or meritocracy, honour, loyalty, and respect. The focus on loyalty is certainly true of MMA and BJJ camps. In BJJ, the term 'Creonte' refers to someone disloyal, a traitor. The name apparently came from a Brazilian soap opera character, and it gained purchase when used to refer to a student who establishes a long-standing relationship with a school, benefits from their support and potentially also their sponsorship, and then switches camps. They take the education, tricks, and skills given to them by one school and betray that trust by transferring their allegiance – and that privileged knowledge – to another.

In these patriarchal fields of mastery, lineage is key. When Jiu-Jitsu practitioners and coaches list their credentials, their lineage is still often featured the same way academic titles show up next to professors' names. If they have a black belt, that might be foregrounded, but often what's important to many is not simply that they achieved this rank, but who bestowed it upon them. Not all black belts are conferred and valued equally, just as a PhD from some small, random college or university does not carry the same social weight as a doctorate from Oxford. Academics are appended to their advisors and mentors like prolific offspring, and the philosophical ideologies and approaches can act like a shared family name. If you include someone's name, you are attaching yourself to their reputation. If you refuse their name, that is a serious political move, as well. But when you abandon your allegiances, that sense of 'belonging' and heredity is forfeit to some extent.

Tight-knit, devoted 'families' are part of what make martial arts practice so rich. There's an intimacy and a camaraderie between training partners and camps that is often layered through struggle and learning. There's a shared vulnerability that comes with it in a way that would be hard to gain outside the bounds of years of close friendship. But under the wrong leadership, or when wielded as an all-or-nothing formulation, these complex, intense, and emotional bonds can also tilt toward the extreme, the fanatic, or even the abusive.

Every community has its own conditions of belonging, whether it's BJJ or a graduate studies program. When choosing affiliations, it's worth asking not 'Will they have me?' but rather 'Is this truly the group to which I want to belong?' As a woman, I have spent years working within the university, and now the martial arts community as well. I don't know why I keep pushing to find my own way to belong within these patriarchal spaces, but there's clearly an equation between masculinity and power, and I don't seem to have been able to get myself fully outside it. At the same time, however, there is power in amassing these skills. As the many simultaneously wonderful, generous, tough, vulnerable, strong women I have encountered in martial arts and the academy and beyond have shown me, we don't need to be pitted against each other, and we don't need to hold each other back. Collecting these tools – from coaches of any gender – and learning to turn them against the structures that seep into us (inside the gym, sure, but also well beyond it), is a lifelong process in itself. But sometimes, especially for women, loyalty comes at a cost.

CLOSE QUARTERS

Women are joining Brazilian Jiu-Jitsu programs in unprecedented numbers. Despite the potential advantages in terms of self-defence and self-confidence, it can still be a hard sell. Learning how to wrestle in this way means rolling around and putting yourself in all kinds of incredibly vulnerable, uncomfortable, and awkward positions, and usually with what are, at least initially, strange men. Jiu-Jitsu is still largely a male-dominated sport. The times I have sparred in Jiu-Jitsu, I came away with the stink of maybe five different men on my clothes, in addition to my own – and to be clear, Jiu-Jitsu sweat isn't like regular exercise sweat. It's something else – stress sweat, the product of *struggle*. It's rank. In 'good' schools, no one comes in smelling that way, but hours into rolling, the air changes. For a person of any gender, taking up BJJ requires surmounting a whole set of major physical and psychological hurdles. And once you make it through the door, don the belted gi uniform (or rash guards for no-gi practice), and negotiate the confusing warm-up ritual, there is the actual training and grappling itself. The most difficult thing to learn, initially, is how not to freak out when, inevitably, someone bigger or more experienced is lying on top of you, controlling you, and (strategically or otherwise) crushing the air out of your body. The most important thing new BJJ students have to figure out is how to exist within incredibly counterintuitive, uncomfortable, and potentially frightening positions – ones that feel like legitimate, immediate, and physically draining moments of danger – and to *relax*. To slow down, stay present, calm your breath, and control the completely natural and reasonable urge to tense up, writhe around, and flip the fuck out.

In order to be able to master even that most elusive but essential of skills (breathing, relaxing, and staying calm) you have to trust that you are, actually, safe. This ability to remain calm under pressure is, of course, one that translates to real life. But none of these exercises work as a training mechanism if they are not practised within a rule set. Without guidelines, this is simply trauma. In BJJ, everyone has the option of tapping out at any point. That's not a detail – it's a fundamental element of practising the sport. It makes the training space a productive one for learning how to manage fears and conflict. If I'm about to be hurt in a position, or feel my airway being cut off by a choke, or am simply having a panic attack and can't control it, all I have to do is tap my opponent with my hand (or verbally say 'tap' if my hands are pinned) and they *stop*. They get up, we break, and I'm whole again. That's the agreement that everyone enters into when they step onto the mat. It's the most sacred rule.

LEVERAGE

With all kinds of exceptions, fighters are not necessarily trained to think independently. Coaches often opt to put their time into someone who will listen to them. In perhaps the same way that teachers reward the students who show they can learn from them, coaches and trainers invest their time and effort in fighters who are not only there to improve but to learn – *their* way. Most head coaches have a 'method' or a 'system' that they have patented (officially or unofficially) as their signature approach. Their fighters go out into the world and are ambassadors for and examples of that system at work, just as academics reflect back on their advisors. Both, especially as they are moving up in the ranks, are products of their coaching lineage.

I am often complimented for being 'coachable.' This is presented as a good thing. I actively try to do what I'm told, both in training and while competing in the ring. When I'm working with a boxing coach, I do my best to keep a boxing stance and to follow the principles they put forward. When I switch (sometimes in the same day, though I don't recommend it) to Muay Thai, I have to reverse a lot of what I've just been doing – from the stance to the rhythm to the approach, not to mention the inclusion of kicking and other tools. I try, with varying success, to do as I am coached. In general, when not ramping up to compete in a specific style, I want to get the most out of each setting, on its own terms. Not only do I want to constantly grow and improve, but I am – as I have been told, lovingly or otherwise – a bit of a teacher's pet. I can't help it. I am a teacher. And I have been a student my entire life. People who do well in these institutions are typically people who have learned how it works and are both willing and able to work within it. I'm like Lisa in *The Simpsons*.

Being a Lisa isn't the worst thing. The desire to improve, and to make sure I'm headed on the 'right' track makes me a hard worker. It also fits my 'Masters' or 'Elite' fighter (age, not necessarily skill – 'Masters' is the category for BJJ competitors aged thirty to forty; as a boxer under forty-one, I fit into the 'Elite' age bracket) and 'lifelong learner' status to some extent. I'm no longer shy about asking for help, the way I was when I was younger. But I have an additional escape hatch that protects me. I am never going to be world champion. I'm not even going to be a pro. I have a profession already, and it requires a certain level of time, commitment, and brain function. There are, therefore, limits to what I'm willing to do. This is not the case for a lot of other fighters, and younger, ambitious female ones, especially. Fighters with the potential or ambition to fulfill their dreams or to make a living through competition are playing with a whole different set of stakes. I have also been fortunate to work with relatively sane, upstanding individuals. But not everyone is so lucky.

In 2013, following a violent attack involving students from his school, coach Lloyd Irvin's reputation was placed in the public eye, and did not survive the exposure. Irvin is a former Brazilian Jiu-Jitsu world champion and the head coach of what was, for a time, one of the top Jiu-Jitsu schools in the United States. Irvin's 'Medal Chasers' team consisted of a group of high-level and high-ranking competitors. In January 2013, three of Irvin's students ran into each other at a New Year's Eve event at a local nightclub. Matthew Maldonado and Nicholas Schultz offered to drive their teammate home, as she had been drinking and wasn't able to drive herself. Instead of bringing her home, as promised, they allegedly raped her, and she eventually collapsed to the ground, hitting her head as she fell. They allegedly then left her unconscious on the pavement, in winter. Eventually, someone else walked by, heard her crying for help, and found her. When this attack was exposed, the whole team was rightly put under a microscope.

One of the facts that immediately came to light was that the man who coached all three of them, Irvin, had himself been charged with rape back in 1989. Irvin had been part of a gang rape of a seventeen-year-old college student, but because he did not technically have intercourse with the woman, he was not convicted like many of the other men involved. Irvin himself (both then and when the story of the assault resurfaced in 2013) admitted to participating in and wanting to be part of the situation. He 'said he *tried to* have sex with her but could not' (my emphasis) – he was struck with a bout of so-called temporary impotence and missed his chance. Not surprisingly, both then and in 2013, Irvin and the other men characterized the woman in question as having wanted the attack; they were convinced her part – what she describes as being lured into a bedroom and then attacked by two men, and then more – was not only consensual, but eager. They referred to her as a 'freak.' And this is the man setting the tone for the environment in which Maldonado, Schultz, and their female teammate learn a sport that trains them how to fight, and dominate, any opponent. Maldonado and Schultz, adults acting of their own free will, allegedly attack and abandon their teammate, someone with whom they have not only shared the ups and downs of training and the close quarters of a shared gym, but also arguably the most intimate physical contact possible in sport. When found not guilty of multiple counts of kidnapping and first- and second-degree sexual abuse, Maldonado released a statement saying, 'My dreams are just to go keep continuing what I was doing before … and try to win as many championships as I can.'

Beyond the completely obvious awfulness of this kind of violent attack, the basis of the relationship between Maldonado, Schultz, and their female teammate is predicated on an agreed set of principles. The rule set itself insists they are all equal. 'At the heart of a fight is a consensual relation to violence,' English professor and sports writer

Jennifer Doyle explains. 'That consensus is not merely an agreement to fight: it is also an agreement to stop fighting when one fighter submits to the other and taps out.' In stark contrast, rape, a violent act intended to assert inequality, 'is a violation of the bonds of trust and dependence that make this sport [BJJ] even thinkable.'

SETTING THE TONE

When the story of Irvin's history surfaced, more discussions of the team and its environment started to stream out. Even within the confines of the gym itself, allegedly, there was ongoing sexual misconduct, in particular the pressuring, coercion, and manipulation of young female athletes. One of the primary conditions for training and working under a coach or within a coaching program is trust. We turn ourselves over to our coaches, to some extent, in order to learn from people who ostensibly know, and have the tools to see, more than we do. Submitting oneself to someone, as a student, is an act of faith. These students were promised that if they followed whatever their coaches told them to do, they would be successful athletes; however, young women were manipulated, abused, and coerced into controlling and sexual activities. They were suffering in silence, unsure about where the bounds of their allegiance could or should lie. In a watershed moment for the gym, one young female student asked an older, more experienced, male colleague for advice. This cross-gender conversation brought to light the contrast in expectations between them and allowed her to see that her coaches were in the wrong, that this was an unacceptable training environment. Both she and her teammate, the man she asked for advice, subsequently left the gym. Her ally – an accomplished competitor and a (now former) leading member of the team – spoke openly online about his departure, as well as his discoveries and misgivings about the gym's dynamic. Thanks to age, gender, and credentials, his words and actions were *heard* in a way that would unfortunately have been impossible for his younger teammate to accomplish on her own.

Around the one-year mark of pandemic shutdowns in Vancouver, Eastside Boxing Club, the home of my Female Fighters team, and the banner under which I fought my first boxing match, faced criticism of its own. Though I have not been back for months, I have been following the controversy, including allegations of bullying and harassment levelled against some male coaches, specifically by female fighters and coach Jaime Ward-Yassin, who have since left the gym. The claims of harassment and bullying are a reminder that we can't be complacent in even the most seemingly progressive spaces. After the #MeToo movement, expectations in all arenas are evolving, including what has been thought of as the traditionally male environment of the boxing gym. I can only hope that in the future, women who fight won't have to fight against their coaches, trainers, and teammates. Meanwhile, I am watching and learning as these spaces continue to change, in real time.

The issues made more visible by the narratives of #MeToo were not available in 2013, however. In response to the New Year's Eve assault allegations, three leading female voices in Brazilian Jiu-Jitsu in the United States, Valerie Worthington, Emily Kwok, and Lola Newsom, issued an article calling on the BJJ community to hold itself accountable for addressing the underlying issues highlighted by this atrocity. They encouraged all readers and community members to create safe spaces in all aspects of their lives, and not to see the problem as something that applies to this violent community, or to certain women, but not to the readers themselves. Their readers are asked to see how they, as individuals, can make a change. The authors referred to the event as a catalyst, but angled away from the discussion of gender or gendered violence. I have read through years of writing by Worthington and Kwok, and these women are clearly smart, thoughtful, and empowering figures. It is worth noting that they were stepping up to open the lines of communication in a time when these conversations were scarce. They were also speaking from the position of athletes who are embedded within the BJJ community. Here, they clearly felt the responsibility to speak out, as women and leaders, but their reticence to be more specific or personal in their comments, and the tendency to point the conversation to a wider lens about people in positions of power outside of BJJ, also suggests a level of distance that marks the discourse of the time. Expressing the mantra that 'grappling is based on trust,' they linked to a previous article by Worthington (pre–January 2013) that outlines '4 Ways to

Be a Good Training Partner: Getting Started in Brazilian Jiu-Jitsu.' Worthington, a coach, BJJ black belt, and PhD in educational psychology, makes clear at the outset of her article that the question of how to navigate and avoid the pitfalls of this martial arts community is 'an issue particularly if you are a woman who trains.' In an interesting turn of phrase, Worthington explains to the reader that her article is intended to 'provid[e] some suggestions for *helping people feel comfortable training with you,* particularly if you are a woman, though they all apply universally.' (The emphasis here is mine.) The onus is placed on the new student – especially the woman – to make herself suitable in the hope of being accepted into a pre-existing, and gendered, community. She has the affective responsibility, in this formulation, of adapting to the space and putting the men at ease with her presence, her appearance, and her desire to train.

This attitude is present in a number of BJJ 'how-to' and 'dos and don'ts' blogs I have found online, with authors ranging from young and semi-experienced female students to instructors and community leaders at some of the highest levels. Every one of these lists I have come across – from as far back as 2013, but also more recent – are written with the female reader in mind. Whereas Worthington's list ultimately provides widely targeted suggestions for any new student starting a BJJ practice – 'Keep it light,' 'Assume the best of everyone,' 'Assume you know less than everyone,' and 'Don't lose your cool' – other lists, often written by younger practitioners, target their advice to women explicitly. Many lists quickly address questions of appropriate attire (with chiding mentions of exposed sports bras, visible thong underwear, and makeup), and the spectre of the woman who is, supposedly, just going into a BJJ or MMA gym looking to find a boyfriend. As I kept coming across these topics in blog after blog, I have to admit I was a little dismayed.

When there are so few women in a field, 'supporting' each other is always complicated. The women who are established have worked hard and put in thousands of hours, years of their lives, and in the case of martial artists, a lot of pain, sweat, blood, and a whole lot of grit, in order to solidify their place and win the respect and opportunities that they deserve. The same kinds of concerns listed in those blogs are also voiced by professional fighters interviewed for sociological studies about women's conception of 'femininity' in 'hard' martial arts. There is a lingering sense that some women who are not serious, or who embody stereotypes that those women have had to dispel, will come in and 'ruin it' for the rest of them. Even at a high level, many fighters worry that they, too, will be lumped in with this behaviour in the eyes of their male training partners, and their work and abilities downplayed or dismissed as a ploy to get dates. The fact that the conduct of certain women is assumed to reflect on all of us (significantly, in the eyes of the men in the room) creates a dynamic that, at its worst, tends to plot women against each other. Even among established fighters, there is no consensus about how to market themselves, for instance. Fighters go back and forth about sexualizing imagery and the public face they put forward in their profession. This tension is not unique to martial arts and combat sports, but the masculine perception of this space heightens the stakes for the women within it, as each can still end up being a representative for their entire gender.

SHOULDS

I started to compete in kickboxing shortly after moving to California post-breakup. Leif and I packed my remaining sliver of possessions into my car and headed out together on the road to Santa Cruz. When we got there, we spent time getting me set back up in my beach shack. We hung out, had talks, shed tears, and made trips to the beach. Then I drove him to the airport and was, for the first time, alone. My life, which had been split in two between Vancouver and California for the past eight months, was now going to be settled in one place. Meanwhile, I had the air of someone who had taken off and joined the circus. The strange narrative presented itself as the idea that I was off in California, far from home, writing books and getting into fights. I avoided calls from my old life. I sat, quiet, on the sand near my flat. I attended to every sunrise I could catch.

I threw myself headfirst into training. I didn't miss a kickboxing class, even if that meant weeping all the way up to the gym door, eyes welling up mid-training (hoping to pass it off as sweat), and then crying the whole drive home. I trained with fervour. I wept bitterly, and often. I took on challenges to externalize my struggle, like signing up to fight, trying to carry my body weight in furniture at IKEA without using a dolly, or taking up alcohol consumption for essentially the first time in my adult life. (With no practice or aptitude for the latter, I was a bit of a wash and it didn't really stick. To my untrained palate, whiskey still just tastes like poison. The furniture carrying, however, was a success. I was, if nothing else, physically strong.) Close female friends came down for long weekends to help bridge my polarized identity between past and present. These were some of the most surreal and memorable visits we'd had. All the while, I kept mostly quiet about what was going on. Almost no one back home knew what had happened, and it was months before I communicated to most of the people that I saw almost every day what had actually changed in my life. Instead, I curled up in the silence. I wore sunglasses to catch spontaneous tears as I walked around downtown. Fortunately, Santa Cruz is often a sunny place, so I assumed my mood swings went unnoticed. Meanwhile, patient friends just happened to keep making a point of inviting me over to watch fights or join their families for dinner.

When I returned to Vancouver to teach for a semester, some months later, I tried going back to my first gym and to training with my first coach, but it was different. Or I was. I spent a lot of time sitting in traffic to get to the gym from my new neighbourhood and twisting my calendar like a pretzel to fit around the gym's limited kickboxing schedule. Even though I had stayed in touch and was always enthusiastically welcomed back to visit when I was in town, the return wasn't simple. I was sensitive. I felt as though I was being treated less like part of the 'family' and more like an outsider against whom my coach could measure his real students' progress. I felt out of place.

It was a hard time in all aspects of my life, and I reverted back to the way I had been when Leif and I first split up; I couldn't control my emotions, even in training. But here there was no softness in the environment to allow for my delicate state. I wanted more classes, and to focus on fighting without being around people I knew, so I tried out another gym on the side as a way to supplement my training. There, I remained anonymous to all but the coaches. I didn't try to make friends, and I'd slink off to the side to avoid the camera when I saw someone recording for their social media account. After all I'd been through, and all the ways I had changed and learned to push myself, I could not figure out how to fit into the boxes from my old life anymore, either emotionally or logistically.

When I moved back to Vancouver more permanently the following year, I didn't go back to my first gym at all. Instead, I started to piece together a new training regimen that would fit my new life. I started training Muay Thai and signed up for boxing. Even with my inability to keep the most important promise I had ever made – till death do us part – still fresh, this secondary breakup from my beloved first martial arts family stung. I felt disloyal to the coach, and the gym, and the life that had formed me. But in all cases, my needs had changed.

It's easy for me to lament the fact that I didn't find my way to fighting until I was already over the hill for a would-be martial artist. What I have learned, along with my love of combat sports and my coaches and training partners, however, is that I have also been fortunate to come into this lifestyle with enough age, distance, and maturity to give myself permission to work hard, to ask questions, and to fight for the training that I want. This also means I have the ability to choose myself over a leader, or an organization, or even a coach. But for me the best coaches, the truest leaders, have never been ones who require that kind of fealty. They encourage their students' growth over their own egos. They earn and inspire trust rather than demanding it. In their video response to the Irvin scandal, representatives of BJJ's Gracie family, Rener and Ryron Gracie, describe the heart of BJJ as one that is, philosophically, about service. While the family (and the sport's) history certainly undercuts the simplicity of that claim, it sure is a nice idea. My hope is that as the popularity of martial arts continues to expand, the power I am finding in my thirties is something others, young women especially, grow up with over their whole lives. The very idea that I could have had that ability as a young girl, to make myself big and strong, to feel protective rather than in need of protection, to feel free to leave a situation that is not serving me or making me better ... seems intoxicating. Just imagine that kind of power at a young age. Whereas some would take powerful young women and try to use their ambition against them, to make them small and quiet, and to secret it away, I love watching the young women for whom that hopefully will never be possible. That next generation is, and will be, formidable.

CONTROL

I took for granted that I was made for simple, straightforward devotion. I'd assumed I'd have a lifetime with one man. And mentor under one coach. But neither was meant to be. Pushing myself into new lives, and uncertain spaces felt counterintuitive. What I learned was that putting almost all aspects of my identity into question made other things possible.

Once the biggest thing, the marriage, broke, the others were still difficult but shrank in comparison. In a similar way, and to only half-intentionally quote *Fight Club*, fighting turns down the volume on a lot of what would otherwise be daily struggle. ('I have to give a talk? … Sure. Is anyone going to kick me in the head while I do it? … No? Huh. Okay.') The loss of my identity, the loss of my partner, and the loss of our planned life together made other shifts – changing coaches, changing countries, stepping into the ring – into small aftershocks of a much more substantial earthquake. Each could cause damage or shift the surface of my world in some way, but none could re-break the earth the way the first shattering tremor had done.

In the process, what had always been the facts (this is who I am, this is what I'm like, this is what I do) suddenly showed themselves to be … choices.

CHAPTER ELEVEN
★
WORK ETHIC

Today is victory over yourself of yesterday; tomorrow is your victory over lesser men.
— Miyamoto Musashi

When I read Sam Sheridan's cult favourite *A Fighter's Mind: One Man's Journey through the World of Fighting*, I get jealous. I think part of Sheridan's allure is the way he makes the reader a vicarious party to things most of us probably would not or could not do. He joins the merchant marines, works as a firefighter, helps to man a yacht, trains Muay Thai in Thailand, studies Brazilian Jiu-Jitsu with the Brazilian Top Team, trains MMA under icon Pat Miletich, trains boxing alongside Andre Ward … and the list goes on. Compared to him, I feel like I've done everything wrong; I should have dared bigger, been tougher, suffered more, bled harder, travelled further.

Sheridan is able to do what he does because he has the social and physical mobility, the cultural capital, and the confidence to pass and play – to belong – in these male-dominated spaces. At the age in his life when Sheridan was sailing around the world and getting in fights with his bunkmates, I was sitting at my parents' kitchen table eating bowls of cereal and, ever the late bloomer, silently congratulating myself on *finally* getting my first bra.

Despite his immersion into 'the world of fighting,' Sheridan isn't really looking to go pro as a fighter himself. A writer first, he self-consciously foregrounds his marginal status, ever careful not to appear to pass himself off as a fighter within the midst of them, while at the same time wanting in some part to belong in that world. He is putting himself through the paces of training and competition and writing his way through it. As he does so, he is woven into that world. He trains like a fighter, with fighters. He fights. Sheridan couldn't gain the access that he has without some considerable Venn diagram overlap between him and the people he studies. He sees some of himself in them and vice versa. Over and over, those worlds invite and accept him into their ranks. Even after Sheridan leaves the gym to move on to the next thing (and despite not winning his MMA fight), coach and former fighter Pat Miletich encourages Sheridan to wear his Team Miletich shirt and 'fly his flag' proudly. They see him as one of their own. It seems that if Sheridan chose at any point to stick around, he could have become a consistent member of any of the communities he trains with. But he's always hungry to learn and collect more, to see more, and each residency ends so he can move on to the next.

It's hard for me to imagine being able – which includes feeling or even imagining I have the *option* – to do any of these things. I can't imagine myself passably living in those worlds, especially as things were almost thirty years ago, when the book was written. Although there are any number of women who can and have taken on activities similar to Sheridan's, for many of us the very idea of most of what he's done is daunting, if not impossible.

Although I can't see myself in the level of mobility that Sheridan enjoys, I find common ground in the ready acceptance that he gets – the way martial arts communities take him in as one of their own, not just because he's a cool, athletic guy but also because he shows them how hard he can work, how much he'll put on the line for it. In general, that part is familiar, and it's not exclusive to men. One of the reasons I fell in love with these communities, and these spaces, is because the people in them saw how willing I was to work; many of them embraced me just for that. I'm not the fastest learner, or the most intuitive. Thankfully, I know how to learn. More importantly, through years of trial and error, I now know how *I* learn. I no longer expect to get something new on the first try, or the second, or the fortieth. But I know I will get it. I will be the one after class kicking the bag a hundred times just to try to refine the angle of my foot. When I finally lock something in, it is mine forever. And I have been fortunate to train in spaces where my approach and needs are not just accepted but also respected. The gyms that I call home accept me not for my status, pedigree, or professional credentials, and not for my speed or power or what I can do for their reputation, but rather because I am willing to work hard. And I keep showing up.

TRAINING SEQUENCE

Maintaining fitness during the pandemic has made many athletes resourceful. There is a resurgence of analogue, low-tech training methods – the increased popularity of simple running or shadow-boxing, for instance – things athletes can do without equipment and all by themselves. With this low-fi approach comes an emphasis on, or a return to, back-to-basics fight training. In the classic boxing movie *Rocky IV*, Sylvester Stallone's title character, the all-American underdog, is on a mission to avenge his opponent-turned-best-friend Apollo Creed's death at the hands of Drago, a Soviet Union power-house. Drago is training in slick, state-of-the-art Soviet facilities, with shiny spandex and dramatic neon lighting. In stark contrast, Rocky bundles up in a heavy coat, toque, and classic grey sweatpants and goes for a run in the snow. He saws a huge log of wood (in the snow), drags a dogsled on all fours (you know, in the snow), chops wood (you see where I'm going here), and does pull-ups in a firelit barn as his small but seasoned training team looks on approvingly. The whole dual montage is blissfully absurd and highlights the auth-enticity of a DIY training regimen that is at least a small comfort for the coachless, gymless fighter. Who wouldn't want to be Rocky (if there's no other option)?

Ross Enamait is the trainer to boxers like Katie Taylor. Taylor is a women's lightweight champion, a two-weight world champion, and an Olympic gold medallist (among other accomplishments). Enamait is a prototypical DIY back-to-basics kind of guy. He'd fit in perfectly out in the snow with Rocky (and indeed, I've watched many an Insta-gram clip of Enamait doing pull-ups on a tree, in the forest, out in the snow). His book *Never Gymless* is a guidebook for training using any space and body weight, which has been of use to both me and the Sams during confinement. As it turns out, this seems to be how

Enamait got connected with Taylor in the first place. As a young aspiring boxer in the early 2000s, Taylor was fighting just to learn and compete in boxing at all. Her father built a makeshift gym in their backyard, and she read Enamait's books to get training tips. After a disappointing second outing at the Olympics and after parting ways with her lifelong coach (her father), Taylor reread Enamait's books. Then she sought him out for her next training camp. They have been working together ever since.

In his characteristic social media editorials, Enamait pitches the value of simple, time-worn training techniques. Speaking to the current moment, he offers, 'If you're in quarantine and looking for low-tech workouts, some of the best ideas you'll find are from old-school boxers, wrestlers, martial artists.' These, he explains, pointing to the street cred of his sources, are 'guys who had limited access to equipment but were training for some real shit … it was their life, so out of necessity, they got pretty good at coming up with simple ways to get in shape … new rarely is better.' These activities – body weight exercises like push-ups and abdominal exercises, hill sprints, and handstands – are, significantly, activities that can be done all alone. (Though not explicitly fight-related, this is, to some extent, the same focus on functional power and fitness that shapes the philosophy of CrossFit.) This emphasis on basics and DIY training makes sense, as the sport of boxing, in particular, has historically been fairly solitary and commonly practised by competitors with little or no income. Even the model of the classic boxing gym itself is one of individual fighters putting in the hours on their own or with one specific trainer. Though trainers and sparring partners are often necessary, the ethos of boxing is largely one of individual struggle. In order to prepare for 'some real shit,' a fighter first has to know they can go that extra mile on their own.

Nobody wants to go into a fight thinking the person they are up against prepared more, or better, or worked harder than they did. More than the fact of preparation, work ethic is a kind of value system, built into the process. This is particularly true of fighting, which sees hard work as a kind of democratizing element. Both opponents have a chance. Who wants it more? Is the element of competition between oneself and another truly the ultimate aim of this kind of hard work? To cast the net even more widely: What *is* work ethic, anyway? It won't look the same for everyone, and it won't necessarily stay the same throughout the course of an individual's life or career. One answer might be that work ethic is the attempt to maximize one's potential, to put in the work to reach the limits of what you can accomplish. Another might be somewhere closer to where I tend, although it reveals a tension I can't seem to resolve: to some extent, work ethic is due diligence, a form of self-defence against failure and disappointment from both internal and external critics. But it is also a love of process over result. Growth, however painful, for its own sake.

In his 1644 manual of strategic philosophy, *The Book of Five Rings*, famed samurai Miyamoto Musashi outlines what makes a warrior. It isn't bravery, athleticism, or even an adherence to any one specific style, master, or school. Rather, as he repeats in nearly every section, 'You must study hard.' In one of my favourite moments of the book, Musashi explains that 'the strategist' – that is, the sword fighter – 'makes small things into big things, like building a great Buddha from a one foot model. I cannot write in detail how this is done,' he states, significantly. 'The principle of strategy is having one thing, to know ten thousand things.' I noted the sentence, laughingly, and it has stayed with me.

What does it take to 'know' your stuff? What kind of training and preparation works, and what doesn't? But more importantly, *why* do it at all? Ambition, and the desire to push and control yourself – mind and body – is double-edged. To be 'hungry' also risks never being satisfied. When it comes down to pursuing a goal at all costs, what are you really willing to do, to sacrifice, to risk? What are you willing to gain? And what happens when your reason for working hard is gone, or when you reach your goal? What drives you then? These last two questions have plagued me since I finished my PhD. When there's no longer a clear finish line, no one is guiding you along, and the results are no longer encouraging, it becomes so much harder to fight off the entropy and stay motivated. Fighters often lie to themselves, telling themselves a story about how they will win. But how do you maintain an aggressive work ethic when you no longer believe your own story?

In an ideal scenario, when a fighter walks into battle (or, to extend the metaphor, walks into their talk, or presentation, or whatever it is – although I admit the stakes are higher for a sword duel) they no longer question or have time to fear failure. They are ready. They have done the work. In fighting, there's an understanding that preparation is the key to survival. Competitors push for repetition and perfection *because* they are nearly impossible. Over-preparing is the minimum of preparation. I have heard it said many times that the training camp should be harder than the fight itself. If that doesn't also sound like over-preparing days or weeks for a ten-minute or one-hour presentation or lecture, I don't know what does. I have also been taught that a fighter should prepare so intensely and drill so many times that their movements become second nature. Fear and doubt are real, and they might have their place in training, but a fighter has to step across the threshold of battle believing they can win. When it's time to walk into the ring, you have to shut the fear and doubt off, and 'trust your training.'

That's what completing a PhD was supposed to give me. My belief was that if I went through all that schooling, then the institutional magic wand would tap me as I was dubbed 'Doctor' (there's power in naming, right?), and all my insecurity would float away.

It did not.

RECONNECT

The transition from 'normal' life to pandemic isolation seemed swift. On Sunday morning, I was at the boxing gym, training and then sparring with Cat. By Sunday night, the city and province had closed up shop. I didn't have gear – I had even forgotten my gloves at the gym, which was now locked and vacant. Like so many others, I scoured websites for ways to make do without gear or training partners. Alone, I completed Radetsky's virtual homework assignments, watched training clips, and took notes for myself.

After about three months in isolation, without access to gyms, punching bags, other people, or some large chunks of my emotional stability, I get my hands on a heavy bag. I have been injured for weeks but am finally on the mend. In the last few months, I tore a quadricep sprinting and developed tendinitis in my Achilles while trail running, two brand new and immobilizing injuries to add to other mildly chronic but still functional ones. I'm not usually very injury-prone, but in isolation I have developed a tendency to get hurt. I've been holed up in my apartment, restlessly completing an obscene daily quota of ab roll-outs and one-leg push-ups (to avoid putting weight on my injured quad), when my friend James offers me use of his garage gym. My leg has been feeling better, I haven't been in contact with another person in months, and I am desperate to punch things. I follow James's instructions to collect the hidden garage key. I find a workspace containing tools, cans of oil, and a DIY weight training area. There's a shelf with gloves, pads, and wraps, and a collection of hand weights, ab rollers, and other training accessories, but I have eyes only for the heavy bag.

This bag is so taut with stuffing that I have to hit it as hard as I can, out of self-defence. A slightly understuffed bag is flattering and obliging; when you hit it, your limbs sink in and it gives way to you. An overstuffed bag like this one, however, forgives nothing. This is like the difference between a beanbag and a block of cement. I tell myself that if I strike it with anything less than my full power, the bag will hurt me more than I hurt it. This is how I convince myself to strike hard objects with force; I trick myself into thinking that the harder I hit, the safer I will be. In truth, there's no space for nuance today. I don't even *want* to focus on anything other than power, and lots of it. I hit the bag for about forty minutes, with no pretense of working any fancy combinations. I keep it simple and throw hard. I don't use a timer. Today, I just need to expend as much force as possible. This rancid combination of stress, grief, and fear has been accumulating in my body for months. Running has helped, but it's not enough.

Alone, I have been shadowboxing for months, but when I finally hit a *thing*, my body meets resistance. I'm not flicking my limbs out at the air; they are smashing into a wall of leather and cloth that has been designed to absorb everything I've got, and more. I feel exhausted in a way that I haven't felt in a long time. This is a deeply satisfying kind of tired. I know I will enjoy it and pay for it later. For the rest of the day, I am radiant. I am refreshed. I remember what it means to make even a small impact on the world around me, how it feels to have power.

When I wake up the next morning, I am reminded of what it means to be stiff, sore, and slow. But I still have access to the gym … so I do it all over again. This time, I branch out a little to work on building patterns in my movement, and do more technical work, but even the attempt to organize myself frustrates me. I take that frustration, add it to the well, and instead throw the idea of control and order out the window. I just kick the bag as hard as I can, as many times as I can muster. I'm sweating profusely. My throat gets raw from vocalizing – exhaling sharply, yelling as I kick, and likely gulping in garage dust in the process. After another frenetic forty minutes or so, I am once again light as air.

My body is getting stronger – I can feel it – but first, it suffers. It's easy to forget how much force translates to the body as shock. Like my muscles, I build power through repeated tearing and breaking. I know this intellectually, but until that tolerance builds back up, this reads to my body only as trauma. I check for any acute pains in the usual spots (none, I am good) and savour this old, familiar feeling. Every bit of tightness, aching, and hurt highlights something I just strengthened.

When the martial arts gyms first reopen temporarily in Vancouver, I hesitate about going back. Instead, I reach out to Diaz for a private session. I return to the gym, which, like everything, looks and feels different. People circulate cautiously. Diaz and I catch up and I explain that I want to refine my kicking technique and get some cues to help me as I continue to train in isolation. I also use the session as an opportunity to squeeze him for shadowboxing tips to carry back into my own little world. Now I have recordings of technique drills and homework from Coach Radetsky, some drills from online boxing Zoom sessions, Diaz's kicking cues and shadowboxing suggestions … and everyone's close friend, the internet.

Social media sites like Instagram and YouTube are a rich source of drills and exercises. The growing community of online tutorials and technique videos enables an exchange of ideas that de-centres any single coach, school, or approach. MMA, by nature, lends itself to this kind of crowd-sourcing method. Because there are so many aspects to the sport, a well-rounded fighter trains with multiple specialists; working across multiple disciplines can require a number of trainers and training partners with different strengths. As pound-for-pound MMA king and arguably the first truly well-rounded MMA fighter Georges St-Pierre claims, combat training and athletics are different now than they were when he was coming up in the ranks. Whereas GSP had to travel from his home in Quebec to a Gracie Jiu-Jitsu academy in New York to learn BJJ, now, he says, he can learn online from a trainer in Australia if he wants to. Fighters and athletes aren't better now, he says. Technology is better. Those training now benefit from greater access and more information. With students no longer under the purview of one teacher or school, there is less emphasis on closely guarded gym-specific trade secrets. As in so many other areas, training online creates opportunities for people who aren't in major centres, who can't afford top schools or high-level seminars, or who for reasons of gender, sexuality, ability, or otherwise, don't feel comfortable in these public gym spaces. This way, a wider range of people can benefit – to a certain extent – from teachers they might never have the finances or the opportunity to meet. As it is, those who have less access or fewer resources often have to find that much more drive to do the work; no one is there pushing them, or invested in their success, and there's no system in place to guide them along.

Any tool can be used well or badly. I've heard instructors joke about BJJ guys teaching themselves at home through online videos without ever drilling the basics in class. The downside to this kind of DIY online-surfing curriculum is the tendency for eager students to choose flash over foundations. These instructors are referring to the students who skip the lesson and come in just for sparring, hoping to use training partners as test cases to try out the new moves they found online. But those skipped steps tend to catch up to them. For everyone else (and this is as true for a mid-level BJJ practitioner as it is for any university student), the online tutorials supplement and deepen their primary work, rather than replacing it. To earn a blue belt (the second ranking level) in BJJ, takes about a year of repetitive, grinding work, for instance. Access to online videos alone does not necessarily create the setting required for that pace and learning curve.

Although the massive scale and potential for interaction through online video platforms is new, this tendency fits within the modern history of martial arts instruction. Whereas martial arts masters once had to travel to other countries and continents to teach their systems themselves (and this approach is still common with expert seminars, one of the ways many martial artists make their money), technology like photography helped to make those instructions move on their own. When Emily Watts released her Jiu-Jitsu instructional in the UK in 1906, for instance, she was doing much the same thing we see online now; she offered skilful, thorough, and more accessible lessons for both women and men who might not be able, or feel comfortable, entering a dojo at that time. Books are mobile (the internet wants to be the new books). When social and geographical access and finances are particularly at issue, these alternative methods provide opportunities for marginalized groups, or those who don't feel comfortable in a traditional gym, to train together in private spaces, for instance. Would-be BJJ students can start their own training groups with a few mats, some floor space, and a Wi-Fi connection.

In addition to accessing lessons and tutorials, many people use their personal platforms to showcase their fitness and martial arts skills, just as others use Instagram to feature their meals, homes, friends, fashion, musical ability, or adventures. Social media, by nature, tends to blur the lines between self-presentation and self-commodification, and the display of martial arts is often commoditized, even for social capital, and shared with friends or posted for a wider public audience. But this idea of training as a kind of public performance is surely older than prizefighting itself. In North America, public training sessions go way back to the old carnival shows, where martial artists would get onstage and show their skills the same way a contortionist or another skilled anomaly would. Incidentally, carnival shows were often the home of a familiar curiosity: the female martial artist. Today, an open workout – where fighters promote an upcoming bout by training and demonstrating their skills (simulating some version of practice with their trainers) in front of media and cameras – is akin to these old travelling carnival martial arts displays. Followers of any televised or broadcast combat sports like boxing or MMA are likely familiar with these open workout sessions as an essential part of the pre-fight hype and promotion. Fighters can also use these sessions to play up their personalities as public figures.

Of course, online videos are reminiscent of the difference between tidy pad work and messy fighting; edited, selected videos provide the satisfaction of repetition and beautiful choreography and technique. Most people don't post the bad or embarrassing parts. Social media is often an exercise in control on top of control, and intention versus execution. Some posts show the struggle of hard work and sweat and mistakes (in reality daily training is filled with ups and downs), but many don't.

Like many other fighters, the Ukrainian boxer Vasyl Lomachenko has invited reporters into his training spaces. He also posts some of his training videos to social media. In training footage, Lomachenko does some of the typical things, like hitting the bag (and yes, it is funny to see one man show off his punching skills while a dozen others crowd around him in awe, cameras in hand). He also includes unorthodox demonstrations of his physical prowess, including walking across the ring on his fists and gracefully punching a tennis ball attached by an elasticized string to his backward baseball cap. Though neither is explicitly boxing-specific, both activities highlight his other-worldly coordination, grace, and speed, features that are essential to his fights. Lomachenko is a three-weight world champion, having competed at junior-lightweight, featherweight, and more recently lightweight (measured at 130 to 135 pounds for men); his fighting style is remarkable for its beauty, movement, sleight of hand, and control. As is characteristic of most lighter weight classes, his style of fighting is fast, with more movement than you see from hard-punching, often slower-moving heavyweights. The boxer also offers some insight into his dancerly style (and indeed, he was famously trained in Ukrainian dancing as a young man in order to prepare him to be light-stepping as a boxer) by demonstrating these DIY reaction and movement drills for the cameras. Seeing Lomachenko do tricks in his gym whets the audience's appetite for the acrobatics he promises to perform in the ring. These performances accentuate his distinct style of fighting, his personal brand.

Approaching the pre-fight open workout from a slightly different angle, MMA fighter Rose Namajunas let her dog onstage for a public media workout in 2017. In addition to hitting pads and showing off her beautiful striking, Namajunas circles and sprawls around Mishka in an endearing display that draws attention for breaking the rhythm of the workouts. It highlights her tendency to stand a bit outside the pomp and circumstance – and the bravado – of the pre-fight buildup. In another UFC media workout in August 2019, Nate Diaz (later a contender for the UFC's infamous one-off BMF – 'Bad Mother Fucker' belt), shows off his swagger – and flexes his excellent cardio – by walking onstage for the open workout and simply lighting up a joint and flexing his arms. As is also true of Lomachenko's videos, in both of these cases, the refusal to show traditional training has the effect of promoting the fighter's persona; Diaz, in particular, is also perhaps hinting that he already works so hard, he's got nothing to prove.

These are largely exceptions, though. The open workout has traditionally been a show of hard work in order to garner interest for the fight and perhaps encourage gambling odds. It's a preview of what the fighter promises to show off in the ring. What it also does, however, is sell the value of hard work as part of the package. After all, if it were easy, anyone could do it.

In 1972, wanting to keep his training camp private and away from prying eyes, Muhammad Ali purchased the land that became 'Fighter's Heaven,' the Deer Lake Training Camp near the Appalachian Mountains. Here, he trained for fights against George Foreman, Earnie Shavers, Joe Frazier (the third time), and others. Ali would invite reporters and cameras onto his home turf, on his terms. These old on-site training videos, common to boxing, have the added effect of showing the fighter in their intimate space – something social media and Zoom videos now do every day – offering a kind of enjoyable voyeurism to viewers who get to feel a little like they are there in the inner circle. We see the colours and textures of the training: boxing gyms with pictures of glorious battles and classic fight photographs posted up, the routes the fighters run, the clothes they wear. These are all part and parcel of the theatre of hard work. (Even if you have only yourself as an audience, is work ethic always, to some extent, performative?)

For almost everyone else who doesn't enjoy the Ali-esque luxury of building their own space, however, training tends to mean doing some part of the work in public. The onlookers are a part of the texture and local colour of these spaces. Hinting at the social geography of a boxing gym, for instance, Katherine Dunn in one essay situates herself 'warming a folding chair against the wall with the other gym rats – retired guys who were there just to get out of the rain, parents and reporters and other such scholars.' The gym might be its own ecosystem, and the work individual, but it is rarely private. People watch you fail and grow in sparring and practise in a way that they don't if you're playing piano at home, for instance.

One fighter who became synonymous with hard work is 'Marvelous' Marvin Hagler, the undisputed middleweight boxing champion from 1980 to 1987. For Hagler, getting into the mindset necessary to prepare for a fight meant, in his words, sending himself to 'prison' – locking in for a rigorous and isolated training camp at Cape Cod with only him and his team. Camp is not just about retreat from cameras and prying scouts. On a deeper level, it is a way to mark a retreat from the comforts and distractions of daily life. The things that make us functional humans who give energy and time to others are also responsibilities and luxuries that can be detrimental to the fighter's ability to maintain the necessary focus and work ethic. Relentless work ethic is (or at the very least resembles) extreme selfishness. Boxer Lucia Rijker once couldn't afford to go away for training camp, so she stayed in a rented house and made it a 'retreat' from her phone and her life, including her relationships. Another champion boxer, Andre Ward, would move out of his house and away from his wife and children during pre-fight camps. There is an ascetic quality already inherent to training. Fighters need to watch their food intake, regulate their workouts, and prioritize health and sleep over all else (so they have the steam to get up and do it all again the next day). These rigours and self-deprivation can be a tool, or a shortcut, to strengthen mental toughness and work ethic.

Even within a professional field defined by hard work, some fighters are particularly known for their work ethic. These include boxing great Ann Wolfe, boxer-turned-MMA-fighter Holly Holm, and more recently China's first UFC Champion, Weili Zhang. The claim that 'my opponent can't outwork me' is a fighting cliché. There are, however, a number of fighters who – beyond being hard workers – have actually developed a personal fighting style built *around* the idea of outworking the person they're up against. Anyone stepping into the cage with the UFC's Max Holloway, for instance, knows a fundamental part of his game plan is to outwork, out-train, and wear his opponent down not with big power punches but with the sheer number of strikes. Sambo specialist Khabib Nurmagomedov wrestles his opponents to the ground just like (vintage video footage shows) he trained by wrestling a bear in Dagestan as a child. Nurmagomedov smothers them with his relentless pressure and by making them carry the force of his whole weight. Not every fighter has the gas tank or physical gifts to fight this way, but for those whose approach is to outwork their opponent, this style complements (or is complemented by) the fighter's own inherent skill and tendencies. A high output plays to their strengths – it is part of their style.

RITUAL

In the first semester of PhD program, my future dissertation partner Sarah and I made a pilgrimage to the thesis defence room. It was locked and imposing. When it came time, years later, for our thesis defences, we booked the space for a 'tech' rehearsal so that we could have access to it in advance. We took inspiration from the Situationist International, a group of mid-twentieth-century artists and revolutionaries who had an idea of radically changing space by using it in ways unrelated or even counter to what was originally intended. So Sarah and I signed out the key and got to work. We dutifully tested our PowerPoint presentations and practised the talks we had to give, to get used to the way our own academic voices echoed within the space. But that was mostly pretense – Sarah and I had other plans. We rubbed good luck charms along the surfaces of the room, climbed on top of tables, and power-posed from above the audience of chairs. We talked, joked, laughed, pumped each other up, and developed a personal relationship with the space as a way to diffuse the power with which it was invested.

When I walked into the space for my defence, it was filled with my committee and teachers, peers, family, and friends, but I could also still see our silliness, our hopes and ambitions – as well as our desire to somehow control the situation. I gave a twenty-minute talk about my research, which was followed by a nearly three-hour grilling by my doctoral committee as the audience watched nervously. We all sat together at a round table at the front of the room and talked while the audience sat facing us. The process is a bit of a blur, but I don't recall it as any shining moment. After years of preparation, I felt stilted and awkward despite being, by definition, the expert in the room on my particular topic.

The defence is a ritual. As in a wedding or a championship belt match, if the ritual is successful, you walk in as one person, with one title, and you leave as another. I walked in as Ms. Dean. At the end of the defence, the committee sent everyone out the door and into the hallway, including me. They took their time to discuss and evaluate in private. When they reached a conclusion, the door opened to the rest of us. Without preamble, the graduate chair poked his head through doorway and called out the magic words: 'Would Dr. Dean please join us inside?'

I followed in a daze, and everyone else shuffled in behind me. I had passed with distinction, the best possible outcome. But even though I had 'won' my PhD defence, it still felt like I lost. As the post-defence celebrations wound down a few days later, I slipped into postpartum sadness. I had been warned about this low phase by others who had also defended dissertations. You go through all of this work, driving toward a goal, and then it's just … done.

Of course, the PhD should ultimately be about the process, not the defence – like a fight, it's the 90 percent training that really matters, not just the 10 percent that everyone sees. But the successful pursuit of any goal creates an ending. As I later realized, it also offers a new beginning.

THE WEIGHT OF IT

Through training, I initially came to love my body not because of how training made it look (aesthetic changes came later) but because it could suddenly *do* things for me. But I also had to learn to coldly assess its strengths and weaknesses.

The struggle for control and perfection begins with the fighter's own mind and body. In combat sports where competitors are organized by weight class, size is a contract and one of the essential terms of the agreement between fighters. Making a promise, asking your opponent to fulfill those conditions in turn – and then not holding up your end of the deal – can also be perceived as a lack of discipline, a sign of disrespect or unprofessionalism.

Fighters generally want to be as big as possible within a weight category. Conventional wisdom suggests you don't want to 'give up' too much weight to your opponent, so competitors generally pick the lowest weight class they can possibly meet, and they aim to come in at the limit of that category. The weight cut, here, signifies the difference between an active, training fighter's weight as they work their way to prepare for competition versus the weight they must hit the day of, or the day before, the fight, depending on when the weigh-in is scheduled. They don't live at the official weight; many are only their weight on paper for a matter of a few hours, or minutes – just long enough to weigh in and then start eating and rehydrating. This process can mean contorting bodies to fit into these strategically selected weight classes. A fighter could weigh in at 115 pounds and have re-absorbed up to 10 pounds by the time they walk into the ring. (Some fights have rehydration clauses limiting how much weight they can take on again in order to avoid a big fluctuation that would make the competition uneven).

Combat sports put bodies on display. The weight, shape, and look of a body register to viewers and commentators as measures of a fighter's work ethic. With the notable exception of heavyweight fighters, who have less pressure to cut, and tend to use their size and power in a different way, making weight is considered a kind of diligence; it's part of the discipline of training and preparation for a fight. There is supposed to be a kind of hungry (pun intended), focused sharpness that gets forged through the process of the weight cut. Priming an animal for a fight. So even when I'm not cutting, I tend to restrict my diet consciously in the week of a fight, in order to signal that something is different. But weight cuts take a much more extreme and controversial form depending on body type, gender, lifestyle, and competitive circles.

In the 2005 inaugural season of the UFC-affiliated reality TV series *The Ultimate Fighter*, a group of male light heavyweight (186-to-205-pound) and middleweight (171-to-185-pound) MMA fighters is housed together and divided into two competing teams. Each side is led by an established UFC fighter who coaches them through physical challenges. In the third episode, light heavyweight fighter Bobby Southworth finishes last in a group challenge and he is told that he will have to pick an opponent from the other team to fight. The terms of the fight are laid out: each competitor will have to show up on weight or be cut from the show. Assuming they both make weight, the winner of the fight will get to stay, and the loser will be sent home. But even before stepping in to fight for his spot, Southworth has to take on the hurdle of his own body. Because it's a reality show, and perhaps is still trying to find its footing in terms of format, the fighters don't know more than a week in advance that they will be required to meet a specific weight that week. When they make the announcement about the fight, Southworth is walking around at 237 pounds. He diets and exercises himself down to 227 but is still nowhere near the 206-pound limit of his weight class. 'I'm not the biggest light heavyweight,' Southworth concedes, 'but I am definitely the fattest.' In a perverse show of pressure, Southworth is forced to lose twenty-two pounds within twenty-four hours in order to avoid immediate elimination.

Though Southworth tells everyone he is determined to make the weight, he appears to drag his feet about getting into the sauna to sweat it out. According to Southworth, this tension is partly selective editing; 'They don't show you the parts where I'm riding the bike in the sauna and I pass out,' he will later say. Edited for maximum drama, the episode instead highlights Southworth's coach, Chuck Liddell, and Liddell's right-hand man, fighter Josh Koscheck, manhandling the big man like a pair of impatient parents attempting to fold their misbehaving toddler into a snowsuit so they can make it to work on time. Hours into his dehydration process, Southworth is understandably depleted and lethargic but (to save him from himself, to save the team from a loss, or both) Liddell and Koscheck refuse to let him fail. At one point, Southworth seems passed out face down on the ground outside the sauna as the other two men look down at him. 'I think we should drag him in there right now for fifteen minutes. Just throw him in there,' Koscheck proposes. At another point, they do literally drag him back into the sauna. Liddell goes from standing outside the door, telling Southworth not to leave, to sitting against it to keep Southworth from escaping. While Southworth doesn't simply give up and walk out the door, viewers are left wondering whether he even *could* have bailed at this point, had he chosen to. He's pretty out of it. 'I was so dehydrated that when I was sitting down if I would just move the wrong way my body would cramp into the fetal position, like literally pull me in,' he will later say. 'Guys on my team would have to grab my legs and shoulders and pull me straight and massage the cramps out of my stomach. It looked like there was an alien inside, that's how crazy my stomach was cramping and moving around inside.'

The situation is orchestrated and then drawn out for the sake of good television – in real life, he would usually have more notice for a weight cut. And if Southworth's cut had gone smoothly, there would be no story. More likely, they saw that he was overweight and targeted him to go through this gruelling ritual for the cameras. The process gets dragged out and its difficulty accentuated as the suspense builds one sauna session at a time. But the fighter's visible weakness and discomfort are real – as is the danger. This is not exactly a good look for Southworth, and probably not the way he'd choose to be shown for posterity.

Given a grace period of a couple of extra hours to extend the cut, Southworth ultimately makes the required weight. He hits 206 pounds right on the button. No one is more surprised by this turn of events than his opponent, who has been smugly watching from the sidelines (he was already easily within the weight limit himself). Rehydrated and determined, Southworth manages to win the fight – he knocks out his opponent – and lives to see another day in *The Ultimate Fighter* house. For non-fighters watching from home, this episode offers a somewhat reckless and dramatized reality-TV version of what is already a fairly bizarre ritual. Not fully aware of what he'd risked until some time later, Southworth would eventually acknowledge the dramatic effect of the cut, telling UFC.com, 'There's a full 48–73 hours that I don't really have a coherent timeline for.' Nevertheless, Southworth doesn't seem to regret the risk. Rather, he's proud of having accomplished the biggest weight cut in the show's history.

Former UFC fighter now bare-knuckle boxer Paige VanZant looks back on her toughest weight cut with a different attitude. In 2016, VanZant went through the process of cutting from 138 pounds to 115 pounds in ten days. Like Southworth, she had to cut almost 23 pounds for her fight, albeit in a week and a half – not a day. Whereas his dangerous cut was partly so alarming due to the short time span, VanZant's was proportionately more dramatic due to her much smaller frame: she cut 16 percent of her total body weight; Southworth cut less than 10 percent. VanZant was extremely lean going in, as well, so there was less room to spare.

VanZant is candid about her process. She – like a lot of fighters who perhaps can't afford nutritionist and medical support – managed the cut herself, with the help of a (non-fighter) friend. The first part of a sharp weight cut, she explains, is to flush her system. VanZant says she drank two gallons of water a day to 'dehydrate [her] body of minerals, which sounds awful but that's what you do.' Flushing results in losing perhaps a couple of pounds per day at first, and then the weight loss slows as the body becomes more depleted. VanZant removed all sodium from her system and limited her food intake to small, clean meals. Once fighters hit the limit on what they can cut simply through flushing and diet, they will focus on sweating out water weight. They lube up with special creams like Albolene that encourage their pores to open, helping them warm up faster and sweat more. They get taped into a plastic sauna suit ('plastics'). They might exercise in this suit leading up to the fight, and a hard weight cut also often means setting up in a sauna in the suit, forcing their body to generate more sweat than usual. VanZant describes her sauna suit routine as thirty minutes in the sauna: one minute out, to cool off and take a breath, then fifteen minutes in, one out, on repeat. For the 2016 weight cut, this process continued until she couldn't walk anymore. The next day she still had almost five pounds left to lose and resorted to other tools, like sitting in a hot bathtub filled with Epsom salt and alcohol to open pores and draw out the sweat. Make no mistake – as anyone can attest who has seen footage of the intimidatingly tough Cris Cyborg bawling in a scalding bath while cutting 26 pounds in an inconceivable three days, this is by no means a warm, relaxing soak.

The other key element to that weight cut, for VanZant, is simple but telling: she prayed. The kind of trauma her body was going through to make weight could kill a person. Fighters die from bad weight cuts, which can cause kidney failure. When her friend found her passed out on the floor of the bathroom, the then-twenty-two-year-old VanZant says, her family staged an intervention saying they would no longer support her if she kept competing at such a low weight. One of the reasons both VanZant and Cyborg were pressured into making such seemingly random and absurd weight cuts is because of the limited weight categories available to women in the UFC, even as of just a few years ago. The general argument for fewer weight classes for women is that there are not enough elite female competitors to fill more groupings. But this can also create a vicious cycle, especially if the women out there can't fit themselves into the limited weight classes made available to them. The pressure to make these cuts is not necessarily about the integrity of the sport or the best interests of the female fighters themselves, in other words; this is about business and the differences in number between professional male and female fighters. Fortunately, the organization has since opened up 125-pound and 145-pound weight divisions, creating the opportunity for more reasonable fighting weights for more women.

There are, nevertheless, fighters with greater access to resources who work more closely with nutritionists, trainers, and doctors in order to manage a safer and more gradual cut. The UFC has never officially had any weight-cut-related deaths, though many fighters have died due to the side effects of bad weight cuts. The practice is widespread across all sports with weight classes, and it remains a controversial practice.

The cut is a battle in itself. It is not a passive process. It's work. The drive to push through this private yet emotionally and physically draining challenge comes after weeks or months of the rigours of a full training camp, and before the next, more public step. Once the weigh-in is done, these athletes have to climb into a cage, or a ring, in front of other people and fight.

Though not an obvious offshoot of work ethic, one element of competitive training that might seem counterintuitive is the physical, psychological, and emotional fallout of years, or decades, spent focusing your life on one specific aspect of your being – whether your mind, or in this case, your body – as a self-defining tool and commodity. The drive and focus required to maintain this kind of dedication has side effects. A person's sense of identity and self-worth can get distilled to specific features and seem inseparable from them. As a result, a number of fighters make reference to imbalanced relationships to their own bodies. After regularly cutting about twenty pounds per fight, VanZant developed an eating disorder. And beyond the more extreme example of pre-fight weight cutting, there's the daily reality of maintaining a general weight while training. Just because someone exercises a lot doesn't mean they can't gain weight; all that work can make a person ravenous, and there's no genetic predisposition in people who like fighting that guarantees they will stay lean. In a 'day in the life' account of preparing for an upcoming MMA fight, Roxanne Modafferi explains the logistical hoops she goes through in order to keep her weight in line: '[I need to] eat in the locker room or out at a restaurant because I have a hard time stopping eating once I start. I think it's the shadow of an eating disorder I developed from dieting and cutting weight over the years. If I'm home, I'll just eat and eat and eat. I can't keep open bags of snacks in the house. I can't have a big pie sitting around. I only buy mini servings of ice cream. I have to portion my meals into Tupperware, eat them out, brush my teeth, and THEN I can go home and not crave anything. That's how I manage.' We are shaped – in good and bad ways – by the activities to which we devote our lives.

The discipline and vigilance required in order to control your body to its fullest physical potential skirt a fine line between controlled order and disorder. And this tension isn't unique to female athletes and competitors. Male wrestlers are also well known for their fraught relationship to weight cutting and disorder. It's difficult to gauge if the pressures that police the aesthetic of female bodies have a greater impact on women fighters than they do on men. Although studies on weight cutting for combat sports tend to focus *only* on men, my guess would be that women's bodies are already so carefully monitored in terms of shape and look, and those opinions about our bodies extend so far beyond the field of play, that it could have more of an effect than many of us would like to acknowledge. But even if the tendency to find disorder in eating is due not to aesthetics but to an imbalance brought on by an extreme relationship to food over time, the effects can be the same.

WORK IT OUT

I was raised to value hard work. I don't think the fact was always obvious to me, but when I look back on it, my parents were (and still are) often working, even at home. Both worked well beyond full time, and after my mother, an elementary school teacher, had worked at school until six or seven p.m., I'd see her toiling away once the rest of the family had gone to bed. If it wasn't work, she'd just as likely be up doing something else: making something, reading a book, or chipping away relentlessly at some problem or other. My brothers, who spent their childhood and teen years making home videos and drawing cartoons, went into filmmaking and animation. There is no separation for them between work and play. Everyone around me was preoccupied with a vocation rather than simply working toward a job.

When I was a kid, my dad used to give me logic puzzles. I can picture his pen jabbing at a line-drawn square on a restaurant napkin as he encouraged me to 'think outside the box.' My mother, for her part, would speak to us using unfamiliar vocabulary. When I complained I didn't understand, she would (with a smile) hand me a dictionary. She wouldn't characterize this as hard work, of course. In her eyes, developing a skill set (and learning the meaning of a word) brings a form of independence. Still, I used to dread getting my parents' help with my homework; the process always felt much more involved than it needed to be. As much as I might have resented the idea, there was never any question to me that the things that matter take time and effort. I realize now how much of this approach (excruciating as it sometimes was) formed who I am and what I value, and how fortunate I was to have that kind of support.

But graduate school, and the academic life in general, is not just about working hard. There are logistical and psychological hurdles as well. Perhaps the PhD is better compared to a marathon than a fight, or a fighting career rather than any single battle. There are small milestones throughout, but it's certainly not a sprint. As in a fighting career, for each competition, you spend months in camp, a few minutes in battle, and then you're done – until the next one.

What most of the people in my life didn't realize, and what I was loath to point out, was that the PhD is not a finish line. Instead, it shows itself near the end to be just another lap. After graduate studies come fellowships, postdoctoral programs (I've done two), the job market (and from there, if you're very lucky, six years of tenure track) … and so it continues. How do you make commitments to the future when where you will live, how much work you will have from one four-month block to the next, and whether you will even have a job at all, are so uncertain? How do you stay strong throughout a race that doesn't end? How do you put everything you have into a fight, knowing you will just have to go into another one a few months later? When the great Muhammad Ali claims, 'I hated every minute of training, but I said, "Don't quit. Suffer now and live the rest of your life as a champion,"' he voices an approach to fighting, and to life, that feels antithetical to my own. How could you devote so much of your life to a process you hate if the only hope is, truly, for one specific outcome? I have aspirations for my hard work, there's no question of that, but the most personal and most compelling part is and has always been the process. My purpose is to keep learning.

In his memoir, Jonathan Gottschall imagines his university firing him from his dead-end English adjunct position because he is an MMA fighter. He fantasizes about his coworkers seeing him through the big windows of the MMA gym across the street as he explores his primal instincts through battle with other men, having been deemed unsuitable for the dignified life of the academy. This is a flight of fancy, to be sure, and a passive one at that. He doesn't want to be an agent. He wants things to happen to him. I can't say I share Gottschall's sense of complacency about getting fired (it's hard to get a stable adjunct position!), though I am intimately familiar with the frustrations of his predicament. It has been painful and humbling to come face to face with my own privilege – the false assumption that because I'm highly educated and work hard, I should get to have the career that I chose. *I did what I was supposed to do,* I think, and that dangerous idea that I deserve, or am owed, something seeps in. And yet.

Gottschall naively sees fighting as a transgression of that same thwarted promise, as opposed to something deeply connected to it. He also wrongly claims that the liberal English department is a 'feminine' space. He believes that this space, where he feels in a sense rejected or underappreciated, is one that he must in some sense undermine the only way he knows how – by becoming a *real* man, a fighter. (This idea alone, that the space that rejects him is feminized and therefore must be defeated is … uncomfortable). As a woman with more than fifteen years in the academy, as both a student and as a teacher, I can think of few spaces that embrace patriarchal and exceptionalist values *more* than the university. An English department is no exception, as a general rule, even though I have had the good fortune of working with many wonderful people. Where Gottschall sees fighting as contradictory to his professional identity, I see them as two parts of the same entity.

But I take his point, inadvertent as it may be. Gottschall wants to be a 'real' man. I, for my part, want to feel some control over my own self, my own life. These might seem like two sides of the same coin. But they're not. He's fighting to prove he is a man. I'm fighting to prove I am a fighter. The stakes are different.

CHAPTER TWELVE
★
IN THE RING

'Do you remember that fish that ran into a wall?' Greg Jackson asks his fighter, Cub Swanson, who sits on a stool in the UFC cage facing his coach. It's the break after the high-impact first round, before Swanson goes back out for the second. Between rounds, fighters have one minute to breathe, get patched up, recharge, and regroup with their team of seconds. But when the broadcast camera follows Jackson and Swanson's interaction in the corner at UFC 206, what the audience gets is more than the usual close-up of an ice pack on the back, latex-gloved hands pressing bruises and lacerations, and coaches speaking to an attentive combatant. They also get this fish joke. Pausing only momentarily at the question, Swanson answers. 'Uh, did he say, "Oh dam?"' 'He did!' Coach Jackson affirms, pleased. 'You're on tonight.'

The middle of an MMA fight is no time for kidding around. But Jackson isn't asking his fighter to repeat an old punchline in order to be funny. This is an evaluation dressed up as a joke. 'It was a mid-fight exam, a little cognitive test devised by one of the most successful trainers in the sport,' Ben Fowlkes explains. Jackson 'wanted to make sure [Swanson's] mind was still moving so that [he] could adjust [his] coaching accordingly.' The fish question is 'a reference to an old joke he'd told Swanson in an earlier fight, something he knew his fighter would remember under normal circumstances.' When Swanson answers correctly, despite the distractions and heightened stress of the moment, Jackson knows he's 'still in it.' This mini-evaluation is efficient and effective largely because coach and fighter have so much history. They share a lexicon, the same way we tend to have shared points of reference, and even old jokes, with old friends and family members. One of the ways Jackson knows Swanson best is by observing him closely in these extreme situations; he has been in his corner for years. There's a grace and efficiency to this interaction. The joke itself is also strangely appropriate. Behind the idea that a wall is a wall unless it's a dam, the pun highlights the way language is, by nature, relative and changeable. Meaning shifts depending on who's speaking and in what context. The same is true for interactions between fighters.

Fights don't really start in the ring. Fighters usually know their opponent and will often build a camp around preparing for that particular person well in advance. They will have them in mind, and tailor their approach accordingly. If they are fighting a taller, longer fighter, they might practise how to get in close and nullify that advantage, for instance. The coaching team might bring in someone of the same height, or who can fight the same style as the future opponent. If an MMA fighter is competing against someone with superior grappling skills, they might practise take-down defence, to try to keep the fight from going to the ground, where they will likely get into trouble. Preparing for his title defence against Sugar Ray Leonard, Marvin Hagler trained wearing a T-shirt with 'Leonard Will Fall' scrawled in what looked like Sharpie on the back, visible to anyone watching. The process of donning the shirt was performative; he reminded himself of his intentions. It was a kind of ritual armouring. For that fight, Hagler would have dissected both Leonard's weaknesses and his own strengths, and then he would try to develop a game plan that meshed the two. Hagler had a particular bone to pick with Leonard, who among other things admitted openly to having come out of retirement to challenge Hagler after the proud champion confided in him that he didn't have the same drive to win anymore. When Hagler sees his reflection in the mirrors around him as he trains, he might catch a glimpse not only of himself, but of that declaration written on his shirt. When he sees himself, he's also visualizing Leonard.

Prizefighters and high-level amateurs are constantly reminded of their opponent in the lead-up to a competition. The spectacle of the fight starts in training camp, or earlier, but extends through social media, face-offs, weigh-ins, the walkout, through the fight, and whatever comes after. The ring or cage is the small but sharply focused centre to a much larger periphery. Building some tension, or even animosity (real or performed) between fighters is a tried-and-true way to sell tickets and pay-per-view orders. Part of packaging and selling a fight is to put forward some kind of narrative. Every big fight needs a story. These can become formulaic, of course – the champion versus the young up-and-coming challenger; the hard-luck underdog in over their head; or the favourite versus a heel. In an extreme example of the latter, boxer Shannon 'The Cannon' Briggs stalked his would-be opponent, then-heavyweight-champion Wladi-mir 'Dr. Steelhammer' Klitschko, interrupting his meals in restaur-ants, yelling at the champ in his press conferences for other fights, and even crashing Klitschko's vacation in Florida. Posing as the heel, a kind of perverse comedian, Briggs pursued Klitschko relentlessly for months, trying to frustrate the boxer into giving him a shot at the belt. He recorded many of these drop-ins and posted them online. (Briggs eventually got his wish, and Klitschko defeated him by unani-mous decision.) In order to promote a fight, and often in order to step into it as one of the competitors, as well, we often feel the need to distill people down to something simple and manageable.

Going into my very first boxing match after competing exclusively in kickboxing, I know the name of my new opponent. It's written on the draft version of the fight card. I look her up, of course. But apart from knowing her general height and whether or not she is right- or left-handed, I choose not to focus on her at all. Her bio lists her as a fitness trainer and boxing coach, which tells me she has good cardio and likely technical skill as well. I don't want to know anything else. Any more information will just get me into my own head, and I have enough going on in there already. I leave the rest up to my coaches and training partners. I won't see her until weigh-ins on the day of the fight.

FIGHT NAME GENERATOR

A few weeks before my fight, after all the other official paperwork is sorted out, I am asked to provide the organizers with my fight nick-name and my choice of walkout song. The request catches me by surprise. The low-level kickboxing matches I have done before were all fairly routine and unceremonious. When my fight was up next, they called out my name and the name of my opponent and said we were 'on deck.' My team and I approached the judging area and waited. When it was time to fight, my coach and I walked up to the table and confirmed my identity. Someone inspected my gloves, checked for a mouthguard, and asked me some questions that I never remembered after the fact. My competitor was doing the same thing at the same table right next to me. Then, we went to our corners and were called into the centre to meet with the referee to review the rules. We touched gloves, backed into our respective corners, and then the bell rang, we met in the middle, and fought. But this boxing business feels like more of a show. The idea that I would have my very own song – which implies some kind of walkout where people are *looking at me*, throws me off. The fight is one thing. A walkout and a nickname are another. To me, this process sounds like a magnifying glass. My nerves start to creep in.

I can't give myself a nickname. I feel strongly that it has to be given to me. At the same time, this idea of alter-egos feels like a quirky and bizarre part of fight culture. The act of naming and being named is a rite of passage. Chuck 'The Ice Man' Liddell got his nickname from his coach, who was impressed by how completely unfazed Liddell was before walking into a cage match. Tommy 'The Motor City Cobra' Hearns transformed into Tommy 'The Hit Man' Hearns when he appeared on the cover of *Ring* magazine dressed like an old-timey gangster, with a Tommy gun and a headline that dubbed him Hit Man. Names can be aspirational or evolutionary, like Claressa Shields's shift from 'T-Rex' to 'G.W.O.A.T' (Greatest Woman Of All Time). MMA fighter Vladimir Matyushenko was an unknown competitor in an international wrestling meet who noticed the mats seemed dirty and decided to clean them off himself in preparation for the next day's matches. When some of the established fighters saw him mopping, they assumed he was the janitor. The next day, this kid comes out of nowhere and plows through the competition. 'You're getting beaten by the Janitor!' the coach yelled at his fighter. Matyushenko won the tournament. And the name stuck, following him through his professional career. In contrast, when 'Marvelous' Marvin Hagler asked to be recognized by his fight name – a name bestowed on him by a journalist back in his amateur days – he was met with resistance. ABC TV refused to introduce him as 'Marvelous Marvin' before his title defence against William 'Caveman' Lee in 1982. The ABC *Sports* executive producer at the time, Alex Wallau, reportedly declared that if Hagler 'wants to be called Marvelous Marvin at ABC,' then 'tell him to go to court and have his name changed.' So he did. Less than a month later, Hagler had legally changed his name from Marvin Nathaniel Hagler to Marvelous Marvin Hagler.

The act of naming is always loaded. (Although, to be fair, I struggle just deciding what to eat for lunch.) I've joined this fight card because it is an exciting opportunity: the Queen of the Diamond is the first all-women's fight card in Vancouver, and the event is being organized by Ward-Yassin. Up to this point, I have only been casually attending her competition class, and I'm not yet a staple in that gym. Joining her team will mean training in a structured fight camp led by the gym's competition coaches. I will be going through the process with a whole group of other women who will also be fighting – a rare experience – on a card of women from teams in Canada and the USA.

Although I've never competed without Radetsky in my corner, these new coaches will be the ones training me for this fight. But they don't know me very well yet. I avoid the whole idea (as is my way) and focus on the practical aspects of preparation instead. Eventually, Ward-Yassin follows up to confirm the name and the song for my walkout, and I have to commit. I go back to the well. I need help from friends and family. I send out an iMessage thread to my Santa Cruz fight family. This nine-person thread, 'Online Fight Name Generator,' begins with an onslaught from Paschel, the human idea machine. He includes offerings such as: Ali 'Tenacious' Dean, 'The Professor,' 'The Snow Weasel,' 'The Saskatchewan Assassin,' Ali 'Ph' Dean, and 'The Introvert.' These are variously hearted or (more prominently) downvoted by the other conversation members. Other suggestions stream in.

As the conversation continues and others contribute and debate, Paschel remains committed to his personal favourite and begins to campaign in earnest. He begins, 'I think you're all missing the bigger picture and the real opportunities here for … the Snow Weasel. (A thread.)' Soon, the feed is swarmed with a litany of GIFs and small low-res photos of white ermine, variously inquisitive, lithe, carnivorous, and monochromatic. With each image, Paschel builds his case: 'Cute … but ferocious' he says, showing a white weasel peeping its head out from underground. My friend Elaina interjects, but her comments are simply met with a long, pasted bubble of text from what I have to assume is a Wikipedia entry describing the animal's ravenous and bloodthirsty nature, its quick, instinctual responses to movement ('counter-two anyone?' he editorializes, pointing to one of my typical moves), and its evasive style. The Snow Weasel is an unassuming-looking predator, he explains. An out-fighter. Plus, a winter animal is perfect for someone from the Canadian Prairies. The Snow Weasel is Ali.

It is by all accounts a ridiculous name, but to his credit, Paschel's characteristic rhetorical prowess actually starts to sway public opinion. If you look into those beady little ermine eyes gazing out at you from the screen for too long, you start to believe it's a good idea, too.

Aaron Shapiro, a friend, teammate, kickboxing instructor, and human fight encyclopedia, steps in with the voice of reason, pointing out a long-held truth: many of the best fight nicknames use alliteration. Consider Archie 'Mongoose' Moore, Jessica 'Evil' Eye, or 'Rowdy' Ronda Rousey, to name only a few. Despite this significant historical insight, our conversation keeps returning to one of the other initial ideas, put forward early by the Sams: Ali 'The Professor' Dean. In training, and in life, Radetsky usually refers to me as 'Doc' or 'The Doctor,' although I was only one of multiple PhD holders at the MMA gym when I arrived (a detail that surprised me a little at the time, but I know now the two categories have considerable overlap). Ultimately, this title – 'The Doctor' – is the one my Online Fight Name Generator selects.

The naming is arguably as much a signal of another persona to the fighter themself as it is for those regarding them. Before signing on for the fight, I deliberate about taking on a boxing match. I want to make sure I have the ability to be a fighter in the ring and not let someone else push me around, especially as this is a new sport, a new team, and a different environment. I'm coming off a recent loss.

With everything going on, I haven't felt resilient lately, and that bad match reminded me what self-defeat feels like. Getting beat up in my recent fight was strangely cathartic at the time. I was so low, and so lost, that getting knocked down in front of my friends actually felt appropriate, like an outward reflection of how I felt inside. But I don't want to walk myself into a situation like that again.

I need to find the right mindset in the ring, regardless of how I feel outside it. In my search for the key to crossing that line, one of the explanations I hear from many fighters and competitors is that there is a necessary demarcation between who they are walking around and who they are inside the ring. There's another version of you, and that is the one who takes over when it's time. That's who you flip the switch *to*. By this compartmentalized logic, I figure it makes sense that the other identity often has their own name. This 'other' self initially sounds to me like delusions of Hulk, until I consider how I take on variations of my identity in different settings; the way I might be Ali walking around with my friends, but Dr. Dean in the lecture hall, for instance. When I'm my teacher self, I look and talk like me … mostly. But there's an element of performance to the role that doesn't carry into other parts of my private life. I do flip a kind of switch when I stand at the front of a classroom or a room full of academics. Fighters seem to have some version of this, although the shift is likely more dramatic. With the title and the name comes the performance of a certain version of themself. Gennady Golovkin seems like an unassuming, regular guy, for instance, but when he is in the ring, 'GGG' carries himself another way. The name authorizes the action, like those people who talk about themselves in the third person. It is all one person, but different facets take over, and perhaps it helps if that body of components has its own name.

Some classic fight names include boxing's 'Golden Boy,' Oscar De La Hoya, and Roberto 'Hands of Stone' Duran. Some say that if you didn't already have a name, opponent Muhammad 'The Greatest' Ali might bestow one upon you in his trash talking. You didn't want that. The nickname of his whim would follow a fighter around the way one bad moment, or a clever (or not-so-clever) bully can attach a moniker to your life in the second grade and you'll still be stuck carrying it around into adulthood. Nicknames range from the silly to the menacing to the religious, with some overlap, from MMA's Wanderlei 'The Axe Murderer' Silva to Yoel 'Son of God' Romero.

Roxanne 'The Happy Warrior' Modafferi and Joanna 'Champion' or 'Violence' Jedrzejczyk are arguably as polarized in temperament and persona as their names suggest. There's also a patriarchal trend, from Christy 'The Coal Miner's Daughter' Martin to Holly 'Preacher's Daughter' Holm. Curiously, both come from the groundbreaking period of modern women's pro boxing in the United States, which – as the early hype around fighters like Laila 'She Bee Stingin'' Ali demonstrates in a very tangible way – is largely tied to women's reputations *as related to* men, and fathers in particular. For the daughters of fighters, last names scream louder than nicknames. In the 1970s, boxer Mercedes Waukago leaned into the 'Indian princess' image projected onto her by a predominately white audience as a member of the White Earth Band of Ojibwe. She named her character 'Princess Tona Tomah.' Adopting a similar persona, likely for similar reasons, Theresa Kibby of the Tolowa Dee-ni' Nation went by 'Princess Red Star.' For her part, Mia 'The Knockout' St. John was unapologetic about her infamous appearance in *Playboy* magazine, however outdated that controversy might seem now, and so the double-entendre of her nickname was likely a playful nod to her claim of both female aggression and sexuality. More recently, overtly femme names from contemporary MMA fighters like Miesha 'Cupcake' Tate and Michelle 'Karate Hottie' Waterson belie both fighters' skill and aggression in ways the women themselves seem to own proudly. But that wouldn't make it any easier to cheer 'Go, Cupcake!' aloud without sounding creepy.

FACE-OFF

The theatre of the pre-fight seems to take on a life of its own. The face-off is an iconic part of this build-up. In a formal face-off in October 2017, Cecilia 'The First Lady' Braekhus and Mikaela Laurén stand eye to eye. The stare-down arguably reaches its furthest logical extent, as Laurén leans in that extra bit and plants a kiss on an unsuspecting Braekhus's lips. Braekhus slaps her opponent out of reflex, and then stumbles away laughing, saying, 'Well, thank you, I haven't gotten that in a while,' before walking away. A similar incident occurs between boxers Ewa Brodnicka and Edith Soledad Matthysse before their WBO world title fight; Brodnicka kisses Matthysse, who slaps her. But when Brodnicka, startled by the retaliation, hits back, the promoter has to jump in to stop them from fighting it out right then and there. Though Braekhus doesn't seem angry leaving the face-off, when asked about the incident with Laurén some months later, she says she was shocked. 'Can you imagine?' she asks. 'You have your opponent, you are filled with adrenaline. You are going to fight! And then she kisses you.' Braekhus acknowledges that Laurén's attempt to throw her off was successful – but only in that moment. The kiss 'didn't affect my fight,' she says – 'well, maybe it did affect my fight a little bit,' she self-corrects, 'because I got a bit pissed … I don't know if I would have knocked her out unless she had done that.'

As I look into these face-off kisses, more surface, and they are as (or more) common with men than with women. I don't know what surprises me more: that this twist on the face-off is something that actually happens, or that this is something that doesn't happen a whole lot *more*. If good fighters project their own fears and weaknesses onto their opponent, as some suggest, then how can there not be some grey area about the person whose being has become, in many ways, your constant companion?

Face-offs that break out into actual, spontaneous fights don't surprise me. The proliferation of face-off *kisses*, however, points to the other side of this coin. Although something like stealing a kiss or simply getting deep into your opponent's personal space is generally presented as yet another way to mess with them, I don't buy this as just a mind game. It lays bare a category confusion that's already deeply embedded in the relationship between fighters. It might suggest an unexplored connection between sexual violence through stealing a non-consensual kiss, especially in a context where the kiss is used as a way to gain power, a psychological edge. While more widely, the idea of establishing dominance is in many ways the aim of fighting, this blurred boundary also highlights the thin line between the intimacy and obsession of going into 'battle' together, even – or especially – as opponents, and that of partners or close friends. Though both sides are trying to posture or lie to the other, no one knows the fighter better than their toughest opponents. They're the only one right there in the ring with them. There's a reason all-out battles like the three between boxers Arturo 'Thunder' Gatti and 'Irish' Micky Ward started with a pair of rivals and ended with two dear friends.

In the first week of January, I return to work from holidays, and go back to the gym for fight camp. As my boxing fight camp starts in earnest at that point, I take a break from Muay Thai classes in order to focus on boxing exclusively. I love the different things I get from both disciplines, and I prefer the thorough training I get from doing both. But as the fight approaches and I am trying to learn the boxing stance and style more intuitively, the clash of styles can be confusing. I decide to approach the last month of camp as an almost total immersion. I have two preoccupations: boxing and teaching.

Unfortunately, the return to teaching for a new semester coincides with the start of an anonymous stalker's campaign, which kicks in, in earnest, about a month and a half before my fight. In addition to the work of teaching in two departments, the beginning of a new semester, and putting myself through five to six days a week of fight camp, I am attending extra meetings with department heads and school administrators and being brought in for consultations with women's violence support organizations, campus security, and more. These discussions are all organized for my benefit. Everyone is mobilizing to support me, and yet the added time, effort, and the repetition of the same narrative for each new audience eat away at me all the same.

I'm wandering through a personal and administrative maze created by a stranger's randomly targeted rage. As it continues, I find myself tipping headfirst into some increasing anger management issues of my own. When I am treading water emotionally and imagining myself stepping into the ring and finally having the space to let it all go, it's really not the woman whose name appears on the card with mine that I have in mind. I'm mad about this harassment, and the way it makes me feel about myself and the people around me; it's even more angering to imagine how much worse it must be for others who don't get the same kind of support I have received. Systems are set in place to deal with physical injury once it has occurred, at best, but there does not seem to be a clear path toward preventing it from getting to that point. The feelings snowball. I'm heavy with unfulfilled promises, heartbreak, fear, disappointment, and how achingly I miss my gorgeous asshole of a cat, Professor, who now lives with Leif (and doesn't even like me anyway). There's the scene from *The Wild One* when a woman asks Marlon Brando's 1950s motorcycle-jacket-clad Johnny, 'What are you rebelling against?' and he replies impassively, 'Whaddaya got?' That's kind of how I feel going into this fight.

EVERYONE PUTS BABY IN A CORNER

Early into fight camp, Tomoko and I are singled out for our boxing technique; apparently, we are both a little too square in our stance or we hold our elbows out too far. We both come to the sport from a kickboxing background, and I occasionally hear coaches gripe 'kickboxers' under their breath to each other as we spar. They advise us that we must make corrections or we will take a lot of punishment in the ring. Our squared stance makes us vulnerable here. As the fights approach, the two of us are forbidden from partnering up in class so that we won't keep reinforcing each other's habits. But because there are only three or four of us in adjacent weight classes (between about 120 and 135 pounds), and the boxing gym is trying to prep us for the size of opponents we will face in the ring, Tomoko and I are still most often paired up for sparring. It's clear, early on, that we are familiar. Despite different builds and differences in our fighting styles, we are close in size, and well aware of each other's tendencies. I'm often both most comfortable and most challenged when I work with her. I can't get away with anything and I don't have any surprises for her.

In sparring, I continue to struggle with being backed up by my opponents, pushed around the ring, and stuck in corners. When students let themselves get backed up in kickboxing, Radetsky quotes Patrick Swayze's cheesy line, 'Nobody puts Baby in a corner,' from *Dirty Dancing*. This silly expression loops in my head. These days, everyone puts me in a corner. On more than one occasion, my partner (*et tu*, Tomoko?) drives me to the ropes and drops me down to one knee by disabling me with a hard hook to the body.

I used to kind of think I knew how to box – I'd taken classes and sparred with only punching (no kicks) plenty of times. But actually boxing – trying to box like a boxer, *with* boxers – is a real challenge. It feels like I'm starting over from scratch. Preparing for a fight means constantly trying to improve, and that includes a lot of critique both from others and from yourself. It takes the built-in humility already inherent in combat sports training and ramps it way up.

A couple of weeks before the fight, I am back in Santa Cruz for a long weekend. At Allied, I meet my MMA gym's new boxing coach, a former pro boxer named Adrienne Alegria. She's technical, matter-of-fact, and generous with her time. I ask her all kinds of questions about technique and grill her about her own experiences. When I ask her how to negotiate emotions and find aggression within the fight, she explains that flipping that switch has never been an issue for her. On top of that, she says, she has never had a fight camp where there weren't other things going on in her life. Pre-fight is never without personal issues, drama, or stresses. There's no getting away from that, she advises. Use it all in the ring. She's not suggesting I become angry or emotional in the ring, but rather she's noting that's it's possible to focus those feelings and turn them into something productive – what that looks like for me, I'm not yet quite sure.

The weekend before the fight, we use our last official female competition team training session to do some light sparring, hit the peak of the training Tabata workout we have been building up for weeks, and do a kind of dress rehearsal to visualize how the fights will go. Our coaches explain to us how we will approach the ring, what kinds of instructions the referee will give us, and how we should respond when certain things occur. We try on shorts and talk about final details. This rehearsal process is helpful, and while it's a little nerve-racking to see things becoming real, having more information rather than less is calming.

Outside the gym, I am still struggling with an onslaught of messages from the stalker and feeling frustrated and hopeless. The communication staff for my department is overwhelmed trying to stay on top of the flood of posts bombarding their social media account day and night. (Every time someone mutes, flags, or reports an account, he creates a new one, sometimes within hours.) Because we are still unable to confirm the identity of the harasser, it is difficult for campus security to know just who to look out for. With each passing day, I seem to be creating more trouble for those around me.

The weeks before my fight are characterized by the laughter and supportive competitiveness of my training camp: the music, the dancing, the hard work and sweat we power through as a group. This training camp has been more joyful than almost any I've experienced. But I also can't separate this camp from the moments between – the gut-punch of threatening messages appearing at any time, and angry walks with my hood pulled heavy over my head to hide a face tightened with anger. I'm a live wire. This burning energy is building, day by day.

I think about Adrienne's advice, to use it all in the ring. One of the problems that keeps me from 'flipping the switch' is, to some extent, politeness, but greater than that, a kind of empathy. I wonder, is it *wrong* to want to take my feelings out on some strange woman I've never met? I'm not talking about engaging in competition. I'm talking about going in with the desire to hurt. I ask friends about the ethics and implications of this kind of physical therapy. She is a willing combatant, they tell me, and she certainly will not be holding back for me. She signed up to fight. It is a sign of respect for her, and for myself, to give it my all. This is the interaction to which we have both agreed. This isn't like a one-sided harassment case, they suggest. This other woman and I are on equal terms. The rule set of the boxing match is a shared language.

But I also know how angry I am, how frustrated I am, how the sadness makes me buzz and count down days and minutes until I am allowed to give it away. I'm disturbed to note that somewhere along the way, the lingering question has shifted from 'Can you flip the switch?' to 'Can you keep it *un*switched until it's time?'

The last days before the fight are meant for tapering – to relax, stretch, and give yourself a bit of a break so you can walk into the ring eager to fight, rather than burnt out. The fight is on Saturday.

Although I'm not allowed to train after Wednesday, I go into the gym on Thursday night anyway, and beg for permission to work for an hour on my own. I climb up into the ring, back myself into a corner, and practise fighting my way out.

THE SOUND OF SILENCE

When UFC (and later boxing, and more) competitions are allowed again after a few months of COVID-19 pandemic shutdown, the competitions feel different than they did before. Because no large gatherings are allowed, the fights take place primarily for cameras, rather than in front of a live audience. The most alarming difference is not perhaps the obvious thing, the visual absence of the crowds in the seats and areas surrounding the cage. When UFC first reappears in May 2020, what stands out is the emptiness of the sound. The silence is, as they say, deafening. Fights seem both more absurd and more brutal when we can hear every heavy breath, every crack of bone on bone, and every word from the coaches and announcers. Some fighters even respond to the announcer's ringside play-by-play and analysis, mid-fight, from *within* the ring. While arenas have long been outfitted with microphones and cameras devoted to the corners at key moments so pay-per-view audiences can listen in on the discussions with fighters in between rounds (this is how we have access to moments like Jackson's fish joke), now the opposing corners, fighters, and announcers can all hear each *other* as well, in real time. The chess game has a new wrinkle.

The team's yelling and cheering has long been a part of the viewing experience. The opponent's team can all likely hear the same things, though the opponent themself might be too distracted to sort through all the voices. For many fighters, thinking about the person in front of them and listening for the cues from their own corner is plenty. When I was new to sparring, Radetsky would yell advice and coaching from the sidelines. Upon hearing his voice, or my name, I'd instinctively turn to look at him – and then get yelled at for it (or hit in the head by my opponent). You can't take your eyes off the person across from you. Tuning into one or two familiar voices in real time when so much else is going on is no small feat.

To protect their strategies and any potential surprises they are plotting, coaches and fighters often adopt some kind of shorthand. Many corners call out a lot of universal shorthand ('one-two!') because their fighter is probably the only one really listening to them. This is not always the case, however. In at least one instance, pre-COVID, despite the noise, MMA fighter B.J. Penn reported hearing his opponent's corners calling for a 'two' (a right hand punch for an orthodox fighter); because the instruction isn't coded, he knew the punch was coming and was prepared to counter it. So, to avoid giving the game away, teams often take their language further. They come up with named combinations and moves ahead of time, to make communicating during a fight more efficient. Coach Duane 'Bang' Ludwig, after his former coach, Bas 'El Guapo' Rutten, uses a whole numbering system that corresponds not to individual strikes but to combinations. In the same vein, before my first kickboxing match, Radetsky worked with me to develop three combinations tailored to my style and strengths. I had to memorize and drill these combinations repeatedly until they could flow automatically. Combos A, B, and C each referred to a four- or five-punch/kick combination that I would try to throw in the fight whenever he called out for it. This kind of coded language is a very simple example of an approach that fighters use all the time, although the more experienced and familiar the team, the more sophisticated their common understanding might be.

For a code or name to work, it must be shared. One of the greater implications of not having a shared language is that it limits access. BJJ coach Eddie Bravo makes a point of naming everything, both moves and the transitions between them. 'To not name every move and not name every transition makes it harder to teach,' he says. Bravo is responding to a tradition in which many of the moves were initially learned in person, by a core group of people, with a specific instructor. The teachers would demonstrate their instruction rather than articulating it. But an already seemingly guarded or privileged and predominately male-dominated society becomes even harder for others to join if they are kept out by those who would be their teachers. According to Bravo (quoting Royce Gracie), 'Helio, the grandmaster of Brazilian Jiu-Jitsu, purposefully didn't name every move, and purposefully didn't name every transition.' 'In a secret society where you don't want the information passed on, maybe [then] it's a bad thing to name everything,' Bravo says. 'But I'm all about sharing and teaching everything.' Naming, in this context – or rather the lack thereof – has a political element. It's about controlling who knows what, how they learn it, and from whom. The names themselves are less important, Bravo suggests, than the act of naming itself. The fact that each name earmarks some combination or transition means that it can be more conveniently codified and taught. At the same time, while including names is a pedagogical gesture, it also has an authoritative element to it (in the authorship sense of the word). Naming something does, to some extent, put your stamp on it.

All that said, in another sense, a lack of shared language isn't insurmountable. Without the assumption of shared verbal language, experienced fighters and trainers can get by fairly well through the perhaps more basic physical language they have in common. I have trained in Switzerland and France, with coaches and teammates who were speaking a mix of French and Thai, for instance. Because I understood the gestures and the context (and some of the French, although I didn't exactly learn a lot combat-specific vocabulary in school), I could still follow along. And consider the fight itself. In the ring, many international competitors don't speak the same language, and yet they seem to understand each other just fine when it comes to the fight. But where successful communication means speaking or gesturing in a way that the other person gets your meaning, fighting tries to do the opposite. Fighters use feints (faking a punch, for instance) to test their opponent's responses and throw them off their game. Fighters use their bodies, movements, and patterns in order to lie. Their skill with body language is often to *mis*communicate successfully. This is another hurdle for me, as I am a terrible liar. But the trick to lies – verbal or physical – is, in a sense, to see them as a kind of performance, or strategic misdirection. Good storytellers do this all the time. My best feints are the ones where I tell myself I mean it and change my mind partway through and switch directions. In time, I've learned to do this more intentionally. That's how I sell it. The best lies are the ones I think are real, too.

Although I struggle with the task of naming myself, I love naming other things. There's a hurdler stretch we often do at the beginning of kickboxing class. You lie flat on the ground with one leg out straight, and the other one bent at the knee and splayed beside your body. Lying there, bent in unnatural directions, we look the way I imagine someone would look from above if they had just fallen out a window and landed on the pavement. To toss someone or something out a window is to defenestrate. Defenestretch. Abdominal exercises? Abcercise. And so on. (I have very patient and indulgent coaches and training partners.) All of my favourite punching bags have names, as do my slam ball and sledgehammer. With those objects in particular – ones that torture me, ones I fight with and against – there's an intimacy and affection, a battle-forged connection, that makes the act of naming seem appropriate.

I have a white whale, though. There's one name I've been trying desperately to get someone to adopt. For years now, no matter how much I ask for it, Radetsky refuses my request to name a combo or a move 'the old switcheroo.' Once, he made a show of yelling it out for me in a fake fight scenario, just to demonstrate how impractical and ridiculous the name is. Apparently, a good code name ought to roll off the tongue for easy use. And it can't be forced. The name has to disclose itself to you.

WEIGH-INS

The fight is approaching, and I can't control my weight. With consistent training, my weight usually stays within a very small range, and I like to walk around near my fighting weight – or rather, I like to fight near my walking-around weight. But the peripheral stresses on my life are messing with my ability to eat enough to maintain the energy to train hard *and* to keep on weight. I haven't dropped a drastic amount of weight, but at this point the loss of every pound seems to show in my face and the fit of my clothes. People at work start to remark on my weight loss with concern. Strangely, instead of evading the conversation completely, I mention fighting – a topic I tend not to volunteer in small talk (it either considerably lengthens or immediately kills the conversation). It seems easier than talking about harassment, which is as much a culprit for my weight loss as the boxing fight camp. I have gotten comfortable with talking about my weight as plainly as I do about my height or shoe size. When you're competing, your weight is everyone's business. So I lean into that response instead.

The day of the fight, I hang out, wander around, and visit. I want to keep my mind off the match. When I show up to the weigh-ins on the afternoon of the competition, I step onto the scale in shorts with my hair still heavy with water from the shower. I have been eating with intention all week in an attempt to put on weight. I am under 120 pounds soaking wet, and my opponent is in the 125-pound range. We had agreed to somewhere between 120 to 125. Close enough, and they give us the green light.

I am expecting nerves to kick in as the fight grows closer, but I retain something that feels pretty close to calm throughout the day. After the administrative part is complete, I sit on the floor near the ring as others complete their weigh-ins, talk to their coaches, and mill around. Facing a mirror, I divide my hair into two halves for French braids and work away at the plaits, with all of the energy swirling around me off to stage left. When you work toward something for a long time, its final approach can be a relief. The event is set up, the wheels are in motion, and there are women all around me, visiting, filling out forms, and gearing themselves up to fight. It is exciting.

BREATHE IN

In a team sport, every player is important, but that's not quite the same as being the *only* one on the field. How do top-level competitors prepare to step into a high-stakes competition, one where a loss isn't just a loss, or where if you have an off day, you might not make the shot or win a medal? How does someone prepare to step into a situation where their life is on the line, as well? This danger factor is at the heart of combat sports, but of course it isn't exclusive to it. The way Emily Cook, three-time USA Olympian in freestyle ski aerials, explains it, danger and risk are relative. Cook acknowledges the danger of flying and flipping through the sky on skis, and yet she doesn't give it as much credence as someone else might. Cook constantly returns to the idea of training: being properly trained, and adequately prepared, counts for a whole lot in terms of mitigating danger and risk. Even though Cook competes in a sport that, by definition, draws in so-called 'adrenaline junkies' (and she is no exception), her approach is analytical, clear-eyed, and reasoned. It seems worth pointing out that 'freestyle' is not as loose as the name might suggest. The search, in this case, is for perfection rather than recklessness. What this kind of extreme sport has in common with fighting is the mindset and the work that goes into it, and – significantly – the high stakes involved in each outing. Stepping into a dangerous arena, whatever it may be, requires diligent, relentless preparation. Emotion is a liability, because it distracts not just your mind but your body as well. For a lot of elite athletes, fighters included, 'imaging,' a multi-sensory approach to visualization – like a deeply meditative form of shadowboxing – is an essential tool. See the moment. Feel it, smell it, and manifest a virtual walk-through of all possible scenarios. Emphasize not only scenarios of success, but also ones where you face adversity and overcome it. By the time you get there, it will feel like you have already done it hundreds of times. You will know what to do, and where and how to make last-minute changes.

Part and parcel with this kind of imaging is learning to identify, face, and then accept the danger and the scariest possible outcomes. Two weeks before her first qualifying Olympics, Cook had a bad landing on a practice jump and shattered both her feet. It took her three difficult years to rehabilitate them. She went on to qualify and compete in the next *three* Olympic games. Imagine the kind of mental work that goes into getting back on the hill with such intimate knowledge of just how wrong it can go. Cook says that in order to compete again, she worked with a mental strength coach (like a sports psychologist but without the rhetorical baggage of the name) to face and accept the fact that she could have the same accident. What if it happens again? If she wanted to continue, she had to decide it was worth doing, even if it meant that kind of catastrophe could reoccur. Without overcoming that fear – and concluding the risk is worth it – there would be no way she could go back out there and keep jumping. This idea of acknowledging the most feared potential outcome clear-eyed, and embracing it, recalls *The Book of Five Rings*. As Miyamoto Musashi says (taking this idea, for better or worse, to its furthest logical extent), 'the Way of the warrior is resolute acceptance of death.'

I have trained as much as I can, and I know my options are either to back out or to trust my training and my coaches and go in accepting the fact that this fight can go any number of ways – some of them bad. Fight day is always some mix of waiting, and waiting, then rushing. I just want to get it done. I mentally prepare for the prospect of getting beaten up. I tell myself I am walking into a brawl, and no matter how hard I get hit, or how much pressure I get, I will hold my ground and fight back with everything I have. I have already made peace with the fact that I might be walking into my lectures this week with a mangled face or a black eye. I will decide later (depending on how bad it is) whether to ignore it completely and not even address it, or to dismiss my appearance casually with a joke and hope no one makes a big deal of it. But if I have to teach with a bruised face, I'd certainly prefer to be able to stand there, shrug, and say, 'Hey, at least I won the fight.'

Though a veteran competitor with ten years as a professional MMA fighter, Julie Kedzie describes the experience of her UFC debut in 2013 (only a year after women were first allowed in the organization) as one that took a little adjustment. In preparation for the media, crowds, noise, and scrutiny that come with this larger competition platform, Kedzie says she practised the walk to the octagon a couple of times. 'I learned the practise to walk to the Octagon from watching some of my teammates,' she explains. She had watched fighters like Donald Cerrone and Georges St-Pierre do their own walk-throughs. 'The night before the fight you kind of mentally prepare,' she says. 'You walk through the cage, you think about what's going to happen. Sometimes you think of touching gloves and meeting your opponent out there, stuff like that.' When she watched Cerrone do his workout, he did the same thing. His 'mental coach was talking him through, like, "Okay, hear the crowd. You're going to feel this; you're going to feel that." I thought, "Damn, I'm going to practise this too."'

Presumably without funding and access to the same kind of coaching staff as Cook and Cerrone, Kedzie took matters into her own hands, putting herself through her own visualization exercises while she was out walking her dog. She walked herself through it, locating herself within the imagined space. 'My dog was almost like my little prop,' she says. 'I was just practising walking down the street … I don't know why I was so scared' about the walk toward the cage. But 'then you get in the cage and I look at her and I'm like, "Okay, cool."' Once she's in the cage, Kedzie says, she likes to 'feel' her legs underneath her. 'I feel blood in them at the beginning of every fight so I can get my movement underneath me – I remember stalking back and forth, getting my usual routine going. And then I remember doing my jump squats, getting ready.' There are all of these incremental steps and personal preparations leading up to and into the ring, long before the next moment, when the bell rings and Kedzie and her opponent make physical contact.

Cerrone's adoption of mental strength strategies like the walk-through make sense, as he finds the pre-fight experience unsteady and emotional. In a recent video interview, he walks through the entire nauseating process:

> Every single time, I'm just as scared, and just as nervous. You're like, 'Man, my legs are heavy, my arms are heavy.' They bring you so early so you're sitting there backstage and you're watching the fights and you're watching the clock because you've got to figure out … when you need to start getting ready but your body's not ready. For some reason, it's the worst night in your life and you're just like, 'I'm sick. My nerves are crazy.' And I go and throw up, I throw up every time, still, to this day. And then they're like, 'All right, Cowboy, let's wrap your hands.' And they start wrapping your hands and you're like, 'Oh my god, man,' and the camera's right there and you gotta kind of smile and make everyone think that's watching, 'Oh, I'm good, I'm happy.' But I'm not, I'm sick and scared.

Beyond posturing for the people around him, Cowboy has to perform in the locker room for everyone watching at home; there's no privacy from the cameras, even before the fight begins. On the day of the fight, the cameras watch the fighters prepare as a way to introduce and build suspense for the matches to come later in the program. And so fighters learn to hide their feelings as a general rule. Opening yourself up to emotion, let alone showing it, is often a liability in the ring. In a pre-fight interview before her match against Amanda Serrano, Heather 'The Heat' Hardy quips: 'Outside I'm calm, but inside I'm like an angry cat.' With no privacy pre-fight, it makes sense that Cerrone would choose to do his visualization and walk-through in relative privacy the night before.

Tickets for our event, the Queen of the Diamond, sell out in less than two weeks, and the card receives a lot of public support and interest. Though I'm free of the scrutiny of cameras, mercurial fans, odds-makers, and the pressure of competition as a professional, the most basic elements still apply. Tonight, the fighters are all camped out in the warm-up area, which is, in this case, a tiki bar underneath the fight venue, repurposed as a kind of green room. The space is dimly lit, like a club long after the party is done, and complete with DJ table (I don't even register whether anyone is using it) and a massage area with body workers on hand to provide free massages or alignments for fighters. Apart from a curtain, there is no real separation between competitors, although our team gathers together on one side of the curtain, and the competitors from other clubs are mostly scattered on the other side with their coaches and friends, or off in a dark corner stretching or warming up. People find spaces to jump rope, but as fight times and orders are staggered, everyone is in their own different stage of pre-fight preparation (or in some cases, post-fight recovery or relaxation). A news crew is covering the event and conducting interviews in the corner of the room, but all I have to do is avoid messing up their shot. In general, once people get through their own match, they clear out and either stay upstairs to watch and support others, or leave altogether. I have my new boxing teammates here. Radetsky and others are texting throughout the course of the day and sharing updates amongst themselves, which creates a nice invisible web of support around me. I haven't really told anyone in town about the fight. My family has a pretty good sense that I am training for a boxing match, but I never tell them which day a competition will take place. Knowing they would worry,

I just send them a photo and a message afterward to let them know that it happened and I'm okay.

As my fight time approaches, I start to get ready for real. I change into my red regulation boxing shorts, a black tank top, and socks. I lace myself up into my soft, high-top boxing shoes. I jump rope for a bit to get my feet moving and my heart rate up. I reinforce my wrists with sports tape and then go through my usual ritual of wrapping my hands. I have a set of hand wraps that I use only for competition. I've worn them ever since my first match, and now it's one thing I repeat consistently. The wraps are a mismatch, one each from two different sets given to me as gifts. On the left hand, the US star-spangled banner design, a parting gift from the first time I left California. On the right, a Canadian maple leaf pattern, a gift in honour of my very first kickboxing fight. I like this combination because it signifies my mixed training and the people who helped to form the fighter I hope to be when I step into the ring.

As this is an amateur fight, one of my coaches will affix the officially sanctioned (red) headgear on my head once I'm in the ring. They will smear both it and my face with Vaseline to help the punches slide off, and so I don't get unnecessary scratches or marks on my skin, and then they will remove my mouthguard from its case and place it in my mouth. Once my gloves are put on, they will be taped and inspected. One coach is upstairs already, and the other is downstairs with me, putting me through some rounds of pad work to help me get warmed up. When we get the nod, we collect our things and head toward the stairs.

Some time before, Paschel got himself a custom mouthguard, to wear during sparring, as a joke. 'It will help you to hit harder,' he said mischievously. The first time I saw it, instead of reacting with surprise or laughter (as he had hoped), I read the script written across it and without thinking, replied with a flat 'fuck you.' When I found out he had one for me, too, I was even less impressed. I tossed the thing in my bag never to think of it again. That is, not until moments before my fight, months later. I am warm, I am ready, and I am halfway up the stairs between the tiki warm-up area and the main room where the fights are taking place. A boxing official checks my gear and asks to see my mouthguard. He then informs me that my mouthguard –

with the design of a red and white Canadian flag, a gift in honour of my very first kickboxing fight in the USA – is not allowed for competition. Red obscures blood, apparently, and so my red maple leaf is, ironically, barred by Boxing Canada regulations. My coach and I stand frozen on the landing. One cold second of panic washes over me and then I realize: I have another mouthguard.

I turn around and run back down the stairs to the warm-up area, rummage madly through my bag, and grab the white case. With it clutched in my cloth paws, I sprint back upstairs to meet my coach. With every step, the irony thickens, and I am shaking my head in disbelief. I'm in the first all-women's fight card in the city, and every time I open my mouth, I will be flashing the word 'PATRIARCHY' in bold capital letters. I tell myself I will keep my mouth closed throughout the fight.

MOMENT BEFORE THE MOMENT

> When I come out, I have supreme confidence, but I'm scared to death. I'm totally afraid. I'm afraid of everything. I'm afraid of losing. I'm afraid of being humiliated. But I'm totally confident. The closer I get to the ring, the more confident I get. The closer, the more confident I get. The closer, the more confident I get. All during my training I've been afraid of this man. I thought this man might be capable of beating me. I've dreamed of him beating me. But I've always stayed afraid of him. The closer I get to the ring, I'm more confident. Once I'm in the ring, I'm a god. No one could beat me.
>
> – 'Iron' Mike Tyson

In footage from one of his very early fights, fifteen-year-old Mike Tyson stands outside with his back to the camera and to his assistant coach, Teddy Atlas. Tyson is dressed for his fight, including the shorts, boxing shoes, and robe so common to the sport. Though he has already had at least a dozen fights up to this point, the young fighter is weeping before going out to compete. Out on the patio of the venue, Atlas is trying to talk him down and get him primed to go in and take the match.

Tyson is famed for his ruthless, aggressive style and relentless power, among his other claims to notoriety. In a later account, Tyson acknowledges the process he goes through before stepping into a fight. He describes the tension between fear and confidence as he approaches the ring, as if the boxing ring itself had magical properties. Like Superman flying toward the Earth's yellow sun, Tyson says he gets stronger the closer he is to the ring's orbit. Perhaps this duality, the combination of crippling vulnerability and the transformation into *something else*, is part of the key to the power he had in the ring for so long.

But no matter how rehabilitated he may be now, I don't think I can separate who he was as a fighter from the violence he committed and power he tried to claim outside the ring – through physical and sexual violence against women, especially. While Atlas is in Tyson's corner early on, the two of them have a falling-out when Tyson allegedly sexually harasses a very young female relative of Atlas's. Then, in 1992, Tyson is convicted of rape and sent to prison. The mind-set Tyson describes is telling. It shows one version of what it looks like to give yourself over to a very specific, and perhaps unnaturally one-dimensional, mode of being. The danger of learning to flip the switch is the inability to function in a healthy way once the switch is supposedly flipped back. But letting in that kind of animalistic mindset (as Tyson himself later described it) and being loved and valued for it, especially from such a young age, as he was, can come at a cost.

Whereas Tyson feels both 'extremely confident' and 'scared to death' at once, Cerrone remains ambivalent at best until the moment the bell rings and 'you run out there and touch gloves. And then it's on, man.' The fighters' candid discussions about their nerves and stress offer a welcome change from a lot of the posturing and cookie-cutter speeches that many fighters give. I appreciate this insight into the way even experienced combatants can be thrown into a self-questioning tunnel as they walk into a fight. Cowboy has a brand, and as his name suggests, it is tied to a persona of rugged toughness and a love of adventure. But he is also willing to speak openly about the emotional stress of going into fights, despite (or perhaps thanks to) the fact that he has done this *so many* times, and often with great success. Unlike Tyson's account, which in many ways sounds the way his fighting looks, Cerrone's description offers a subtle view of someone who shifts into another gear for the fight but doesn't claim any kind of deification or invincibility.

Still, Cerrone's admission raises a question, even for me. If it's so miserable, why do it? 'I love fighting,' he explains. 'It's … the scariest, most intense, fun feeling … I couldn't even explain it to you … Holy shit. Six weeks [of preparation]. And it's here. And it's now. And I've been on the edge of a plane about to jump out. And I've been on top of mountains. And nothing puts that fucking hair-on-the-back-of-my-neck feeling like walking into that fucking octagon, and they shut that door, and … there's only two ways this could go, right? In or out.'

THE WALKOUT

The walk to the ring is always a performance of some kind, but it hasn't always been as theatrical as it sometimes is now – particularly in boxing matches, although some MMA fighters like ONE Championship's Stamp Fairtex have been known to sing and dance their way toward the cage. On a very basic level, the walkout is a simple logistical step; the fighter literally has to get to the ring. At one point, fighters didn't take the lead, but rather put their hands on the trainer's shoulders and let themselves be led to the ring. Fighters walked out without any kind of music or fanfare – just the sounds of the crowd. As author and award-winning boxing journalist Thomas Hauser explains, this convention slowly started to change in the 1950s and 1960s. When boxer Ralph 'The Cajun Ghost' Dupas entered the ring, he often did so to blues music. And late in his career, Muhammad Ali 'broke new ground by entering the ring to face Earnie Shavers to the majestic sound of the theme from Star Wars.' At one point, Premier Boxing Champions apparently tried to standardize walkouts by having fighters come out to 'a theme written by Academy Award–winning composer Hans Zimmer. But the practice was abandoned after criticism that the music was too sterile and deprived fighters of their individuality.' The persona of the fighter is becoming a bigger part of the show. In more recent years, walkouts for boxing and other organizations, like Pride or One, have become more theatrical and elaborate, with big digital screens and light shows.

In this context, Tyson's ring walks, which involved him stalking out with no music, wearing no special outfit – just a T-shirt, his shorts, and maybe a towel and a mean look – had a stark and menacingly bare-bones quality that stood out from the pack. But others embrace the walkout, for various reasons, as part of their bigger 'Performance.' Claressa 'G.W.O.A.T' Shields dresses up for her ring walks, including a walkout to the sound of Beyoncé's 'Run the World (Girls)' in which she dons a crown and dresses more like an Amazonian goddess from *Wonder Woman*'s Themyscira than anything as relatively prosaic as a boxer.

Tyson 'Gypsy King' Fury leans toward outrageous pageantry, from a bombastic Uncle Sam get-up to an elaborate Mexican-inspired outfit he claims is a tribute to Mexican Independence Day. In his 2019 rematch against Deontay 'The Bronze Bomber' Wilder, Fury took his entrance to another level when he dressed up as a king, complete with crown and regalia, and had himself carried in on a throne to the sound of Patsy Cline's classic song 'Crazy' (which had to play twice because the 'walk' took so long). But Fury's throne was preceded by almost fifteen years by Floyd 'Money' Mayweather, who was brought out on a throne carried by faux Roman centurions to meet his match with Arturo Gatti. In an example of a 'Performance' actually taking away from the fighter's performance, boxer 'Prince' Naseem Hamed put on a show as he entered the arena to fight Marco Antonio Barrera ('Assassin El Barreta'); as Hauser describes it, Prince Naseem had himself 'strapped into a rig and "flew" down to the ring' from the top of the arena, 'with a backdrop of smoke, flashing lights, flame-throwers and a virtual waterfall made of sparklers.' As if simply being put into a rig weren't enough of a distraction and an ordeal in itself, his descent was almost three minutes long and drew his 'concentration from the task at hand. Adding insult to injury, someone threw a plastic glass filled with beer' that hit its target, the airborne fighter, just as he was entering the ring.

I don't know what to expect from my walkout, exactly, but I know it won't involve pyrotechnics or a zip-line. An amateur competition doesn't have that kind of money (or any money) behind it, and this isn't that kind of show. As it is, I'm definitely more a member of the 'get it over with' school of thought than I am a Performer. I have no reputation to establish and nothing to gain from rustling up some hype. What's the point of any of it if I can't back it up in the fight?

On deck, I am fitted into the regulation ten-ounce boxing gloves (that's six ounces lighter than the ones we wear for sparring), and my coaches give me a few final reminders. Before I know it, the announcer speaks my name: 'In the red corner, Alison 'The Doctor' Dean!'

Then my song, 'My Way' by Frank Sinatra, starts.

I have been putting myself through behavioural conditioning with this song for weeks. While the fight name was a question, the choice of walkout track was intuitive and immediate. I knew this was my song, even before I knew I had a fight. I always react to it the same way. I laugh, I get proud, and I get ready.

'I had two characters when I was fighting,' boxer Bernard Hopkins recounts. 'The first was The Executioner. The second was The Alien. They came to the ring in different ways. The Executioner was angry … he was all about inflicting pain and destruction' but 'The Alien came later in my career and was about, "Look at me. I'm as old as the hills and beating guys half my age."' As Hauser explains, Hopkins walked toward the ring singing along to 'My Way.' I didn't learn that until well after my fight, however. The song is about a man nearing the end of his life, looking back unrelenting and unrepentant. I get The Alien, although the green plastic mask that Hopkins wears to accompany the song and name look like … a lot. Still, the idea of walking out to fight at the wrong stage of life – and for me, of turning such an indulgently masculine song upside down and claiming it for my own – just feels right.

I step out and through the crowd, flanked by my coaches, Jaime and Andy. The audience parts to let us through, but I can't focus on any one person; the crowd is a blur. My coaches press the ropes down to make space for me to step over and into the ring. The whole production is well orchestrated. I have told myself not to get attached to the timing or lyrics of the song and not to put any weight on the performative aspect of the walkout. I don't need more things to get hung up on, and I don't want to be precious about ritual, because there are so many variables at play. But as it turns out, there is no need to worry. As I land firmly in the ring, one of the song's big payoffs shows up, right on time.

To my own surprise, I am singing along with Sinatra, my arms raised triumphantly. Like magic, I'm already lighter just for being in the ring. I'm in the space I have been fixating on for months. Among other things, this moment gifts me one of my favourite photographs of me. The image shows me in the ring, facing my coaches, with a smile across my face. I think they're just about to put my headgear on and the fight is about to start, but in this moment, I look unexpectedly happy. I am just where I want to be. There's nothing else to do, no more time or pressure to prepare, and no more waiting. This is it. As one of my favourite Toni Morrison narrators says, albeit in a very different context: 'Look where your hands are. Now.'

IN THE RED CORNER

There are three of us in the ring. My opponent, the referee (a smiling blonde woman in a tie), and me. I am fixated on the question of when we will touch gloves. It feels like an important cue, and I don't want to misread it. One of my favourite aspects of fights is when the competitors demonstrate sportsmanship. I like knowing that the competitiveness and brutality can coexist with that common act of acknowledgment. Strangely, our ritual glove touch gets overlooked in the final rules review. My opponent and I don't make eye contact, and the ref doesn't call for it. I come out at the bell thinking we'll touch gloves then, and ready to take that opportunity if it presents itself. If you watch closely, when competitors come out and touch gloves after the bell – and this seems fairly common in MMA – it's not entirely spontaneous. One person holds their glove up to indicate to the other that's how they want to start, and so they agree to walk in and touch hands on neutral terms for that first brief connection. But we haven't set up that agreement. When the bell rings and we each move toward the centre, the fight is on.

Many fighters have mantras that follow them into the ring. Like the alternate personas, these words help to narrow their focus toward the task at hand. Before she sends herself vaulting into the air to flip and twist on skis, Cook repeats a set of three key words to herself, cues that change depending on the run and the routine. Before Jackson asks Swanson to finish the fish joke, he prompts the fighter by asking, 'What am I telling you?' And they recite together: 'Head movement. Hands up. Pressure.' Other mantras are less technical and more psychological. Some people psych themselves up saying, 'This is mine. You can't take it.' My training partner Ale repeats, 'Ten toes down,' to ground and ready herself. (Embarrassingly, I never manage to get this right in real time. Before her first BJJ tournament, I kept trying to cheer her on by saying, 'Twelve toes down!' and could not, for the life of me, figure out why she thought I was joking.) Once, Hauser reports, when an undercard-level lightweight 'with a losing record' met Muhammad Ali, he admitted his own mantra. 'Mr. Ali, when I'm going to the ring for a fight, I get real nervous,' he began. 'So I say to myself, "I'm Muhammad Ali. I'm the greatest fighter of all time and no one can beat me."' Ali leaned toward the fighter and whispered, 'When I was boxing and got nervous before a fight, I said the same thing.'

As I step into the ring, my own phrase presents itself to me, although I have to say, it is wholly unexpected and by no means a conscious choice. After months of feeling the frustration, the sense of powerlessness, embarrassment, and anger brought on by the constant harassment – not to mention the heartbreak of divorce, goodbyes, and the stress and loss associated with multiple moves – I feel ready to flip the switch and be whoever I need to be in this moment. I expect to be rushed and backed up. This is my chance to try to finally hold my ground and throw my weight into it when I am tested. No small part of me is looking forward to being deep in that struggle. But instead of telling myself to 'take what's mine' or 'be first,' or some other mantra I have heard before, my mind goes blank except for the phrase, sent from somewhere deep in my subconscious (or, more likely, from the lyrics of my fight song) out toward the blue figure across the ring: 'I'm going to eat you.'

My opponent is light on her feet from the first bell all the way through, and she is constantly moving. As we throw out the first few strikes, her punches aren't landing. I can't figure it out. She is moving and throwing punches, but they just aren't connecting.

Though we are about the same height, I seem to have a longer reach, and the way I fight at long range seems to confuse the issue. Within the first few seconds of the fight, it dawns on me that she can't find me; she isn't able to measure where I am. Because she can't establish her distance, she can't hit me.

Everything slows down. I am in control. And I have time. I don't have to struggle. When she moves toward me, I am not simply backing myself up. More than that, I am driving forward and cutting angles. I'm going after her. I have been gearing myself up to dig in and fight at close range – to take punches and retaliate in turn. But I don't have to. I get to pick my range, and my pace, and use the long, clean punches that I prefer.

I've been advised to land a hard 'two' (right hand, a power punch) very early on, to establish it as a threat in my opponent's mind. If you listen to announcers during fights, the idea of respect comes up a lot. If two established fighters seem like they are being very safe and conservative with each other, it's often because each 'respects' the other's power. They're not underestimating their opponent by being reckless or wild. As heavyweight-champion-turned-writer Michael Bentt puts it, 'Oftentimes what determines whether or not a fighter is reduced to what the great Sonny Liston described as "a man reaching for the alarm clock while he's still asleep" depends on how much respect you give your opponent.' To respect your opponent doesn't simply mean recognizing that they are a decent person, the way we might assume; it means acknowledging that the other has the ability to hurt you, and fighting accordingly. I'm not exactly known for my power, but the right straight (two) is a good punch for me. It makes sense to consciously try to set it up as a threat. On the other hand, if a fighter lands their hardest punches and they don't hurt their opponent, then they've essentially shown their cards. If you've experienced their best shot and truly feel your opponent can't hurt you, you might be inclined to be looser, to give their power less respect.

I can hear both my coaches and the crowd as I fight. I know when I've landed a good shot partly from the feeling of the way my gloved fist connects with her face and how her body responds to it, and partly from the audience's reactions. At some point mid-round,

Jaime yells out, 'Don't love your two!' or at least that's what I think she's saying. My mind races to sort out the meaning as I fight – 'Am I bringing my hand back too slowly? Am I admiring the punch after I throw it?' But as it turns out, she was yelling, 'Double up your two.' We have a shared language, but at the moment I'm not entirely fluent; I have to do some mental math. I eventually figure out the call, though, and I comply by throwing a second two right after the first. I can also hear Evelyn in the crowd yelling 'one-two-one' so I throw the combination of left-right-left, and it works. This combination lands more than once. The stabbing left hand seems to catch her by surprise, popping in after the bigger right-hand punch. I'm not mixing things up very much; the basic ones, twos, and long left hooks (threes) are doing the bulk of the work for me. This continues for the first two rounds.

At the end of the second round, the bell rings again. When I return to my corner, now for the second time, my coach pulls out a stool for me to sit and kneels before me, at eye level, as she did the round before. I open my mouth dutifully and she pulls my mouth-guard off my teeth, like I'm a child, gently feeds me water, and tells me to just go back out there and have fun. 'You've won the fight,' she says. 'Now mix things up, try out different combinations and techniques.' I listen and nod, my eyes trained only on her. The ref calls us back and I stand up abruptly as they yank out the stool from beneath me. My coach's hand reaches out and I open my mouth to receive my mouthguard. I'm no longer thinking about what's written on it. The third round begins.

While I feel confident, I don't really manage to improvise. I want to mix it up, but my long punches continue to land, and they leave me at a controlled distance. I'm still in survival mode to some extent, in spite of myself, so I keep throwing them. All the while, my opponent keeps coming, keeps moving. No matter how many times I hit her, she persists. Close to the end of the third round, instead of cutting an angle as I have been, I let her back me up for a second, straight toward the ropes. Although I throw a check hook to get myself back into the open space (I turn a corner stepping backward while throwing a hook at the same time – a move I drilled in antici-pation of spending time against the ropes), this return to backing myself up instead of moving forward tells me I'm starting to lose some steam.

But then the bell rings. It's done.

We immediately hug and then return to our respective corners to have our gear removed. We stand in the centre with the ref between us holding our wrists as we await the judge's announcement. It's a unanimous decision in favour of the red corner. As the judge lifts my arm, I am not trying to control my expression at all, as I have with other wins. Often, I feel myself trying to stay stoic. But today I have no trouble owning the smile on my face. The ref turns us around and raises my hand again for the other side of the room.

I start to notice more of my surroundings, including the 'ring boys' in cut-off belly shirts (the first of their kind any of us had ever seen – a playful touch for an inaugural all-women's fight card). When I come back up later to watch the fights that follow, I'll see them hold up number cards and breakdance in the centre of the ring between rounds. I pose for a photograph with the ring boys, who are boxers themselves, then I go to my opponent's corner to hug her again. I shake her team's hands as she visits my corner to do the same. I collect my things and leave the ring with my coach. All of this takes only a few minutes. As I walk back through the crowd, the blur breaks into various individual faces as people stop me with their congratulations.

Reader, I did not eat that woman. I didn't even take her down or likely hurt her much. (I think I spotted her from afar at a pub later that night and she seemed nothing if not intact.) My version of consuming someone is, as it turns out, technical and measured, and – I admit – more than a little bit joyful. Vital. But not wild or out of control. So far, anyway.

This is, frankly, a pleasant surprise. I love a technical fight. And I want to actively take control, even if it's only for six minutes.

BREATHE OUT

As I break away from the crowded area, I have a couple of small orders of business – a triumphant photograph with Jaime and Evelyn with my 'Queen of the Diamond' trophy in hand, and a final check-up from the fight doctor. He approaches me, exclaiming, 'Where did *you* come from?' He has seen most local competitors fight before, but today has been our first meeting. 'You're a doctor, too!' he continues affably, referring of course to my fight name. 'I am! Of English!' I reply. He leans in conspiratorially. 'I have to pretend to check you out now to make sure you're okay. But this feels like a technicality,' he jokes. 'Did you even get hit?' I shrug, wild-eyed, grinning. He asks me the official checklist questions about my head and my vision, congratulates me, and we part ways.

It occurs to me then that I should hurry back downstairs. Tomoko is up soon, and we're supposed to be sharing the only size-small pair of women's red competition shorts.

I run downstairs, quickly change into jeans and a T-shirt, and snag an apple from my gym bag. I rush back up to the main room in time to be near Tomoko. I film her walkout with my phone and cheer her on from as close to the ropes as I can get without climbing in after her. As she takes to the ring and the fight begins, I am yelling, choking on my apple (basic-human-function overload), and calling out encouragement and advice, though it's impossible to tell if anything I am saying is of any real use. That's not entirely true. I'm pretty certain that my senseless croaks of '*HIT HER*, TO-MO-KOOO!' (with apple bits sputtering all over the people next to me) were not helpful to anyone involved. They were, however, extremely enthusiastic and deathly sincere.

Tomoko is a smart, athletic, and technical fighter. Tonight, she is in the ring with a windmill – a young, aggressive woman who throws her weight forward and swings relentlessly. This is Tomoko's first fight, and she's not used to this style – no one at our gym fights this way, and Tomoko does not tend to get pressured onto her back foot anyway – but here she is negotiating an offence that is very different from what she has practised. Tomoko evades punches well with her head movement, and her footwork is sharp and fast, and yet here she's dealing with the same issues I have been struggling with in practice for months. Her opponent wants to back her up. It's a hard-fought match right from the start, and I quickly give up on my apple (much to the relief of the people around me, I'm sure). I'm just so excited to see my beloved friend fight. Since my very first day of training, I've been watching and echoing her in the studio mirror or when we were partnered. I'm always trying to be more like her. And now here we are, together, even if we're taking our turn in the ring one woman at a time.

Because my fight is very early on in the card, I get to spend the rest of the evening watching my teammates compete. As we are visiting and packing up at the end of the night, I pause to check my Instagram; it has been flooded with notifications for most of the evening, and I am heartened to see all of these lovely posts and clips and congratulations from people who were watching the fights. But as I continue to scroll, my smile is jolted from my face. The wave of positive messages is matched with an equal inundation of threatening and harassing posts from the stalker. Fortunately, he doesn't even know about the match – my account is and has always been set to private, and he hasn't tracked me to this new gym's account yet. The timing is just a coincidence. But still. *This fucking guy.* I just won my fight. I am happy, and relaxed, and light, for the first time in a long time. I did the hard thing. I exorcised the anger. And yet here he still is. I bracket the feeling, the very thought of it, and put my phone back in my pocket. Not tonight. I collect my things and join my friends to celebrate.

Later, I wonder how different things would have been if I had found myself up against someone who had insisted on a messy fight, instead of agreeing to a 'boxing' match. I have more things I want to know, more questions I want to ask myself in the ring. I imagine (I hope!) I'll have more chances to find out.

Continuing the Fight Name Generator, Paschel and I try to decide what we would call him if he decided to take on a fight. When practising Jiu-Jitsu, he had been called NyQuil. 'Because you go to bed early,' I reasoned. 'No,' he corrected, half pretending to be offended. 'Because I put people to sleep.' And now? Well, Paschel is a silver-haired athlete. He changes stances a lot, shifting fluidly between right-handed (orthodox) and left-handed (southpaw) as he spars. Always trying on different looks, he doesn't feel like he has a specific style of his own. An evasive fighter, he sets himself problems and plays them out but never rests too long on one identity. He's the kind of person who makes a good training partner, because he can imitate other fight styles easily. 'Chameleon?' I ask. He shakes his head no.

And then a lightbulb clicks on above his head as he declares happily: 'The Old Switcheroo.'

EPILOGUE
★
YOU'VE CHANGED

Every now and then, I hear some reference to Kintsugi, the Japanese art of repairing broken pottery. In Kintsugi, the cracks are mended using a lacquer often made of gold. The object goes from whole object to broken thing, and then back to a solid whole. Through that breakage and repair, it takes on a new life; it becomes something beautiful in a different way when pieced back together with precious metal.

Kintsugi reminds me of the idea of worship through use – the way a favourite pair of shoes has worn itself to the shape of my feet, or the familiar pattern in which my notebooks become tattered and ragged from living inside my unruly purse. I've nuzzled and clutched my favourite heavy bag more affectionately than I do most flesh-and-blood friends. When I close my eyes, I can conjure the texture of its torn seams, taped patches, and misshapen stuffing. I think I absorbed some of this attitude from my best friend, Lara, who has always had a fondness for a random hole or snag in an otherwise perfect piece of cloth. It's one of my favourite things about her. She's much more loving toward flaws than I am.

The same principle, worship through use, applies to the body. This includes the mental, emotional, and physical. I think on many levels the idea of strengthening and gaining new and ultimately greater value through breakage is true. In Kintsugi, the gold fortifies the cracks in a way that is stronger than the original ceramic. And, after all, that's also how you build muscle, or strengthen your shins for kicking. Thousands of small tears and microfractures ultimately make for stronger tissue and bones. But on another level, a break is a break. For better and worse, it signals a change and a turn, a loss of uninterrupted wholeness, or an end of innocence, from which one version of you just doesn't come back.

I have been learning about breakage, slowly. It has been one of my companions these past few years. As this time in my life has shown, once something breaks, it's not just the thing in name that ends. In divorce, as in becoming a fighter, there was who I was, and there's now who I am going to be. I am becoming retroactively acquainted with who I used to be, in that life, but now the suture is also part of the identity I will carry with me forever. Fighting remakes me. I am told by others that I am the one who changed in my marriage, while I had thought for sure it was both of us. No matter. I have changed. What's left now is a beautiful, broken thing I fight every day to fill in with gold.

When a round ends in a match, the fighter's support team is allowed to run in, set down a stool, and surround the fighter. They use this short reprieve to coach, give water, press down bumps, patch up cuts, and ice the back or chest – whatever the fighter needs in order to go on. This team is called 'seconds.' I had always thought 'seconds' referred to a hurried unit of time. Actually, seconds are people. This team is integral. They support the competitor up until and through-out their fight. But when the interim between rounds times out, the team must collect their things and step back out, leaving the fighter in the space without them. 'Seconds out!' the official calls, signalling this moment when, no matter how dedicated the fighter's team, they have to leave the ring and the fighter has to go forward, taking the tools and help they've been given, and do the rest on their own.

I have spent no small amount of time studying and interrogating fight culture, poking around in its dark corners. I question and complicate, but not out of a desire to cut it down. This is an act of gratitude. Like anything I love, I want to see it clearly. I want to keep my eyes open, so that I may know it for what it is – both the good and the bad. Ultimately, fighting has taught me that I am still learning my own strength and my own resilience. I haven't hit my limit yet. My hope is that others will find some version of the same. Although not everyone can take up athletic pursuits, there are other ways these lessons apply. It's also possible to press these sports and practices into use, if desired, to make them fit *you*, rather than trying to contort yourself to fit an image of what others think they, or you, ought to be.

Boundaries are hard to set and harder to enforce. Change is painful. Fighting is difficult, and it's messy. Fighters train to be perfect *because* perfection is impossible.

The thing about fighting – like life, I suppose – is that in the end it is not a team sport. You bring your training and the support of your team with you, and your seconds are there to step in when they can. But no matter how amazing your corner or supportive your cheering section, when you have to fight, you climb into that ring alone. Each fight changes you permanently, and can break you, but you can also come out the other end stronger, and more beautiful.

REFERENCES

Chapter Two: Histories and Futures

This chapter is deeply indebted to the work of L.A. Jennings, particularly *She's a Knockout: A History of Women in Fighting Sports* (Washington: Rowman & Littlefield, 2014), and Wendy L. Rouse's *Her Own Hero: The Origins of the Women's Self-Defense Movement* (New York: NYU Press, 2017).

Quoted Sources

Erdman, Corey. 'Yosh Wagoner Helps Heal Her People through Boxing.' *Vice*, February 9, 2017. https://www.vice.com/en/article/kbxee3/yosh-wagoner-helps-heal-her-people-through-boxing

Gerrity, Diana. 'Miss Superfist,' *Atlantic Monthly* 225 (March 1970): 91–92.

Grand, Sarah. 'The New Aspect of the Woman Question.' *The North American Review* 158.448 (March 1894): 270–276.

NBC *Sportsworld*. 'Women Who Fight.' February 23, 1985. https://youtu.be/-mU9S-8dyUg

Thrasher, Christopher. 'Disappearance: How Shifting Gendered Boundaries Motivated the Removal of Eighteenth Century Boxing Champion Elizabeth Wilkinson from Historical Memory.' *Past Imperfect* 18 (2012): 53–75.

van Ingen, Cathy. '"Seeing What Frames Our Seeing": Seeking Histories on Early Black Female Boxers.' *Journal of Sport History* 40, Issue 1 (Spring 2013): 102.

Watts, Mrs. Roger (Emily). *The Fine Art of Jujutsu: With 141 Action Photographs by G. W. Beldam*. London: William Heinemann, 1906.

WYNC *News*. 'A History of Women's Boxing.' January 29, 2012. https://www.wnyc.org/story/183864-history-womens-boxing

Other Referenced Sources

Byron, Peg. 'A Former Lightweight Boxing Champ Said Sunday She … ' *UPI Archives*, April 26, 1987. https://upi.com/4947475

Fox, Sue T.L. 'Lady Tyger Had a Dream … A Female Boxer from the 70s and 80s.' *Women Boxing Archive Network*, May 15, 1998. https://www.womenboxing.com/tyger.htm

Jennings, L.A. 'The Women Boxers Who Fought for Their Right to Be Pro.' *Vice*, June 13, 2016. https://www.vice.com/en/article/aebv9b/the-women-boxers-who-fought-for-their-right-to-be-pro

Kurchak, Sarah. 'Edith Garrud and the Jiu Jitsu of the Suffragette Movement.' *Vice*, October 7, 2015. https://www.vice.com/en/article/pg5j48/edith-garrud-and-the-jiu-jitsu-of-the-suffragette-movement

The Olympic Museum. 'Women's Wrestling Super 8.' January 14, 2015. https://www.olympic.org/museum/explore/programming/in-archive/womens-wrestling-super-8

Rossen, Jake. 'Lady Ali: How Jackie Tonawanda Changed Women's Boxing.' *Mental Floss*, October 2, 2017. https://www.mentalfloss.com/article/504460/lady-ali-how-jackie-tonawanda-changed-womens-boxing

Ruz, Camila, and Justin Parkinson. '"Suffrajitsu": How the Suffragettes Fought Back Using Martial Arts.' *BBC News Magazine*, October 5, 2015. https://www.bbc.com/news/magazine-34425615

Wickens, E. 2016. 'Boxing.' *English 330: Eighteenth-Century Literature: University of Warwick*, 2017–2018. http://eighteenthcenturylit.pbworks.com/w/page/10195 6858/Boxing

Williams, Lena. 'Woman Boxer Set to Meet Male Foe.' *New York Times*, June 1, 1975. https://www.nytimes.com/1975/06/01/archives/woman-boxer-set-to-meet-male-foe.html

Chapter Three: Self-Defence

This chapter is also informed by the many coaches, training partners, friends, and family members who answered my questions about self-defence.

Quoted Sources

Gracie Breakdown. 'Women's Self-Defense That Actually Works! (Gracie Jiu-Jitsu).' YouTube video, January 7, 2016. https://youtu.be/pndPbpHLpos

Gracie University. 'Women Empowered.' https://www.gracieuniversity.com/Pages/Public/Information?enc=FMtOnZSK59l%2bIJqsLOgYQQ%3d%3d

Hollander, Jocelyn A. 'Does Self-Defense Training Prevent Sexual Violence Against Women?' *Violence Against Women* 20.3 (2014): 265.

———. 'Why Do Women Take Self-Defense Classes?' *Violence Against Women* 16.4 (2010): 466–469.

Markus, Hazel Rose, and Paula S. Nurius. 'Possible Selves.' *American Psychologist* 41 (1986): 954–69.

McCaughey, Martha. *Real Knockouts: The Physical Feminism of Women's Self-Defense*. New York: New York University Press, 1997.

Mierzwinski, Mark, and Catherine Phipps. '"I'm Not the Type of Woman Who Does Yoga": Women, "Hard" Martial Arts and the Quest for Exciting Significance.' In *Global Perspectives on Women in Combat Sports: Women Warriors Around the World*, edited by Alex Channon and Christopher R. Matthews. New York: Palgrave MacMillan, 2015.

Chapter Four: Look the Part

This chapter responds to the work of Joyce Carol Oates in *On Boxing* (Toronto: Harper Perennial, 2006), pp. 59, vii, 73; the boxing writing and stories of Ernest Hemingway; and Jonathan Gottschall's *The Professor in the Cage: Why Men Fight and Why We Like to Watch* (New York: Penguin, 2015), p. 55.

Quoted Sources

Cyborg, Cris. 'ESPN's Dana White UFC RNC Says Cris Cyborg Looks Transsexual Joe Rogan Says Cyborg Has a Dick.' YouTube video, July 29, 2019. https://youtu.be/ lBYOsLfNlsM

Forsyth, Janice. 'Bodies of Meaning: Sports and Games and Canadian Residential Schools.' In *Aboriginal Peoples & Sport in Canada: Historical Foundations and Contemporary Issues*, 25. Vancouver: University of British Columbia Press, 2012.

Hargreaves, Jennifer. *Heroines of Sport: The Politics of Difference and Identity*. London: Routledge, 2000.

HBO *Sports*. 'Real Sports with Bryant Gumbel: Fallon Fox Web Clip.' April 21, 2014. https://youtu.be/fstJQJk2WoY

Hill, Amelia. 'Ali v Frazier IV: The Daughters Strike Back.' *Guardian*. June 10, 2011, https://www.theguardian.com/world/2001/jun/10/ameliahill.theobserver

hooks, bell. 'Oppositional Gaze.' In *Black Looks: Race and Representation*, 99. New York: Routledge, 1992.

Jones, Josh. 'Ernest Hemingway's Delusional Adventures in Boxing: "My Writing is Nothing, My Boxing is Everything."' *Open Culture*. 7 October 2013. https://www.openculture.com/2013/10/ernest-hemingways-delusional-adventures-in-boxing-my-writing-is-nothing-my-boxing-is-everything.html

McBee, Thomas Page. *Amateur: A True Story About What Makes a Man*. Toronto: Scribner, 2018.

Merz, Mischa. 'All Men Are Welcome: The End of Gender in Boxing.' *Offset* 16 (2016): 2,3.

Noble, McKinley. 'UFC Champion Ronda Rousey Rips Transgender MMA Fighter Fallon Fox.' *Bleacher Report*, April 10, 2013. https://bleacherreport.com/articles/1600520-ronda-rousey-not-a-fan-of-fallon-fox-doesnt-want-transgender-ufc-womens-champ

———. 'UFC's Matt Mitrione Says Transgender Fighter Fallon Fox Is a "Disgusting Freak."' *Bleacher Report*, April 8, 2013. https://bleacherreport.com/articles/1597393-ufc-matt-mitrione-says-transgender-fighter-fallon-fox-is-a-disgusting-freak

Rosenblatt, Josh. 'Why Are Writers Drawn to Boxing? Albert Camus, Norman Mailer, and Me.' *Lit Hub*, March 14, 2019. https://lithub.com/why-are-writers-drawn-to-boxing/

Ross, MacIntosh, and Janice Forsyth. 'A Good Fight: How Indigenous Women Approach Boxing as a Mechanism for Social Change.' *Journal of Sport and Social Issues* 1.26 (2020). DOI: 10.1 177/0193723520919817

Snowden, Jonathan. 'UFC 1, 25 Years Later: The Story Behind the Event That Started an Industry.' *Bleacher Report*, November 12, 2018. https://bleacherreport.com/articles/2804552-ufc-1-25-years-later-the-story-behind-the-event-that-started-an-industry

Sugar, Bert R. 'I'd Rather Poke Out My Eye with a Sharp Stick.' *Bert Sugar on Boxing: The Best of the Sport's Most Notable Writer*. Guilford, Connecticut: The Lyons Press, 2003. 12, 13.

Trimbur, Lucia. *Come Out Swinging: The Changing World of Boxing in Gleason's Gym*. Princeton: University of Princeton Press, 2013.

Watthanaya, Frances. 'First Transgender Fighter Competes at Thailand's Oldest Stadium.' *Vice*, June 9, 2017. https://www.vice.com/en/article/new3mm/first-transgender-fighter-competes-at-thailands-oldest-stadium

Other Referenced Sources
The documentary *Game Face*, dir. Michiel Thomas, 2016.

Glock, Allison. 'The Remarkable Life (and Near Death) of Boxer Christy Martin.' *ESPN*, June 17, 2020. https://www.espn.com/boxing/story/_/id/29315414/the-remarkable-life-death-boxer-christy-martin

Chapter Six: Anywhere but the Face

Quoted Sources

Gottschall, Jonathan. *The Professor in the Cage: Why Men Fight and Why We Like to Watch*. New York: Penguin, 2015.

McDonald, Archie. 'Tough to Get Used to Women in Boxing Ring: Women's Boxing Growing on Local Scene.' *Vancouver Sun*, April 19, 1996. Retrieved from http://proxy.lib.sfu.ca/login?url=https://searchproquest.com.proxy.lib.sfu.ca/docview/243019906?accountid=13800

Muay Ying (@muay.ying). Instagram post, June 2, 2020.

Rivera-Parr, Angela (@AngelamParr). Instagram post, June 4, 2020.

Rovira, D. 'Nak Muay Ying(s): Female Fighters in Thailand.' *News Muay Farang*. 3 January 2019. https://news.muayfarang.com/2019/ 01/03/nak-muay-yings-female-fighters-in-thailand/

von Duuglas-Ittu, Sylvie. 'Caring for Stitches in Thailand – Muay Thai Cuts, Aid, Healing, Training, Fighting, Scars.' *8 Limbs US*, November 4, 2015. https://8limbsus.com/muay-thai-thailand/stitches-cuts-stitches-thailand-cuts-care-healing-training-fighting-scars

———. 'Risking Your Beauty – Female Muay Thai, Brutality and the Beauty Aesthetic.' *8 Limbs US*, March 1, 2014. https://8limbsus.com/blog/risking-beauty-female-muay-thai-brutality-beauty-aesthetic

Other Referenced Sources

FightLiveTV. 'Parr's Scars.' YouTube video, October 13, 2015. https://youtu.be/pKnrOU8dsfk

Parr, John Wayne (@johnwayneparr). Instagram post, October 6, 2015.

And a number of combat sports–related Instagram accounts and YouTube channels.

Chapter Seven: Mental Toughness

Quoted Sources

Bieler, Des. 'UFC 224 Fighter Says She's "Done" But Her Corner Sends Her Back Out in Brutal Beating.' *Washington Post*, May 13, 2018. https://www.washingtonpost.com/news/early-lead/wp/2018/05/13/ ufc-224-fighter-says-shes-done-but-her-corner-sends-her-back-out-in-brutal-beating/

DAZN Boxing. 'Rory MacDonald: "I Don't Know If I Have That Same Drive to Hurt People Anymore."' YouTube video, April 28, 2019. https://youtu.be/zmFW-XPPV50

ESPN. 'Henry Corrales KOs Aaron Pico After Wild Exchange: Bellator 214 Highlights.' YouTube video, January 26, 2019. https://youtu.be/ HfMLA8xLfxo

Fowlkes, Ben. 'The Stories Fighters Tell Themselves – and What Happens When They Stop Working.' *MMA Junkie*, February 12, 2019. https://mmajunkie.

usatoday.com/2019/02/the-stories-fighters-tell-themselves-and-what-happens-when-they-stop-working

Jung, C. G., Gerhard Adler, and R. F. C. Hull. *The Collected Works of C. G. Jung, Volume 9 (Part 2): Aion: Researches into the Phenomenology of the Self*. Princeton: Princeton University Press, Revised ed. 2014.

MacDonald, James. 'The Science Underlying the Fighter's Chin.' *Bleacher Report*, June 10, 2013. https://bleacherreport.com/articles/1668009-the-science-underlying-the-fighters-chin-what-makes-a-fighter-durable

Mailer, Norman. *The Fight*. New York: Random House, 2013.

PBC *on Fox*. 'Wilder on First Career Loss: "I Wish My Corner Would've Let Me Go Out on My Shield."' YouTube video, February 23, 2020. https://youtu.be/lFmpwTo7btA

Slack, Jack. 'The Life and Fights of Muhammad Ali: A Ballet of Stubbornness.' *Vice*, June 6, 2016. http://fightland.vice.com/blog/the-life-and-fights-of-muhammad-ali-a-ballet-of-stubbornness

Ward-Yassin, Jaime. Personal (filmed) Zoom interview, May 7, 2020.

Other Referenced Sources

Alarcon-Swaby, Jorge. 'Unfortunate Deaths in the Ring Within the Last 10 Years.' *Bleacher Report*, August 7, 2011. https://bleacherreport.com/articles/794374-10-unfortunate-deaths-in-the-ring-within-the-last-10-years

CBC *News*. 'Female Boxer Dies After Bout.' April 5, 2005. https://www.cbsnews.com/news/female-boxer-dies-after-bout/

Goldberg, Suzanne. 'Punch Kills Woman Boxer.' *Guardian*, April 6, 2005. https://www.theguardian.com/world/2005/apr/06/usa.boxing

Laffoley, Steven. *Shadowboxing: The Rise and Fall of George Dixon*. Nova Scotia: Pottersfield Press, 2012.

Radiolab. 'Limits.' April 4, 2010. https://www.wnycstudios.org/podcasts/radiolab/episodes/91709-limits

Chapter Eight: Built for It

This section draws, in particular, on the work of Caroline Criado Perez in *Invisible Women: Data Bias in a World Designed for Men* (New York: Abrams Press, 2019), especially chapters 7 and 10; and Katherine Dunn's chapter 'The Knockout: Lucia Rijke,' in *One Ring Circus: Dispatches from The World of Boxing* (Tucson: Schaffner Press, 2009).

Quoted Sources

Bostwick, J. Michael, and Michael J. Joyner. 'The Limits of Acceptable Biological Variation in Elite Athletes: Should Sex Ambiguity Be Treated Differently from Other Advantageous Genetic Traits?' *Mayo Clinic Proceedings* 87.6 (June 2012). DOI: 10.1016/j.mayocp.2012.04.002

De Souza, Mary Jane, Kristen J. Koltun, Emily A. Southmayd, and Nicole C. Aurigemma. 'The Female Athlete Triad.' In *The Exercising Female: Science and Its Application*, eds. Jacky Forsyth and Claire-Marie Roberts. London: Routledge, 2018.

Dreger, Alice. 'Redefining the Sexes in Unequal Terms.' *New York Times*, April 23, 2011. http://www.nytimes.com/2011/04/24/sports/24testosterone.html

Government of Canada. 'The Canadian Charter of Rights and Freedoms.' Last modified on November 21, 2019. https://www.justice.gc.ca/eng/csj-sjc/rfc-dlc/ccrf-ccdl/resources-ressources.html#copy

Kutner, Jenny. 'World Boxing Council Decides to Shorten Female Matches Because of Periods.' *Salon*, October 22, 2014. https://www.salon.com/2014/10/22/world_boxing_council_decides_to_shorten_female_matches_because_of_periods/

Loosemore, Michael P., Charles F. Butler, Abdelhamid Khadri, David McDonagh, Vimal A. Patel, and Julian E. Bailes. 'Use of Head Guards in AIBA Boxing Tournaments − A Cross-Sectional Observational Study.' *Clinical Journal of Sport Medicine* 27.1, (2017): 86–88. DOI: 10.1097/JSM.0000000000000322

McAlpine, Kat. 'How Does CTE Impact Women?' BU *School of Medicine* (blog), July 11, 2019. https://www.bumc.bu.edu/busm/2019/07/11/how-does-cte-impact-women/

Morse, Ben, and Becky Anderson. 'From Fighting 'As a Boy' to Undisputed Champion. How Katie Taylor Boxed Clever.' CNN *Sports*, August 7, 2019. https://www.cnn.com/2019/08/07/sport/katie-taylor-boxing-spt-intl/ index.html

Percyz, Robin, and Elizabeth Kissling. 'Boxing and Bleeding.' *Society for Mentrual Cycle Research* (blog), December 2, 2011. https://www.menstruationresearch.org/2011/12/02/boxing-and-bleeding/

Pfeiffer, Sacha, and Katie Barnes. 'South African Runner Loses Appeal over Restriction of Testosterone Levels in Athletes.' NPR, September 9, 2020. https://www.npr.org/2020/09/09/911188426/south-african-runner-loses-appeal-over-restriction-of-testosterone-levels-in-ath

Rosenblatt, Josh. '(Male) Olympic Boxers Will No Longer Wear Ridiculous and Dangerous Headgear.' *Vice*, March 3, 2016. http://fightland.vice.com/blog/male-olympic-boxers-will-no-longer-wear-ridiculous-and-dangerous-headgear

Schonbek, Amelia. 'The Fight for Women's Boxing Rights.' *Pacific Standard*, April 15, 2015. Updated 14 June 2017. https://psmag.com/social-justice/the-fight-for-womens-boxing-rights#.77vqzm76v

World Boxing Association. 'Female Boxing.' February 15, 2009. https://www.wbaboxing.com/box-medical-articles/female-boxing

Other Referenced Sources

Beaubier, Dean M., Shannon A. Gadbois, and Sheldon L. Stick. 'The Pasternak Case and American Gender Equity Policy: Implications for Canadian High School Athletics.' *Canadian Journal of Educational Administration and Policy* 120. 6 (April 2011). https://files.eric.ed.gov/fulltext/EJ923620.pdf

Glick, Ira D., Todd Stull, and Danielle Kamis, eds. *The ISSP Manual of Sports Psychiatry*. New York: Routledge, 2018. https://www.routledge.com/The-ISSP-Manual-of-Sports-Psychiatry/Glick-Todd-Kamis/p/book/9780415792509

PINK Concussions (blog). https://www.pinkconcussions.com/pageus

Stern, Robert A. 'What Is Chronic Traumatic Encephalopathy (CTE)?' *Cure PSP*, YouTube video, August 24, 2018. https://youtu.be/rJM372Pztfl

Williams, Nancy I., and Kaitlyn M. Ruffing. 'The Menstrual Cycle and the Exercising Female: Implications for Health and Performance.' In *The Exercising Female: Science and Its Application*, edited by Jacky Forsyth and Claire-Marie Roberts, 25. London: Routledge, 2018.

World Boxing Council (blog). 'Science not Sexism.' April 17, 2019. https://wbcboxing.com/en/science-not-sexism/

Chapter Nine: Crying in Combat Sports

Quoted Sources

Allen-Cottone, Kate, et al. 'Female Muay Thai on Facebook.' Facebook post, September 18, 2013. https://www.facebook.com/groups/27801291615/permalink/10151653218051616/

'Crying After First Time Sparring.' Posted to r/amateur_boxing, archived. Reddit, 2019. Posted by u/OddishVapor. https://www.reddit.com/r/amateur_boxing/comments/b6c547/crying_after_first_time_sparring/

'Question about Women's Psychological and Emotional Breakdown after Sparring.' Posted to r/martialarts, archived. Reddit, 2017. Posted by u/[deleted]. https://www.reddit.com/r/martialarts/comments/4yjjyk/question_about_womens_physiological_and_emotional/

Sanchez, Josh. 'Daniel Cormier Explains Why Patrick Cummins "Made Him Cry."' *Fansided*, Yahoo Sports, October 19, 2013. https://fansided.com/2014/02/17/daniel-cormier-explains-patrick-cummins-made-cry/

Stets, Michael. 'UFC 170 Video: Barista Patrick Cummins Claims He Made Daniel Cormier Cry in Wrestling, Heated War of Words Erupts on FOX *Sports Live*.' MMA *Mania*, February 14, 2014. https://www.mmamania.com/2014/2/14/5410960/video-patrick-cummins-pretends-to-cry-mocks-agitated-daniel-cormier-fox-sports-live-mma

von Duuglas-Ittu, Sylvie. 'There Is Crying in Muay Thai – Emotional Training.' *8 Limbs US*, September 15, 2013. https://8limbsus.com/blog/crying-muay-thai-emotional-training

Ward-Yassin, Jaime. Personal (filmed) Zoom interview, May 7, 2020.

Other Referenced Sources

Channon, Alex, and Christopher R. Matthews, eds. *Global Perspectives on Women in Combat Sports: Women Warriors Around the World*. New York: Palgrave MacMillan, 2015.

'Daniel Cormier Did Cry after Training Session, But It's Not Because of What You Think.' *Yahoo Sports*. February 19, 2014. https://sports.yahoo.com/news/daniel-cormier-did-cry-after-training-session--but-it-s-not-because-of-what-you-think-193604600-mma.html

Follo, Giovanna. 'A Literature Review of Women and The Martial Arts: Where Are We Right Now?' *Sociology Compass* 6.9 (2012): 707–17. DOI: 10.1111/j.1751-9020.2012.00487

———. 'Does Age Matter in Sport: Differing Experiences Among Women in

Rugby and Martial Arts.' *Advances in Gender Research* 14 (2010): 275–95. DOI: 10.1108/S1529-2126(2010)0000014016

Gottschall, Jonathan. *The Professor in the Cage: Why Men Fight and Why We Like to Watch*. New York: Penguin, 2015.

Miller, Shane Aaron. 'Making the Boys Cry: The Performative Dimensions of Fluid Gender.' *Text and Performance Quarterly* 3.2 (2010): 163–82. DOI: 10.1080/10462931003658099

Tolvhed, Helena. 'Sex Dilemmas, Amazons and Cyborgs: Feminist Cultural Studies and Sport.' *Culture Unbound Journal of Current Cultural Research* 5.2 (June 2013): 273–89. https://www.researchgate.net/publication/269681230_Sex_Dilemmas_Amazons_and_Cyborgs_Feminist_Cultural_Studies_and_Sport

Chapter Ten: Lineage

Quoted Sources

Crocker, Ronnie. 'Verdict Delayed in Gang-Rape Trial.' *Daily Press*, April 21, 1990. https://www.dailypress.com/news/dp-xpm-19900421-1990-04-21-9004210056-story.html

Doyle, Jennifer. 'What Happens When a Teammate Rapes a Teammate.' *Deadspin*, November 7, 2013. https://deadspin.com/what-happens-when-teammates-rape-a-teammate-1460111117

'Matthew Maldonado Found Not Guilty of Sexual Abuse, Kidnapping.' *ABC/WJLA News*, October 28, 2013. https://wjla.com/news/local/matthew-maldonado-found-not-guilty-of-sexual-abuse-kidnapping-96055

Worthington, Valerie. '4 Ways to Be a Good Training Partner: Getting Started in Brazilian Jiu-Jitsu.' *Breaking Muscle*. https://breakingmuscle.com/ fitness/4-ways-to-be-a-good-training-partner-getting-started-in-brazilian-jiu-jitsu

Worthington, Valerie, Emily Kwok, and Lola Newsom. 'When Trust Is Broken: How to Pick Up the Pieces.' *Breaking Muscle*. https://breakingmuscle.com/ fitness/when-trust-is-broken-how-to-pick-up-the-pieces

Other Referenced Sources

Brookhouse, Brent. 'Team Lloyd Irvin Crippled by Mass Exodus of Top Students after yet Another Scandal.' *Bloody Elbow*, March 5, 2013. https://www.bloodyelbow.com/2013/3/5/4066506/team-lloyd-irvin-sex-abuse-cult-power-medal-chasers-exodus

Gracie Breakdown. 'The Moral Responsibilities of Jiu-Jitsu Practitioners.' YouTube video, January 18, 2013. https://youtu.be/iTxAjN1XSso

Moskatelo, Dino. 'Creonte – Loyalty, Disloyalty, and Traitors in Brazilian Jiu Jitsu.' *BJJ World*, September 28, 2017. https://bjj-world.com/creonte/

Chapter Eleven: Work Ethic

Quoted Sources

Enamait, Ross (@rosstraining). Instagram post, April 29, 2020.

Dunn, Katherine. 'Epilogue: Imagine a Square.' In *One Ring Circus: Dispatches from the World of Boxing*. Tucson: Schaffner Press, 2009.

Modafferi, Roxanne. 'A Day in the Life of UFC Fighter Roxanne Modafferi.' *Bloody Elbow*, April 10, 2019. https://www.bloodyelbow.com/2019/4/10/18291613/ufc-fighters-perspective-roxanne-modafferi-st-petersburg-camp-antonina-shev-chenko-syndicate-training

Musashi, Miyamoto. *The Book of Five Rings*, 7. 1644. http://www.holybooks.com/wp-content/uploads/The-Book-of-Five-Rings-by-Musashi-Miyamoto.pdf

Rondina, Steven. 'UFC's Paige VanZant: "I Was Giving Myself an Eating Disorder to Make the Weight."' *Bleacher Report*, March 19, 2018. https://bleacherreport.com/articles/2765409-ufcs-paige-vanzant-i-was-giving-myself-an-eating-disorder-to-make-the-weight

The Ultimate Fighter. Season 1, Episode 3. Aired January 31, 2005.

Other Referenced Sources

'Cris Cyborg's History with Weight Cutting. OTL Archives.' *ESPN*, December 12, 2018. https://youtu.be/ACuiQFSQ5Jo

'Georges St-Pierre: Royce Gracie is MMA G.O.A.T.' TMZ *Sports*, July 26, 2020. https://www.tmz.com/2020/07/26/georges-st-pierre-royce-gracie-mma-goat-ufc-jon-jones-conor-mcgregor-khabib/

Gottschall, Jonathan. *The Professor in the Cage: Why Men Fight and Why We Like to Watch*. New York: Penguin, 2015.

'Paige Vanzant: UFC Gave Me an Eating Disorder.' *BBC*, March 17, 2018. https://www.bbc.com/news/newsbeat-43442629

The Player's Tribune. 'UFC Fighter @PaigeVanzantufc discusses the dangers of weight cutting in @mmaFighting ahead of this weekend's fight. #ufcSTL.' [Video] Twitter. January 13, 2018. https://twitter.com/PlayersTribune/status/9522004 28028088320?s=20

Sheridan, Sam. *A Fighter's Mind: Inside the Mental Game*. New York: Grove Press, 2010.

Van Wey, Walker. 'Bobby Southworth Defied the Odds on TUF Season 1.' *UFC News*, June 1, 2020. https://www.ufc.com/news/bobby-southworth-defied-odds-tuf-season-1

Chapter Twelve: In the Ring

This chapter draws on the history outlined by Thomas Hauser in 'The Evolution of the Ring Walk: Key Moments That Changed Boxing Introductions Forever,' *Sporting News*, November 14, 2018. https://www.sportingnews.com/us/boxing/news/greatest-boxing-ring-walks-music-evolution/xjbud3xfr2bx18ti7r4g8kzpy

Quoted Sources

Bentt, Michael. 'Anatomy of a Knockout: How It Feels to Be KO'd.' *Fight Game*, Fall 1996.

Bohn, Mike. '"Cowboy" Cerrone Passionately Describes "Scariest, Most Intense, Fun Feeling" of Fighting.' *The Blue Corner*, February 16, 2018.

Fowlkes, Ben. 'Why Did Greg Jackson Tell a Joke About a Fish in Cub Swanson's Corner at UFC 206?' MMA *Junkie*, December 12, 2016. https://mmajunkie.

usatoday.com/2016/12/why-did-greg-jackson-tell-a-joke-about-a-fish-in-cub-swansons-corner-at-ufc-206

Kedzie, Julie, as told to Josh Rosenblatt. 'What It's Like to Fight Your First UFC Fight.' *Vice*, August 12, 2013. http://fightland.vice.com/ blog/what-its-like-to-fight-your-first-ufc-fight

Musashi, Miyamoto. *The Book of Five Rings*, 4. 1644. http://www.holybooks.com/wp-content/uploads/The-Book-of-Five-Rings-by-Musashi-Miyamoto.pdf

Nack, William. 'What's in a Name?' *Vault*, October 18, 1982. https://vault.si.com/vault/1982/10/18/whats-in-a-name

Palmquist, Chris. 'Why Eddie Bravo Names Everything.' *Mixed Martial Arts*, March 4, 2013. https://www.mixedmartialarts.com/news/why-eddie-bravo-names-everything

Raffali, Mary, quoting Heather Hardy. 'Women in the Ring: Female Boxers.' *Sunday Morning*, CBS *News*, November 17, 2019. https://www.cbsnews.com/news/women-in-the-ring-female-boxers-heather-hardy-amanda-serrano/

Thaboxingvoice. 'Cecilia Braekhus: On the Infamous Kiss Incident with Mikaela Laurén.' YouTube video, December 8, 2017. https://youtu.be/iItHmwbBhwQ

UFC – Ultimate Fighting Championship. 'Cowboy Cerrone Describes His Emotions Walking Out for a UFC Fight.' YouTube video, January 10, 2020. https://youtu.be/SrDUxogE1Dc

Other Referenced Sources

Morrison, Toni. *Jazz*. New York: Vintage International, 2004

Ross, MacIntosh and Janice Forsyth. 'A Good Fight: How Indigenous Women Approach Boxing as a Mechanism for Social Change.' *Journal of Sport and Social Issues* 1–26 (2020). DOI: 10.1 177/0193235209198`7

UFC 206. 10 December 2016.

ACKNOWLEDGEMENTS

I am always drawn to a book's acknowledgements section because I like to imagine the invisible connections, voices, readers, and acts that are folded up within the making of a thing. Here, however, my list of 'seconds' is long and I'm afraid I'll just be scratching the surface.

I am indebted to the Coach House and Cursor staff, especially my editor and fellow fight fan, Alana Wilcox, who has been kind enough to share her warmth, intelligence, and sharp scissors with me.

There's no adequate way to thank my training partners and teammates, of all genders, who have been as generous with their friendship as with their fists. Special thanks to Katia Schwerzmann, Reem Bazzari, and Jenni Patrick, who took the time to share their experiences with me. Thank you to Elaina Ramer for taking me under her wing, for loving as ardently as she fights, and for fighting for everything she believes; Rebecca Fowler for walks, weights, and writing talks; and Alejandra Flores and Mia Venuti, who (near or far) are always right in it with me.

Allied MMA is as much a home as almost any other I've had. I have benefited from the kindness, skill, and expertise of my coaches, especially Aaron Oreb, Aaron Shapiro, Domonique Speight, Scott Anderson, Jeff Maldonado, Dustin Moore, and Adrienne Alegria. I am grateful to the Allied community who welcomed me into their ranks. We also share the memory of Xavier Cortes, who will be dearly missed.

Thank you to Ryan Diaz, Lamsongkram Chuwattana, and all the coaches, staff, and members at DCS gym for providing warmth, fun, and remarkable instruction – and for giving me something to look forward to at the end of the day, especially on days when I needed it most.

Thank you to the Female Fighters team and coaches at Eastside Boxing Club. Special thanks to Jaime Ward-Yassin, Evelyn Calado, Andy Mavros, Iva Jankovic, Sigrid Løhre, Catherine Accardi, Rachel Warner, Meghan Elliot, Sarah Common, Audrey Angchangco, Jay Basgabas, Tora Hylands, and the members of mixed competition classes.

Roy Duquette and the Spartacus kickboxing family will always hold a special place in my heart. I am also grateful to a number of gyms and trainers who were kind enough to take me in, including Tarin Carr and Marcella Davalos at Activated Boxing Fitness, Chris Buron and Garth Taylor Jiu Jitsu, High Caliber Jiu Jitsu, Justin James's East Van Militia back-alley fight club, James Finn's Garage, Old Man Gym, and my trusty pandemic partner, Stanley Park. (I would be remiss if I didn't also give a nod to the long-suffering Squishy, Squishimus, Giles, Bouncimus, and Smashimus.)

Tomoko Yanagibashi has been a kind, patient, and inspiring presence for me since my first day of kickboxing. Beyond providing a fantastic model for technique, she has also shown me what goes into being a great training partner.

I am deeply grateful to my friend Jordan Scott for so many things at this point that I've nearly lost count. Thank you to Emily Cook for taking the time and talking openly with me. Coach Trevor Wittman and Steve Eovine at ONX Sports provided me with both inspiration and the best boxing gloves I've ever worn.

I have benefitted from the kindness and advocacy of many coworkers/friends and institutions. I am grateful to Sharla Reid, Carolyn Lesjak, Clint Burham, Jennifer Scott, and the tireless Andrea Ringrose. I need to acknowledge Dalya Israel at the Women Against Violence Against Women Rape Crisis Centre and thank Hilary Murfitt for connecting me with her (among other things). When I was experiencing harassment, WAVAW (www.wavaw.ca) was ultimately able to help in ways other organizations could not. Thank you to WAVAW, and others like them, for their important work.

Thank you to Maria Ko for her constant scheming, Meagan Dallimore for her friendship and for getting me through the door, Micah Ranallo for eating all the leftovers, Mike Vann for being Mike Vann, Chessa Adsit-Morris for sharing her puppies, her home, and her massive first aid kit, Phillip Teachout for trying to fight like a 130-pound woman for me, and Lyn Guy for always having my back. As always, I am bolstered by the love and support of Linda and Doug Thorseth, the Donnellys, the Fosters, Christy Wels and the Gowans, the Deans in Canada and in Trinidad, and the lovely Cathy Bettschen.

Thanks to Nicolle Nugent and Carey Shaw, Niall MacKenzie, James C. Kent, the wonderful Danielle O'Byrne and Erin Mclauchlan, the always inspiring Amy Juschka and Heather McNabb, and the powerhouse that is LeeAnn Croft.

I have had bruiser and all-around brilliant dissertation and writing partner Sarah Creel by my side since 2009, and I cherish her more with every passing year. Among many other things, she reads with me, writes with me, and drafts difficult emails on my behalf. I am grateful to the good Doctor for her unending love and support.

Rachel Nelson is a constant source of inspiration, and as ruthless as she is loving. She was in my pocket through this whole process, and it doesn't feel like an overstatement to say this mid-pandemic book might not have materialized without her encouragement, enthusiasm, daily writing quotas, and jokes.

Thanks to my family, my beating heart. My parents are the original 'seconds' and they have always sought to give us everything we could need. At my very best, I am a blend of Vivian and Edward. My brothers, Lowell and Adrian, are always in my corner, and I am grateful to them for their feedback and help, but mostly for their love. Thanks to Erin Dean, Danielle Masters, and the radiant Liv Dean. Thank you to the Professor for sitting with me through late nights and post-training baths. And as always, thank you to Leif Thorseth for being wonderful, constantly believing in me, and for the honour of growing up together as a family.

Thank you to Lara LeMoal (for everything, always).

When I work with Sam Radetsky, I am reminded of why I fell in love with kickboxing in the first place. He is a wonderful coach, mentor, father, collaborator, and friend, and has set me on the path to finding my own way as a martial artist. When I watch Sam Paschel move through the world, I learn how to challenge myself more, be more generous, and get more out of every minute. Thank you to the Sams for their overwhelming support, and the countless hours of training, talking, reading, cooking, laughing, problem solving, and working with me to help me grow. Thank you for teaching me, inspiring me, and bringing so much joy.

Thank you to my opponents, for helping to motivate me to be the best fighter I can be. Thank you to the many women who fought to make room for us.

This book is in many ways about power and consent. Even though the connection is not always explicit, colonial and patriarchal histories, among others, underlie everything in here. With that in mind, I want to give thanks and acknowledge that this book was written while living, working, and training in Vancouver on the unceded territories of the the xʷməθkʷəy̓əm (Musqueam), Sḵwx̱wú7mesh (Squamish), and Səl̓ílwitulh (Tsleil-Waututh) Nations; and in California on the unceded territory of the Awas-was-speaking Uypi Tribe, the Amah Mutsun Tribal Band, comprised of the descendants of Indigenous people taken to missions Santa Cruz and San Juan Bautista during the Spanish colonization of the Central Coast.

ABOUT THE AUTHOR

Alison Dean has a PhD in English from Simon Fraser University and is an alumna of the School for Criticism & Theory at Cornell University and the Whitney Museum of Modern Art Independent Study Program. She is a lecturer in English Literature and Histories of Photography. Her academic research focuses on the politics of portraiture and the portrait's opposite – images of atrocity and torture. Alison currently trains and competes in kickboxing and boxing. She has a bad habit of dropping her left hand and her best punch is a straight right.

Typeset in Albertina and Knockout.

Printed at the Coach House on bpNichol Lane in Toronto, Ontario, on Lynx Cream paper, which was manufactured, acid-free, in Saint-Jérôme, Quebec, and it was printed with vegetable-based ink on a 1973 Heidelberg KORD offset litho press. Its pages were folded on a Baumfolder, gathered by hand, bound on a Sulby Auto-Minabinda and trimmed on a Polar single-knife cutter.

Coach House is on the traditional territory of many nations including the Mississaugas of the Credit, the Anishnabeg, the Chippewa, the Haudeno-saunee, and the Wendat peoples and is now home to many diverse First Nations, Inuit, and Métis peoples. We acknowledge that Toronto is covered by Treaty 13 with the Mississaugas of the Credit. We are grateful to live and work on this land.

Edited by Alana Wilcox
Designed by Crystal Sikma
Cover design by Ingrid Paulson
Author photo by S. R. Paschel

Coach House Books
80 bpNichol Lane
Toronto ON M5S 3J4
Canada

416 979 2217
800 367 6360

mail@chbooks.com
www.chbooks.com